140 Great Hikes
in and near
Palm Springs

Text and Photography by
Philip Ferranti

with

Hank Koenig
Cartographer

WESTCLIFFE PUBLISHERS
www.bigearthpublishing.com

ISBN 978-1-56579-625-6

Text, Maps, and Photography Copyright: Philip Ferranti, 2003, 2007, 2008.
All rights reserved.

Copy Editor: Nancy Hall
Reprint Editor: Kelly Smith, Jenna Browning, Ali Geiser
Designer: Rebecca Finkel
Production Manager/Illustrations: Rebecca Finkel

Published By:
Westcliffe Publishers, Inc.
a division of Big Earth Publishing
3005 Center Green Drive, Suite 220
Boulder, CO 80301
1-800-258-5830
bigearthpublishing.com

Printed by Hing Yip Printing, China

The Library of Congress has cataloged the earlier edition as follows:
Ferranti, Philip, 1945–
    140 great hikes in and near Palm Springs / text and photography by Philip Ferranti;
with Hank Koenig, cartographer.
        p. cm.
    Includes index.
    ISBN 1-56579-490-7
        1. Hiking—California—Palm Springs Region—Guidebooks. 2. Palm Springs Region
(Calif.) —Guidebooks. I. Title: One hundred forty great hikes in and near Palm Springs.
II. Koenig, Hank. III. Title.

GV199.42.C22P3455 2003
917.94'97—dc21
                                                                        2003049703

For more information about other fine books and calendars from Westcliffe Publishers,
please call your local bookstore, contact us at 1-800-258-5830, write for our free color
catalog, or visit us on the Web at **bigearthpublishing.com**.

Cover Photos (clockwise from top left): Canyon Oasis; Tahquitz Peak; Joshua Tree National
Park; Little Utah Canyon, Mecca Hills
Back Cover Photo: Ocotillo, Joshua Tree National Park

Please Note: Risk is always a factor in backcountry and mountain travel. Many of
the activities described in this book can be dangerous, especially when weather is
adverse or unpredictable, and when unforeseen events or conditions create a hazardous
situation. The author has done his best to provide the reader with accurate information
about backcountry travel, as well as to point out some of its potential hazards. It is the
responsibility of the users of this guide to learn the necessary skills for safe backcountry
travel, and to exercise caution in potentially hazardous areas. The author and publisher
disclaim any liability for injury or other damage caused by backcountry traveling or
performing any other activity described in this book.

Dedication

This book is dedicated to my beloved dog-friend Skitts (1991–2002),
who hiked these and many other trails with me with love and enthusiasm.
Thank you, Skitts.

Acknowledgments

Special thanks to Les and Shirley Larson for first introducing me to the local trails.

Many thanks to Sheila Koenig for her artistic map layouts.

Much appreciation to all the hike leaders and support volunteers in the Coachella Valley Hiking Club for sharing the joy of hiking these magnificent trails.

Bruce and Denice Hagerman deserve special recognition for their contributions to the first version of this book, *75 Great Hikes in and near Palm Springs and the Coachella Valley,* published by Kendall/Hunt Publishing Company, Dubuque, Iowa.

Contents

San Jacinto Mountains *(continued)*

Santa Rosa Mountains 188

Joshua Tree National Park... 203

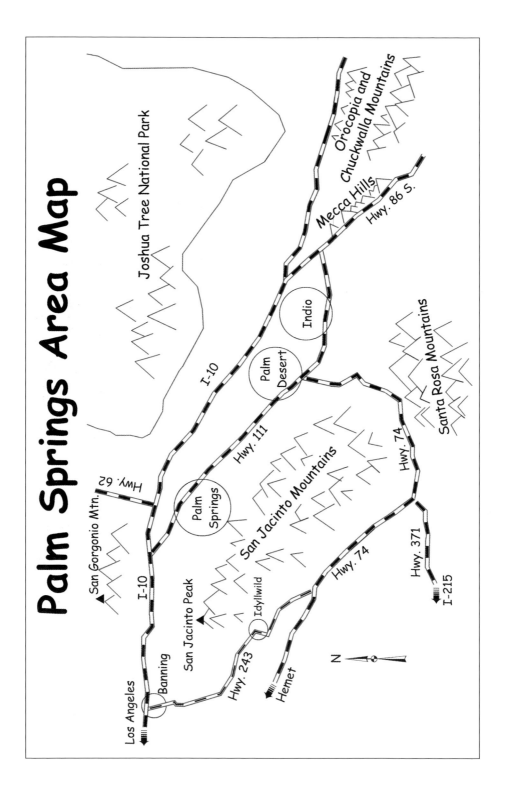

Palm Springs Area Map

Introduction

The Topography

This hiking guide takes you into the interior of Southern California, where the mountains slope down into deserts and reach out into canyons and the surrounding low foothills to form the 60-mile stretch of land known as the Coachella Valley. The San Andreas Fault cuts through this valley, contributing to its formation while causing those infamous earthquakes.

Tahquitz Peak and South Ridge Trail

The northwest area of the Coachella Valley is bordered by the San Bernardino Mountains, with Southern California's tallest peak, San Gorgonio (11,501 feet), acting as the sentinel guarding the San Gorgonio Pass which ushers visitors into the valley from the west.

The southwestern-to-west boundary of the valley is marked by the towering San Jacinto Mountain Range and San Jacinto Mountain, whose 10,800-foot massif fills the whole western skyline above Palm Springs. These same mountains provide the granite bedrock upon which the Desert Divide Ridge has been married to the Pacific Crest Trail (PCT), allowing hikers to traverse the entire 60-mile length of the mountains above the valley, all the way to Idyllwild, past San Jacinto Mountain and eventually across the pass to the awaiting San Bernardino Mountains.

Looking south by southeast, one sees the Santa Rosa Mountains, with the twin peaks of Santa Rosa and Toro dominating the horizon above La Quinta and Palm Desert. Lesser foothills carve their way along the valley floor to enfold the cities of Rancho Mirage and Cathedral City and the eastern side of Palm Springs.

To the north, the Little San Bernardino Mountains, Indio and Mecca Hills, and the Cottonwood and Orocopia mountains complete the border of the Coachella Valley and provide an abundance of canyons and interesting geological formations for hikers to explore.

Both the Santa Rosa and San Jacinto mountains are relatively new, perhaps 20 million years old. They were formed when the Pacific Plate began to push against and into the North American Plate, causing forces deep within the crust to uplift these ranges, while dredging up 500-million-year-old rocks to cover their slopes as granite boulders and sharp escarpments.

Across the valley, along the Mecca Hills, the San Andreas Fault has contributed to the valley formation by pulling the floor away

The Red Canyon, nearly 12 miles in length, is at the heart of the Orocopia Mountain Wilderness.

from the southern mountains, thereby widening the valley, which acts as a receptacle for the sand deposits from the surrounding mountains' eroding granite and quartz rocks.

Thus, within 70 miles of Palm Springs, more then a dozen mountain ranges and foothills provide the raw material for 750 miles of hiking trails, making this area one of the premier winter hiking destinations in the United States.

Climate and Weather

The Coachella Valley represents the furthest reaches of the Colorado Desert. The mountains surrounding the valley to the west effectively block Pacific storms from unleashing their full potential. Annual rainfall amounts may reach 3 to 5 inches, whereas Los Angeles receives 15 to 25 inches. Hikers need to respect the desert conditions in planning where they will hike, at what altitude, and when. What begins as a comfortable 70 degree sunrise hike, might end up at 100-plus degrees by late afternoon.

Usually hikers can begin comfortable day hikes on the valley floor and in the lower foothills by November. The moderate temperatures allow hikes up to 6,000 feet in elevation all winter long, with only scattered, thin snow conditions at worst. By April, hikes should be planned for the higher elevations only. Short hikes from sunrise until morning heat sets in can safely be done along the desert floor and in the mountain canyons through late spring.

From June to mid-October, hikers can comfortably do all the 6,000- to 10,000-foot-elevation hikes. Sometimes during the dead of summer, when the Coachella Valley experiences 110 degree days, hikers can enjoy the many hikes along the PCT, and the Desert Divide Ridge overlooking the valley, in 70 degree weather provided there is a cool, onshore Pacific breeze blowing and the marine layer has penetrated inland from the coast.

In the Idyllwild–San Jacinto Mountain region, summer storms can suddenly gather and deliver a cold rain, even hail, upon unprepared hikers. It is always wise to check the local forecast for weather that might affect the day's hike. Still, the combination of mountains and

San Gorgonio Peak, from Mission Creek, Pacific Crest Trail

adjacent deserts allows year-round hiking within 70 miles of the Coachella Valley—following the simple rule of thumb, "as temperatures rise, climb to higher elevations to hike."

Flora and Fauna

The Coachella Valley and nearby mountains reward the hiker with a generous diversity of plant and animal life. Dozens of cactus species, yucca, ocotillo, sage, smoketree, and desert flowers sweep up from the valley floor to the surrounding foothills and join with ribbonwood, manzanita, juniper, and scrub oak. They, in turn, eventually encounter pine, fir, cedar, and oak, which blanket the mountains and provide an incredibly distinct and fragrant "desert-mountain" scent that is unique to this area.

Bighorn sheep, coyotes, golden eagles, red-tailed hawks, rabbits, deer, and even mountain lions are just a few of the animals found along our trails. Visits to the Living Desert yield a rich educational experience for anyone wanting to learn about the local plant and animal life.

Trail Closures

As of this printing, the Bureau of Land Management (BLM) and other agencies have encouraged partial trail closures to protect the bighorn sheep during their annual lambing season. For the most up-to-date information, please call the BLM office at (760) 251-4800 or the Santa Rosa & San Jacinto Mountains National Monument Visitor Center, (760) 862-9984.

Trails affected by the closures include: the Skyline Trail (Cactus-to-Clouds), Clara Burgess, Dry Wash, Fern Canyon, Vandeventer, Hahn Buena Vista, Cathedral Canyon, Art Smith, Carrizo Canyon, Schey, Bear Creek Canyon, Bear Creek Oasis, Guadalupe, and Boo Hoff Trails. Trails that might be affected include: The Araby, Shannon, Berns, Garstin, Wild Horse, Goat, Eagle Canyon, La Quinta Cove to Lake Cahuilla, Morrow, and North Lykken (north of Desert Riders Park). The Art Smith and Boo Hoff Trails may be open for several days a week during this restricted times, which spans from January 15 through September 30.

The Santa Rosa & San Jacinto Mountains National Monument

On October 24, 2000, a large section of the Santa Rosa and San Jacinto Mountains became protected and designated as **The Santa Rosa & San Jacinto Mountains National Monument.** Visitors to the desert and nearby mountains can learn about the Native Americans who first settled this area as well as the area's flora, fauna, trails, and recreational opportunities by visiting the Santa Rosa & San Jacinto Mountains National Monument Visitor Center. This facility includes a bookstore and is just left off Hwy. 74, 4 miles south of Hwy. 111, in south Palm Desert. The visitor center is open daily, from 9 a.m.–4 p.m., except on Christmas and New Years, and their phone number is (760) 862-9984. The bookstore's number is (760) 862-9084.

The National Forest Adventure Pass, required for parking in the San Jacinto Mountains, is available at the bookstore. Big 5 Sporting Goods stores in Palm Desert and Palm Springs, and Desert Map and Aerial Photo (73-612 CA 111, Palm Desert, (760) 346-1101) also carry this pass.

Other local resources on this area include: The Idyllwild Ranger Station, (909) 659-2117; Tahquitz Canyon Visitor Center, (760) 416-7044; San Jacinto California State Park Visitor Center, (909) 659-2607; and the Palm Springs Aerial Tram, (760) 325-1391.

Using this Book

At the top of each hike is found useful information for planning your hike. This mini-guide includes:

Dramatic uplift, Coffee Bean Canyon area

Length: Either given in round-trip mileage or one-way. If a shuttle is necessary, this is indicated in the text.

Season: The best time of year to hike a given trail in relative comfort. Please understand, however, that desert hiking is an iffy proposition—we have seen 95 degree temperatures in February and 70 degrees in April! A good precaution during the warmer months is to start early, thereby avoiding the possible surge in temperatures by mid-afternoon.

Hiking Time: An estimate based on a 2 to 2.5 mph pace with some time considered for breaks and lunch. We have found that going uphill takes at least 25 percent longer than going downhill. This calculation is included in estimated times. Note that most hikes in this guide end by going downhill.

Information: Provides the name and current phone number of the agency where you can obtain maps, guidebooks, and advice for your hike. (The California Desert Protection Act of 1994 affects your access and use of Bureau of Land Management land. Consult with the *Oak Glen Nature Trail* BLM agency in Palm Springs for additional information.) Some hikes lack phone numbers for getting information. This is because many hikes are not "trails" as such, but follow canyons, ridges etc. There are no agencies, therefore, that have these kinds of "hikes" in their jurisdiction, or are "trails" that the agency has built.

Elevation Gain/Loss: Measured from the beginning of the hike to the end, including the return. Hikers need to know their own stamina, endurance, aerobic conditioning levels and the like, before attempting any hike—especially the strenuous ones.

Difficulty: A relative term, but considers all of the above factors. This book uses the Coachella Valley Hiking Club standards as follows:

> *Easy:* up to 500 feet elevation gain and up to 6 miles in length.
>
> *Moderate:* between 500 and 1,800 feet elevation gain and between 6 and 10 miles in length.
>
> *Strenuous:* over 1,800 feet elevation gain, and between 8 and 15 miles in length, or longer.

All hikes in this book are "day hikes," but many can be taken over several days if the hiker wishes to camp out.

Some trails are deceptive in their demands. A hike 6 miles in length is usually considered easy, but when most of the elevation gain comes during the return portion's last 2 miles, it might be regarded as a moderate hike. On some hikes the strenuous portion is at the very beginning, while the remaining 80 percent is moderate or even easy, for example, the Zen Center Trail. Some hikers find steep downhill sections more difficult than uphill, because of knee or toe stress.

Using Your GPS Receiver with this Book

The maps in this book were created by hiking the trails with a handheld Global Positioning System (GPS) receiver.

On many of the hikes the trails are obvious, and you need do no more than use your eyes. Some hikes, however, take you off trail where markers are not clear. This is when a GPS receiver can be useful. Any inexpensive ($100-$150) receiver (Garmin, Eagle, Magellan, etc.) will work just fine.

All points of interest have latitude (LAT) and longitude (LON) coordinates shown. These coordinates can be entered as waypoints into your GPS receiver. You can then navigate to each point. You can also use the coordinates to locate the points of interest on a topographic (topo) map.

Important: A datum is a reference surface on which a map is drawn. Be sure to set your GPS receiver to the *North American Datum of 1927.* This matches the datum of the local topo maps and is the datum used in developing the maps in this book, which include LAT and LON coordinates in areas that are particularly difficult to navigate. If you use any other datum, your GPS receiver will display wrong positions—wrong by several hundred feet!

Set the units of LAT and LON on your GPS receiver to degrees, minutes, and decimal minutes. This method is much easier to use than degrees, minutes, and seconds. Incidentally, the third decimal place of minutes (0.001') equals about 8 feet of horizontal distance. The second decimal place (0.010') equals about 80 feet.

Unavoidable errors: You may find that when you stand at a point of interest, your GPS receiver displays coordinates that differ from the coordinates in this book. The difference could be as much as 3,000 feet horizontal (0.040') but is usually less.

This difference is unavoidable and does not mean that your GPS receiver has been zapped by aliens or that the mapmaker was under the influence of illegal substances. The difference is due to a security system devised by the U.S. Government. The data collected while making the maps were subjected to differential correction, which gets around the security system. If the idea of differential correction really interests you, see Appendix 4 for a detailed discussion.

If you just want to hike and enjoy the security of knowing where you are, get out the boots, call your favorite hiking partner, fire up the GPS and start walking.

Safety

Desert hiking requires more safety than a casual walk along a national park trail. Water is essential to survival, and no hiker knows what events await on the trail. I suggest carrying at least 2 quarts of cool water for hikes up to 6 miles, and more water for longer distances. During the hot season you might try freezing 50 percent of your drink—for example, Gatorade or a sport drink—then adding the remainder of cool liquid the morning of the hike. This ensures a cool drink all day!

"Chocolate sundae" hills, Painted Canyon area

Protect your head with a hat of some sort, use sunscreen, and carry extra food and water, sunglasses, a windbreaker for the higher elevations, and basic first aid essentials like aspirin, tweezers, Band-Aids, moleskin, and anything else you feel supports your personal safety. Carry a comb in case you brush against a cholla cactus (guide the comb down through the thorns and flick off the entire ball of cactus).

The beauty of these areas demands respect. If you pack it in . . . pack it out!

It's always a good idea to have a map of the area where you are hiking, as well as a compass to assist in land navigation. The Coachella Valley Trails Council with the BLM has published a good trail map of the area.

It's always a good idea to hike **with someone else!** In case of injury or if you get lost, two or more hikers are better than one. Let someone know where you are going and when you expect to return. The Coachella Valley Hiking Club, (760) 345-6234, conducts guided hikes all year long and has hiked every trail mentioned in this book. Give them a call for information and consider accompanying them on a hike as a guest.

Wild animals present little hazard. Snakebites are best avoided by looking carefully around wherever you intend to sit, rest, or eat, and be sure not to put your hand under logs, rocks, and bushes. Wearing long pants is another protection against snakebites; despite hitting you in a strike, the snake may be unable to get enough clean leverage and angle to pierce your pant material. Mountain lions have been observed in the desert and mountains nearby, but again, traveling in numbers almost ensures that no harm will befall you.

During the hot summer months, hiking at higher elevations can be quite pleasant with temperatures reaching into the low 80s. In August and early

Flowers found in the San Jacinto Mountains

September, however, summer storms can blow up quickly over the mountains. Rain gear and a warm, long-sleeved, light jacket will prove ample protection.

The Coachella Valley Hiking Club (CVHC)

In October 1992, the Coachella Valley Hiking Club was formed for the purpose of organizing hikes into the magnificent deserts and mountains surrounding the Coachella Valley, and educating the public about the availability and nature of the great hiking trails found there. The club welcomes visitors as guests for day hikes. For more information: (760) 345-6234, www.cvhikingclub.net. CVHC is very active and sponsors over 300 hikes a year.

A Hiking Philosophy

Hiking is what our ancestors did effortlessly as part of their daily routine. Hunting and migrating to new pastures, warmer climates, and homelands are part of the psyche of human beings. We feel "home" where nature draws us into her beautiful deserts, mountains, canyons, prairies; along seashores, lakes and rivers; under star-canopied skies . . . wherever the plant and animal kingdoms engage the nurturing earth.

The advent of civilization has greatly impacted our commune with nature. Cities enclosed us. Still, the call of the wild is meant for all people, eliciting primeval stirrings and beckoning us to the peace of the land's quiet beauty. Hiking is our entrée into the nurturing embrace of nature. We shed the stresses, the onslaughts of media encroachments, and the demands and noise of "civilization" when we hike out into nature and release their demanding grip on our longing hearts and spirits.

Santa Rosa Plateau

Hiking is best approached as a way of life, a creative lifestyle, part of the daily fabric of existence. To walk each day somewhere touched by nature's gentle hand, to hike each week into the calming embrace of nature . . . these are goals worthy of those pursuing a high quality of life. Trails are like a collection of recipes that only nourish when acted on; they are meant to be walked, not merely acknowledged.

The rewards are great. A moderate hike burns almost 400 calories per hour. Six hours on the trail goes a long way towards firming, toning, and weight reduction. Hiking rejuvenates and energizes the hiker mentally, emotionally, physically, and spiritually. It offers us the needed beauty of nature, teaches us her quiet lessons, and reminds us that there awaits a shelter from any of life's storms.

Hiking is a metaphor for life itself: We climb our inner mountains and seek quiet meadows within our souls, following whatever *Flowers displayed along the Mission Creek Trail* guide proves worthy of our allegiance. Unlike so many modern activities, a day on the trail has a set beginning, middle, and end. By trail's end we accomplish something of real value while participating in an activity free from pretense, contrivance, and bravado. Hiking is honest.

Along the trail we can share something of ourselves with our fellow travelers. The community of humankind is built on small but precious acts of sharing such as those that take place while on a hike.

This book is therefore an open invitation to visit those unique and beautiful desert, canyon, and mountain trails in and near the Coachella Valley. Ask any hiker who has been there, "What is out there?" Come see for yourself. Come reach beyond your daily routine and enjoy!

"If you pick 'em up, O Lord, I'll put 'em down."

Anonymous
The Prayer of the Tired Walker

Mecca Hills / Box Canyon

HIKES 1 – 29

*T*he Mecca Hills lie in the northeast corner of the Coachella
Valley, along the boundary of the North American Plate. Here
the San Andreas Fault converges with several other earthquake
fault lines to form the uplifted low hills known as the Mecca Hills.
These hills, along with the surrounding mountains resemble a
lunar landscape, especially under the soft light of a full moon. By
day, this contorted, compressed land is blessed with a profusion of
vibrant color.

NOTE Most of the hikes in the Mecca Hills & the Orocopia Mountains are wilderness and off-trail type hikes. Often canyon bottoms
or ridges form the "trail" and should be done by hikers comfortable with these kinds of trail conditions. Land navigation skills,
following book directions and noted landmarks are helpful on
these hikes.

Hikes 1 – 10

Trailhead Locations in the Mecca Hills/Box Canyon

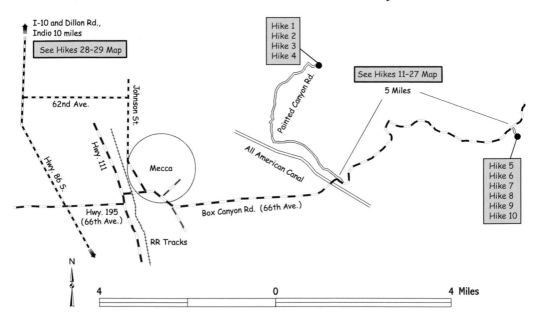

Painted Canyon/Ladder Canyon Loop

1

(see map on page 21)

LENGTH: 5 miles

HIKING TIME: 3 – 4 hours

ELEVATION GAIN: 450 feet

DIFFICULTY: Easy/moderate

SEASON: October to April

INFORMATION: BLM Office, Palm Springs, (760) 251-4800

Cutting through the middle of this colorful, twisted, exotic landscape is Painted Canyon, accessible in all its mystical beauty by a loop hike using a series of ladders to reach the uplifted Painted Canyon area.

A WORD OF CAUTION: The ladders in Ladder Canyon are sometimes maintained by volunteers. Be very careful climbing them, and if you judge something unsafe or doubt your ability, try doing the Little Painted Canyon Loop instead. It is safest to have your group's best "ladder climber" proceed up the tallest ladders first, then lend a helping hand to climbers below. Also, be careful not to get too close to the rim to look down into the canyon. Sand can be loose and slippery.

DIRECTIONS

TO REACH THE MECCA HILLS, Painted Canyon and Box Canyon area, take I-10 several miles past Indio heading east. Take the 86 S Expressway exit towards Brawley; this new, down-valley expressway bypasses the old Hwy. 111. After turning right onto the 86 S Expressway, travel nearly 10 miles to 62nd Avenue. Turn left onto 62nd Ave. and drive several miles until reaching Johnson St. Turn right and drive several miles to 66th Avenue. There turn left onto 66th Ave. (Box Canyon Rd.). Proceed almost 5 miles past many grape and citrus ranches, cross over the All American Canal, and look for the green sign on your right indicating Painted Canyon. Turn left onto this dirt road and proceed almost 4 miles. The sign indicates passibility only for 4WD vehicles, but in dry years the road can be driven safely with a car. Check with the BLM Office in Palm Springs for road conditions at (760) 251-4800. The last mile of Painted Canyon Road passes through the beautiful and exotic canyon entrance to this area and actually crosses over the San Andreas Fault as you enter the canyon, ending at a turn-around parking area with a sign posted "End of Maintained Road."

Little Utah Canyon, the Mecca Hills

Begin the Painted Canyon/Ladder Canyon Loop Trail by walking into the large canyon marked by steep, dark, lilac-colored walls located right of the road sign and behind the BLM sign. After walking 0.25 mile up the canyon, you will notice a signpost to the right that points across the canyon to the left. Walk across the canyon as the signpost directs and climb up the right side of what looks like an impassable rock slide. This trail follows the collapsed canyon along its right side until you quickly reach the first and tallest ladder. At the top the trail then takes you through a magnificent slot canyon, so named because of its thinness, and continues rising toward the top of the canyon after you've negotiated several smaller ladders.

After another .25 mile the canyon splits. Take the obvious split to your left into a canyon that winds for .5 miles, always staying in the largest canyon, avoiding any side canyons (footprints of previous hikers will help guide the way). The canyon slowly rises, taking many turns. Eventually you will reach several more small ladders. Climb these and continue hiking until you top out at a large pile of rocks, with spectacular views of the Salton Sea Basin and the surrounding Mecca Hills. Continue north on the trail as it climbs up to another top and joins with another trail. Turn north (left) and follow the trail as it skirts the edge of Painted Canyon on your right. Eventually you will see a group of large radio towers to the north, and after almost a mile take the trail that drops right and down into Painted Canyon.

Hikes 1 – 4

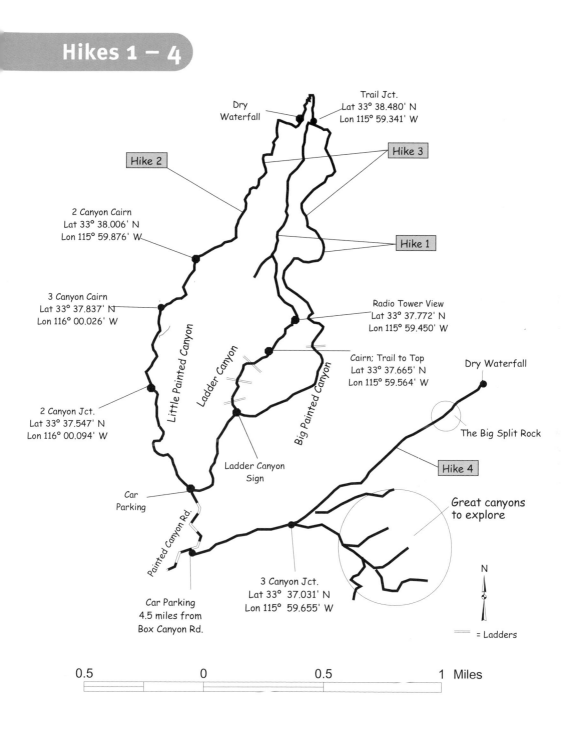

Dry
Waterfall

Trail Jct.
Lat 33° 38.480' N
Lon 115° 59.341' W

Hike 2

Hike 3

2 Canyon Cairn
Lat 33° 38.006' N
Lon 115° 59.876' W

Hike 1

3 Canyon Cairn
Lat 33° 37.837' N
Lon 116° 00.026' W

Radio Tower View
Lat 33° 37.772' N
Lon 115° 59.450' W

Little Painted Canyon

Ladder Canyon

Big Painted Canyon

Cairn; Trail to Top
Lat 33° 37.665' N
Lon 115° 59.564' W

Dry Waterfall

The Big Split Rock

2 Canyon Jct.
Lat 33° 37.547' N
Lon 116° 00.094' W

Hike 4

Ladder Canyon
Sign

Great canyons
to explore

Car
Parking

Painted Canyon Rd.

3 Canyon Jct.
Lat 33° 37.031' N
Lon 115° 59.655' W

N

Car Parking
4.5 miles from
Box Canyon Rd.

= Ladders

0.5   0   0.5   1   Miles

Once in Painted Canyon, proceed down canyon, taking the right fork at any junction. The geology of this area is colorful and invites close examination of the many varieties of rock found uplifted and exposed all along the return route. After a mile the canyon narrows sharply, and hikers are challenged to descend the last several ladders to a lower canyon below. Follow this last 0.75-mile section until you are back to your starting point at the car parking area.

2 Little Painted Canyon Walkabout

(see map on page 21)

LENGTH: 4 – 5 miles

HIKING TIME: 3 – 4 hours

ELEVATION GAIN: 300 feet

DIFFICULTY: Easy

SEASON: October to April

INFORMATION:
No information available

This hike was designed for hikers who are uncomfortable climbing the ladders through Ladder Canyon that take hikers into the main and largest canyon of the Painted Canyon complex of colorful rock and geological formations. With this hike you will be able to enjoy the Painted Canyon experience without the ladder climbing.

DIRECTIONS   Follow the directions for Hike 1.

After you park your car near the turn-around, begin walking into the large canyon just past the sign indicating the end of the road. The canyon begins to turn left after 0.25 mile. Stay to the right and leave the main canyon by hiking into the large canyon area to your right. There is another canyon to your left, but by staying right and hiking into the large canyon, you will be on the right track. Do not be fooled into walking into the little side canyons before this turn. Once you veer right, after another 0.25 mile you will again come to a major canyon juncture where the canyon splits into three large canyons, the width of their mouths being 20-30 yards. Again veer to the right, taking the canyon to the far right. I've marked this with a rock cairn just next to the far right wall of the canyon (GPS), but you cannot be sure that this marker will still be there (a large 5x6-foot dirt boulder lies just back of the cairn). Once into this canyon, you are now hiking Little Painted Canyon. As the walls narrow, you will begin seeing

Typical rock color found in the Painted Canyon area.

spectacular, colorful rock formations. Most of this hike is an easy walkabout through the canyon (stay right in the main canyon except for one obvious left turn).

After 2-plus miles the canyon narrows into a difficult-to-negotiate dry falls. You can proceed farther by retreating 20 yards and then walking left up and over this dry falls or trying the more difficult rock scramble to the right of the dry falls. After another half mile you will probably want to turn back and retrace your route back to your vehicle, staying to the left as you proceed down canyon.

3 Little and Big Painted Canyon/ Ladders Loop (see map on page 21)

LENGTH: 5 miles

HIKING TIME: 3 hours

ELEVATION GAIN: 400 feet

DIFFICULTY: Moderate

SEASON: October to April

INFORMATION:
No information available

With this loop hike it is possible to experience two parallel "Painted Canyons" and descend the easier set of ladders while avoiding the more demanding first ladders and the scramble to the top ridge of Painted Canyon.

DIRECTIONS
Follow the directions for Hike 1.

After following Little Painted Canyon to the dry falls (2.5 miles from the start), negotiate the dry falls by either retreating 20-30 yards and scrambling up the slope to the left of the falls, or do the more difficult scramble to the right of the dry falls.

From either position, once above the dry falls look up toward the sloping small cliff above you (if you are below the falls looking directly at the dry falls, this cliff is directly to the right and above the falls area). Scramble up this slope where it appears easiest. For some this might mean going up the small gully to the left. Once at the top, depending on from where you scrambled up to the top, walk for a few yards until you notice the trail along the ridge that winds sharply down the other side and into Big Painted Canyon (GPS). Descend into the larger Painted Canyon. At the bottom, looking south down canyon, notice that the darker, more colorful rock begins to be exposed beneath the sandstone and top-covering soil and dry mud. Proceed south down Big Painted Canyon, examining the incredible, colorful, and diverse rock formations along the way. By always staying to your right you will eventually arrive, after 1-1.5 miles, to a rock area highlighted by white, chalky material and dark striped rocks that some refer to as Zebra Rocks. The last ladder of Painted Canyon lies around the corner as the canyon comes to an abrupt narrowing.

Descend the taller of the two ladders, then the smaller one if it is there. If not, just scoot down the last 6-foot rock face. From the bottom of the canyon look back to enjoy the spectacular drop out of Painted Canyon. Continue hiking the canyon along its sandy bottom for another 0.75 mile until you eventually empty out onto the road where your vehicle is parked.

"The Ladders" —Ladder Canyon Loop

4 The "Big Split Rock" Slot Canyon Walkabout (see map on page 21)

LENGTH: 6 miles

HIKING TIME: 3 hours

ELEVATION GAIN: 100 feet

DIFFICULTY: Easy

SEASON: October to April

INFORMATION:
No information available

This is a "fun" adventure, especially for kids and those who still want to be! The colors, rock formations and interesting slot canyons, including the interesting "Big Split" make for a Utah kind of hike without driving the 500 miles.

DIRECTIONS Follow the directions for Hike 1.

After turning left off Box Canyon Road (Ave. 66) drive 4.5 miles on the Painted Canyon dirt road (as of this printing the road is passable for cars even though the sign says 4wd vehicles). You will come to a very colorful and narrow part of the canyon, a winding section that goes right then left and straight again (4.5 miles from the Box Canyon paved road). As the road widens and opens up, note the brilliant silver, grey, orange, and cream rock formations to your left. This trail is best done early in the morning and on a sunny day for maximum enjoyment and effect. Turn off the dirt road just as you come to that colorful explosion of rock on the left (4.5 miles), and take the smaller jeep trail towards and alongside the hills for 100 yards. Park just before reaching the large canyon opening in front of you, one marked by a profusion of colorful soil and rock. If you overshoot this area

Exotic rock formations, Big Split Rock, Slot Canyon Walkabout

and go 0.25 mile to the road's end at the Painted Canyon Trailhead, just drive back and go into the first large canyon to your left.

Begin hiking into this at-first narrow canyon opening. Note the colorful rocks and rockslides to your right, where large muted orange-colored boulders have broken off and fallen down from the mountain top above you to the right. Disregard the first small canyon you come to on your left. After 0.3 mile you will reach a fork in the main canyon (which is the large canyon veering right). Take the fork to your left, which breaks into two parallel canyons. Stay in the larger canyon to your left. You will soon pass a small slot canyon on your left, which you are free to explore, but return to the canyon you just entered.

I call this "The Big Split Rock Slot Canyon," and it continues for almost 0.5 mile. As you proceed, the canyon narrows, as a slot canyon does. In places you climb up small rock chutes or over boulders and even sometimes under them! You'll see great rock falls and large mountain chunks. It's a slot canyon that claustrophobic individuals should avoid. Large dogs might be challenged, but small adventurous ones (and kids!) will have a blast! You finally arrive at... "The Big Split" which is obvious, and can be negotiated carefully before the canyon again widens a bit and seemingly ends at a tall rocky dry falls. Return to where you entered the canyon. The next canyon to your left is also a slot canyon and can also be explored partway. Return to the main canyon, heading left into the large open wash bottom canyon that slowly curves around the large mountain above you. Note the interesting rock formations sculptured above you every 0.25 mile or so.

After hiking 1.25 miles through the main canyon, you will come to the first large canyon opening to your right. You may explore this canyon, but the better

choice is to stay in the main canyon and take the next canyon going right, its opening marked by a large, thorny cat's claw bush. This canyon winds past interesting rockslides, Utah-like sand sculptures above you, and other worthwhile geological sights. After 1.5 miles in the main canyon you may take either split in the canyon, exploring as you like before returning back to your vehicle the same way you came. This hike really "pops" in early morning sunlight and entices you with multiple canyons you will want to come back to and explore.

Slot canyon near Big Split Rock

5 The Grottos

(see map on page 28)

LENGTH: 5 miles

HIKING TIME: 3 – 4 hours

ELEVATION GAIN: 300 feet

DIFFICULTY: Easy/moderate

SEASON: October to April

INFORMATION: BLM Office, Palm Springs, (760) 251-4800

At the eastern flank of the Mecca Hills Wilderness area east of Box Canyon Road, lies the Western section of the Orocopia Mountain Wilderness. Within this upheaval of sandstone, mud hills, and washes are two cave systems formed when an ancient river cut through sandstone mountains. Earthquakes then forced the collapse of parts of these mountain systems to buttress against each other at their tops, leaving the bottom hollow or cavelike in appearance. The hike to the caves offers a stunning view of the Salton Sea and the eastern Santa Rosa Mountains, suggesting Lower Baja California's Sea of Cortez. For this hike, as well as for the 2nd Grotto, bring a good flashlight.

DIRECTIONS Follow the directions for Hike 1 up to the sign indicating Painted Canyon to the left off Hwy. 195. Continue driving on Hwy. 195 exactly 5 miles past the Painted Canyon sign until you can turn right off the road at the tall signpost marked Sheep Hole Oasis. Drive 100 yards to the trailhead located against the mud hill just off the road.

Begin hiking behind the trail sign found at the parking area. The trail leads east up a small water channel for 30 yards before climbing alongside a small hill. Within a few hundred yards you arrive at an overlook of the Salton Sea Basin, before continuing up to the top overlook in another 0.1 mile. From here the trail drops down along a ridge for 0.5 mile. To the left and down in the canyon is a small cluster of palm trees marking Sheep Hole Oasis, a water collection spot for bighorn sheep. The trail then drops down into a canyon where you have two options to access the main canyon, Hidden Springs Canyon.

You can turn right as you reach the canyon floor and hike 100 yards to the main canyon, where you will then turn left and proceed east for 0.6 mile until coming to the narrow canyon entrance. Or you can take the "post route" into Hidden Springs Canyon by following the iron posts found in the canyon that you first drop down into as the trail crosses the small wash, climbs a low hill, then drops down into Hidden Springs Canyon; then you'll continue post to post

Hikes 5 – 8

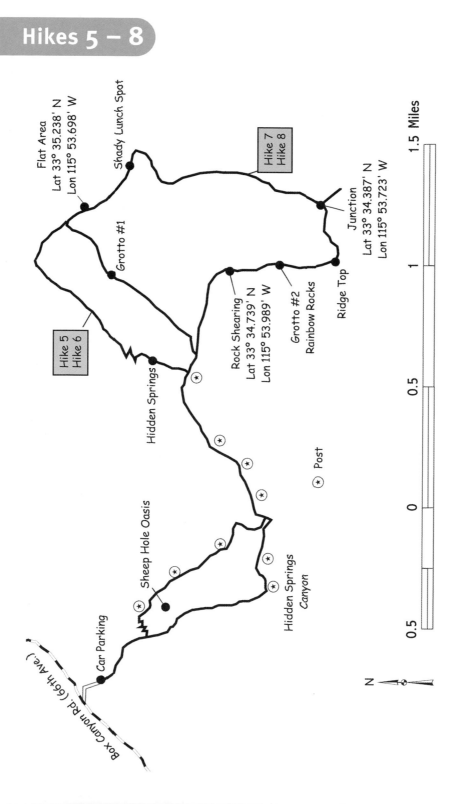

Flat Area
Lat 33° 35.238' N
Lon 115° 53.698' W

Shady Lunch Spot

Grotto #1

Hike 7
Hike 8

Junction
Lat 33° 34.387' N
Lon 115° 53.723' W

Hike 5
Hike 6

Rock Shearing
Lat 33° 34.739' N
Lon 115° 53.989' W

Grotto #2
Rainbow Rocks

Ridge Top

Hidden Springs

Post

Sheep Hole Oasis

Hidden Springs
Canyon

Car Parking

Box Canyon Rd. (66th Ave.)

N

0.5   0   0.5   1   1.5 Miles

Santa Rosa Mountains from trailhead, Big Colorful Canyon

until arriving at the narrow canyon entrance. From here, hike into the increasingly more dramatic canyon for 0.25 mile until coming to a colorful rock formation on your left, a small canyon entrance that leads to Hidden Springs Oasis found 100 yards from the entrance. Note the explosion of colorful rocks on the right side of the canyon as well. After exploring the oasis, return to the main canyon and continue hiking for 100 yards until coming to the first large canyon to your left, marked by a large cluster of trees and bushes. Turn left here and follow the narrowing canyon until it ends in what looks like a rock slide. This marks the entrance to the 1st Grotto cave system.

Carefully climb up the right side of the slide, entering the cave system by dropping down a small ladder after crossing a wooden plank. As you crawl or move about the cave system, be careful not to rise up too quickly, or you might painfully encounter a low-hanging rock! After carefully negotiating the several cave systems found here and exploring up the narrow canyon you exit into, return to your vehicle by following the same route you took back through the Grottos. Be sure not to forget the flashlight! This hike provides some interesting camera shots, so photo enthusiasts will want their cameras as well.

6　1st Grotto Loop to Hidden Springs

(see map on page 28)

LENGTH: 5 miles

HIKING TIME: 3 – 4 hours

ELEVATION GAIN: 400 feet

DIFFICULTY: Moderate

SEASON: October to April

INFORMATION:
No information available

DIRECTIONS　Follow the directions for Hike 5.

Trail above 1st Grotto

After negotiating through the cave area, instead of backtracking through the caves, continue hiking the narrowing canyon that exits from the Grottos. After less than 0.5 mile you will notice to your left a steep jeep road coming down into the canyon. Hike up and out this sharp incline. At the top, notice the road turning left. Follow it up another very sharp incline (plenty of quick aerobic exercise in this section) until it almost tops out on a hill. Take the faint trail to the left and slightly down, (it will begin moving toward the south/southwest). This trail becomes more defined and offers great valley vistas as well as sweeping views of the Salton Sea and its basin.

After 0.75 mile the trail begins to follow a narrowing ridge until it is above Hidden Springs (you can see the palm trees below you). Carefully descend the ridge, a rough bushwhack and scramble, until you are at Hidden Springs Oasis.

This is a great lunch stop. Continue south through the narrow canyon until you empty out into the same large canyon you first hiked up to get to the Grottos. Turn right and proceed down canyon for at least a mile until you notice the large canyon that you entered from earlier in the day. Be especially careful to note this canyon entrance. Upon entering it you will, after 100 yards, come to a large iron-wood tree to the left. The trail up the ridge is now visible and will take you back to the vehicle parking area.

7   2nd Grotto/Rainbow Rocks Walkabout

(see map on page 28)

LENGTH: 7 miles

HIKING TIME: 5 hours

ELEVATION GAIN: 800 feet

DIFFICULTY: Strenuous

SEASON: October to April

INFORMATION:
No information available

DIRECTIONS   Follow the directions for Hike 5.

After coming to the canyon leading into the 1st Grotto, continue past this entrance and instead follow the same canyon you've been hiking in for the last several miles. In another 0.5 to 0.75 mile you will come to a narrowing of the main canyon (Hidden Springs Canyon). Along the way you will notice many colorful formations to your right. Feel free to enter these small side canyons and examine the rainbow display of soil and rock. At the very end of the main canyon, look to your left for a narrow opening (an Alice-in-Wonderland kind of entrance). Crawl into this narrow entrance (flashlights are necessary) and begin negotiating this cave system. After a while you will come to a rock wall that requires careful climbing. Many hikers will feel uncomfortable doing this rock wall and can backtrack out of the Grotto and return down

Red-orange explosion of color, Big Colorful Canyon

canyon to the trailhead. If you choose to continue, upon exiting above the wall, notice the rainbow array of rock and soil surrounding you. Take the larger canyon to your right. Feel free to explore the trail system before returning to your vehicle by returning through the 2nd Grotto, following the route you came in on back to your vehicle.

8 2nd Grotto/Rainbow Rocks/ Hidden Springs Loop (see map on page 28)

LENGTH: 8 miles

HIKING TIME: 5 hours

ELEVATION GAIN: 1,000 feet

DIFFICULTY: Strenuous

SEASON: October to April

INFORMATION:
No information available

This hike takes you to the second cave system in the Box Canyon area known as the 2nd Grotto, past colorful rainbow rock formations, to the tops of several mountains for some great vistas, and back to Hidden Springs via a cross-country bushwhack. This is an adventurous hike, physically demanding, with steep uphill and downhill rock scrambles and vertical drop exposures down into deep canyons. In short . . . be prepared, be careful, and be willing to challenge yourself, mentally and physically. This hike is best suited for experienced hikers with land navigation skills.

DIRECTIONS   Follow the directions for Hike 5.

After parking at the trailhead, follow the trail just in back of the sign. It begins by hugging a low hill to your right, climbing quickly to the top of one great vista overlook, then another. From the top the trail, head down for 0.5 mile along a ridge offering you spectacular views of the lower Salton Sea Basin, the Santa Rosa Mountains to the south, and the Box Canyon foothills. Note the palm trees down in the canyon to your left. This marks the spot for Sheep Hole Oasis, a small opening in the ground where water is available most of the year for bighorn sheep.

From the ridge the trail eventually drops down into a canyon. As a variation on other hikes into Hidden Springs Canyon and eventually to the 2nd Grotto (GPS), follow the iron posts in the wash as they lead you up to a small hill overlook and

The Salton Sea, as seen from above the Mecca Hills

then down into Hidden Springs Canyon. This "post route" can now be simply negotiated by following the posts as they lead through the main canyon to where the canyon narrows.

Note the rock formations on either side of the canyon, especially the ones on the left where the softer base rock has eroded, allowing the harder stone it supports to break and fall down the hillside. After passing into the canyon entrance and hiking for 0.25 mile, observe the two sentinel-like dark purple rocks guarding a narrow opening to the left. This marks the entrance to Hidden Springs Oasis, from which you will exit on your return.

Along the route of the next half mile and to your right, you will enjoy a series of colorful "rainbow rock formations," which you can examine by walking a few yards off the main canyon. Along the same route you will also come to a rock formation on your right where uplift and possible severe rock shearing forces have broken off pieces of rock in a dramatic fashion (GPS).

As the canyon ends in an intensifying explosion of color, take the entrance to the left into the 2nd Grotto. You begin this part of the hike by crawling through the small opening into a series of chambers. You must negotiate narrow rock blockages until coming to "the wall," a 12-foot vertical rise that demands careful rock climbing. Once at the top you are "through" the 2nd Grotto. Follow the canyon for 30 yards until you turn right at the first opportunity. This narrow canyon leads slowly upward, in a stair-step fashion. When you come to the big boulder sitting on the ledge to your right, stay left in the still-narrow canyon, then right at the next junction, hiking up toward an ocotillo on the upper right ridge above you. In a few yards, veer left past the nearby ocotillo, then left of the large rocky upthrust, aiming for the large, shiplike rock above you to your left. Climb up the 4-foot-high ridge to your left, then make for the top of the mountain by scrambling up its steep sides until you reach the top (40 yards).

At the top, turn left, being especially careful of the exposure and narrow trail conditions. Enjoy the views, but not while you are hiking! Stop first, then take in the magnificent scenery. After about 150 yards, veer right, heading toward the three rock cairns atop the mountain east of you. After another 100 yards you will come to the last ridge junction (GPS). Do not take the trail to the cairns. Instead, follow the steep trail leading sharply down on the left, a trail that demands extreme caution because of loose rock and steep drops. After another 75 yards, veer left and then right to the faint trail that summits the steep hill due north. From atop this hill, head north by slowly and carefully stair-stepping your way down the north face of the hill until coming to a small saddle. Drop down left into a wash then head for the next steep hill to the northwest, following the jeep trail up to the top.

By now you're wondering what possessed you to ever consider taking this hike in the first place . . . but persevere, your land navigation skills will see you safely home!

From the top of this next hill, follow the jeep road down its steep north face, eventually coming out into a large wash accented by many palo verde trees—the trees with the green bark. Continue left down the wash for 0.25 mile until coming to a large palo verde that makes a shady lunch/snack stop. Stay in the wash for another 0.25 to 0.5 mile until you see a large boulder, to the right of which a jeep trail climbs steeply out. If you continue to follow the wash, it quickly becomes a narrow canyon leading directly into the 1st Grotto.

After taking the steep jeep trail out of the wash, you summit onto a flat area. Look left and then follow the jeep trail that drops down and then quickly up onto another steep hill climb. Just a few yards from the top look for a faint trail veering left. This bighorn sheep trail leads you up to the hilltop and almost joins the jeep road to your right. Stay on the narrow trail as it turns left and then south away from the jeep road, following a ridge for the next 0.5 mile and offering beautiful vista views of the Salton Sea and Rainbow Canyon/Rocks to the left.

The trail will narrow to a steep ridge just above Hidden Springs Oasis. Take it down, to the left, to the oasis, then out the narrow canyon, where you will negotiate more rock obstacles. Once back in the main canyon, follow the post route until it climbs the first hill. The trail up and to your right will take you down into the wash, where you turn right to access Sheep Hole Oasis, about 0.5 mile up canyon. One final steep trail left of the second set of palm trees leads you to the high ridge trail you first came in on. At the top, turn right and follow the trail back to your parked vehicle.

This demanding hike requires an adventurous attitude, land navigation skills, and physical stamina. It rewards the hiker with a sense of accomplishment, the fun challenges of following a bushwhack route, plenty of awesome vista views of the Salton Sea Basin and Rainbow Canyon/Rocks area, and a generous scattering of magnificent quartz specimens. This hike is best done on a sunny day, early in the morning, and before the temperature reaches into the 80s.

9 Back of the Grottos Ridge Loop
(see map on page 36)

LENGTH: 5 miles

HIKING TIME: 3 hours

ELEVATION GAIN: 500 feet

DIFFICULTY: Easy/Moderate

SEASON: October to April

INFORMATION:
No information available

DIRECTIONS
Follow the directions for Hike 5.

Begin hiking past the BLM sign, following trail directions as you would for the Grottos Hike #5. As you come down off the high ridge that offers great vista views of the Salton Sea Basin, you will enter a wash. Hike right for a few hundred yards until you enter the very large Hidden Springs Canyon. Turn left and hike in the wash or beneath the cliffs to your right to gain the shade on a hot day. After 0.75 miles you will notice the wash leading toward a canyon opening. Before reaching the canyon walls that on your left would confine you in Hidden Springs Canyon, turn left into the wide wash bordered by plateaus where large pieces of rock have broken off and gathered on the down-sloping cliffs. Stay towards your right for 0.25 mile, then hike towards and into the canyon on your right.

This canyon narrows and begins winding turns. At the first canyon entrance on the left (2.15 miles from the trailhead), a narrow affair, turn left into this canyon. You are in the right canyon if you pass through a narrow opening after a few yards into a larger canyon. Continue hiking to the right as the canyon

Hikes 9 – 10

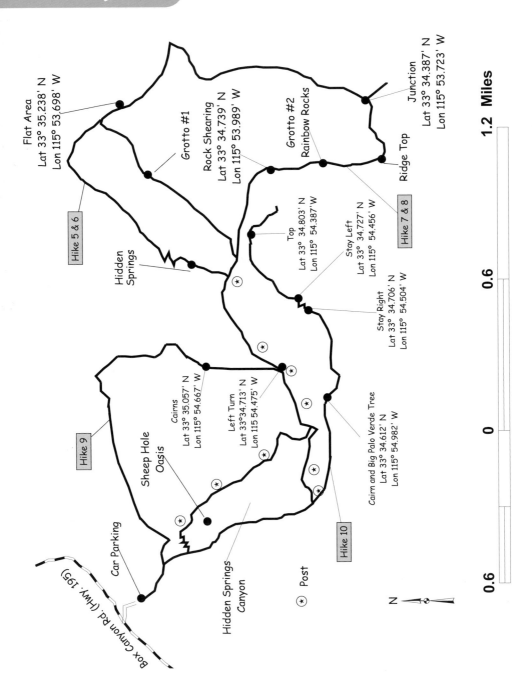

Flat Area
Lat 33° 35.238' N
Lon 115° 53.698' W

Grotto #1

Rock Shearing
Lat 33° 34.739' N
Lon 115° 53.989' W

Grotto #2
Rainbow Rocks

Junction
Lat 33° 34.387' N
Lon 115° 53.723' W

Ridge Top

Hike 5 & 6

Hidden
Springs

Top
Lat 33° 34.803' N
Lon 115° 54.387' W

Stay Left
Lat 33° 34.727' N
Lon 115° 54.456' W

Hike 7 & 8

Stay Right
Lat 33° 34.706' N
Lon 115° 54.504' W

Hike 9

Cairns
Lat 33° 35.057' N
Lon 115° 54.667' W

Left Turn
Lat 33°34.713' N
Lon 115 54.475' W

Sheep Hole
Oasis

Cairn and Big Palo Verde Tree
Lat 33° 34.612' N
Lon 115° 54.982' W

Hike 10

Car Parking

Box Canyon Rd. (Hwy. 195)

Hidden Springs
Canyon

Post

N

1.2 Miles

0.6

0

0.6

In the Mecca Hills, entering Painted Canyon

wash turns to the right and stay in the main, largest canyon. After another 0.35 mile the canyon undergoes a noticeable split. Take the canyon to your left, looking for rock cairns that have been strategically placed to indicate the trail heading up a rocky, uprising narrows. As you go higher you will continue to see rock cairns marking the trail. After 0.20 mile the trail heads steeply upwards towards a large rock marker. Scramble up-slope until gaining the top, then continue hiking left and up past the rock marker until you reach a small trail at the top. The feel of this hike is a "what's next" kind of adventure.

Once you access the small ridge trail, turn left and continue following this trail. When the trail splits and divides both right and left around small hilltops, take the trail to the left. This ridge loop offers some of the best vista views of the Salton Sea Basin and the Grottos area of any trail in the area. It will continue heading west as it ups-and-downs all the way to where you first went down the large ridge at the beginning of the hike. As you hike west, see if you can spot this juncture. Finally the trail ends on top of the ridge just minutes from the trailhead. Turn right and down, hiking back to your vehicles just around the hill.

10 Grottos Overlook Trail

(see map on page 36)

LENGTH: 5 miles

HIKING TIME: 3 hours

ELEVATION GAIN: 500 feet

DIFFICULTY: Easy

SEASON: October to April

INFORMATION:
No information available

DIRECTIONS   Follow the directions for Hike 5.

This hike is short, but oh, so sweet! The overlook vista views at the top are magnificent, showing the canyon of the 1st Grotto, as well as the canyon into Hidden Springs Oasis, along with Salton Sea Basin vistas. This hike has a lot of short segments to it that are each unique in the ambience and scenic offerings. Caution! At the top the trail is narrow, with exposure to sheer drops. This hike is best done in a group, or at least with a friend.

This trail begins at the Sheep Hole Oasis Trailhead and follows the trail in back of the BLM sign up to several great vista overlooks of the Salton Sea Basin. The trail then drops down along a ridge heading south, finishing in a wash next to a large Ironwood tree. Turn right and hike several hundred yards into the large Hidden Springs Canyon, then turn left and head towards the right side of the canyon and the cliffs. After 1.4 miles from the trailhead note a large green Palo Verde tree growing next to the cliff and marked (at least at this time) by a large rock cairn. Hike in back of this large tree and climb up the small chute trail to your right. At the top, head down, then right into a small wash for 100 yards until arriving at the faint trail climbing left over the short hill. On the other side turn left and hug alongside the hills and the wash that may follow the hills. Hike towards the large green Palo Verde tree several hundred yards ahead. Notice the wash and flat ground heading east at about a 60-degree compass bearing. Follow the wash alongside the low hills that border it on the right, then as the wash turns left, follow it as it eventually turns right into a large canyon area. To get your bearings, at the first large Palo Verde tree mentioned earlier, note the light yellow or amber soil on top of the higher mountains due east. The canyon that takes you towards this area is the one you will follow.

As the wash climbs it effectively ushers you into a narrowing canyon. Stay in the main canyon, left, as it eventually winds its way higher along a narrow and often cool enclosed area. After a mile from leaving Hidden Springs Canyon, the canyon you are in will narrow at a dry falls. Note that to your left is a "rock chute" of colorful rocks, with a light lilac outcropping highlighting the top. Hike up this easy "stair-step" formation to the top.

At the top note the large deep canyon beneath you to your right...the 1st Grotto! To your left an explosion of lavender and brown rocks mark the entrance to Hidden Springs Oasis below. Carefully take the faint narrow trail up to your right and explore the wonders of "rainbow ridge" for 0.5 mile or more. But use extreme caution, as this trail is narrow, slippery, and very exposed! Return the same way that you came.

Uplift and rock strata, the Mecca Hills

11   1st Canyon Walkabout

(see map on page 41)

LENGTH: 7–9 miles

HIKING TIME: 3 hours

ELEVATION GAIN: 200 feet

DIFFICULTY: Easy

SEASON: October to April

INFORMATION:
No information available

DIRECTIONS

FOLLOW THE DIRECTIONS FOR PYRAMID CANYON, Hike #13. However, as you come into the curve in Box Canyon, look for the open space to your left, just as the canyon opens up at 2.2 miles past the green Painted Canyon sign. The dirt to the left of the road has been flattened due to past flash floods and is hard packed and easy to drive on. Drive off the road and park on the left, at 2.2 miles past Painted Canyon sign. You will pass another canyon on your left (close to the road, and blocked by several boulders) just before you get to the "real" first canyon. Drive just past this canyon that goes nowhere.

The Coffee Bean Canyon "look," Coffee Bean Canyon Walkabout

I named this hike "1st Canyon Walkabout" because this is the first viable and large enough to hike canyon on the left that you find along Box Canyon Road after passing Painted Canyon Road. Many branch canyons come off this canyon, which makes for a nice walkabout experience. The hike begins by entering the small gap 20-30 yards north of the road (in a 330 degree direction) and to your left. You will enter a private canyon where unfortunately some trash has been dumped. Continue up the canyon as it winds around. After 0.3 and 0.5 mile you'll see your first and second noticeable canyon openings on your right. On your way back these are canyons you may want to explore during this walkabout.

Continue in the main canyon for 0.8 miles from your starting point. Note the much larger canyon to the right, marked with a rock cairn. This canyon differs from the smaller notch-like canyons previously seen, as it appears as a separate canyon in its own right. Explore this canyon, staying in the main canyon on the left, for 0.4 mile where the canyon divides left and right. Explore either or both canyon branches, then return to the main canyon, turn right, and continue up-canyon until the canyon narrows. This last section of 1st Canyon becomes a small slot canyon before dead-ending at a sheer hillside. This hike shows you the possibilities that come from just hiking into a seemingly nondescript canyon and finding its many side-canyon adventures.

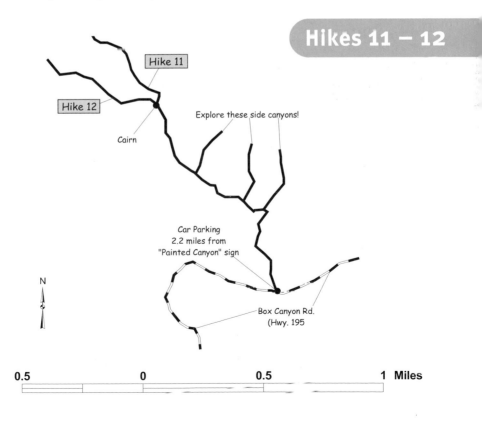

Hikes 11 — 12

Hike 11

Hike 12

Explore these side canyons!

Cairn

Car Parking
2.2 miles from
"Painted Canyon" sign

N

Box Canyon Rd.
(Hwy. 195

0.5   0   0.5   1 **Miles**

12 Silt Canyon

(see map on page 41)

LENGTH: 5–6 miles

HIKING TIME: 3 hours

ELEVATION GAIN: 500 feet

DIFFICULTY: Easy

SEASON: October to April

INFORMATION:
No information available

DIRECTIONS   Follow the directions for Hike 11.

This canyon has a few "surprises." Begin the hike into 1st Canyon, staying in the main canyon as it veers left. After 1.3 miles look for a canyon opening on your left. I've placed a pile of rocks (cairn) to the left and above the entrance. I

Desert Poppy in the Mecca Hills

call this "Silt" canyon because the past few floods have washed down generous amounts of silt onto the canyon floor, making this one of the easiest-on-your-feet hikes around.

The draw of Silt Canyon is to be found in the many "where-does-this-go?" side canyons that branch off the main canyon. As you go up this canyon, stay in the largest canyon to your right. We've tried to mark it with rock cairns. It will "surprise" you as to its meandering up-climb. How far does it go? Can we get out and over the top into the next canyon? See for yourself!

After finishing the main canyon, on your return, explore the many smaller side canyons...just to see where they go, too! Silt Canyon is a good example of the fun that one can have exploring the many exotic canyons found in the Mecca Hills area.

13 "Pyramid Canyon"

(see map on page 45)

LENGTH: 6.5 miles

HIKING TIME: 3 hours

ELEVATION GAIN: 800 feet

DIFFICULTY: Easy

SEASON: October to May

INFORMATION:
No information available

The canyons of the Mecca Hills empty out into Box Canyon and provide hikers with many opportunities to explore without the need of technical equipment. These canyon hikes are, for the most part, easy, though some offer rock scrambles to the tops of ridges with spectacular views of the Mecca Hills, the Salton Sea basin, and agricultural areas of the Coachella Valley. The colors that highlight these canyons—burnt sienna, beige, rust, white, dusty mauve, and occasionally green—are at their best on clear, sunny days, and early in the morning. All these canyon routes make great winter hikes.

DIRECTIONS

FOLLOW THE DIRECTIONS for Hike 1. After reaching the green sign for Painted Canyon, continue driving on Box Canyon Road (66th Avenue) for 2.5 miles. Park along the road or continue to the left on a short dirt road ending in front of a line of boulders that block vehicles from accessing the canyon.

Begin hiking Pyramid Canyon (designated by the author and not so named on any topo map) by heading north and entering the first canyon on your right, favoring the right side of the canyon for the first 0.25 mile. The hike meanders along a wash, past canyon walls. After 1.4 miles of hiking in the main (left favoring) canyon, you will come to a grouping of smoke trees. You will also notice that farther down canyon the hill formations are more contorted. After less than a half mile, you will notice a hill on your left that inspired this canyon's name, but you must walk past this hill for at least 50–70 yards and turn around, looking south in order to see its pyramid shape. Walk another 200 yards, then turn into the first large canyon on your right. (A variation of this hike continues down canyon as far as possible, following the canyon as it bends to the right, and then continuing to its end. Return to your car the same way you came).

After turning right into the large canyon just past the pyramid, hike until you come to the second canyon on your left. Turn into this canyon and continue as

The Pyramid in Pyramid Canyon

far as possible, noting that the canyon will narrow as it rises. When you can go no farther, you can either turn around or scramble up the steep slope on your left. Be very careful if you choose the slope, as the rocks and soil are loose. The view from the top is spectacular, revealing the Salton Sea basin with its many green agricultural areas and the dozens of colorful canyons making up the Mecca Hills. You can return by carefully going down the same steep slope you came up or by walking another 100 yards up the ridge, then carefully descending into the narrow canyon on the west side of the ridge. This canyon descent is challenging, with bushes and brush partially blocking the way as well as steep 4–6-foot dry falls. When you reach the canyon bottom, hike into the larger canyon, bear left, and continue for 0.5 mile back to the pyramid-shaped hill. From here, you can proceed down canyon and return to your vehicle.

Note: On these canyon-to-ridge-top hikes, several side canyons provide possible return routes. Simply remember that nearly every canyon return will be down hill, as all of the canyons in the Mecca Hills empty out onto Box Canyon Road, and this fact should allay your fear of getting "lost" in an unfamiliar canyon.

Hikes 13 – 26

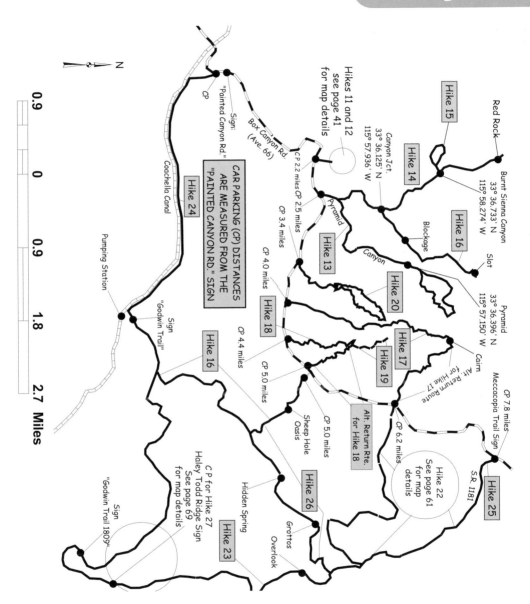

N

Hike 15

Red Rock

Hike 14

Burnt Sienna Canyon
33° 36.733' N
115° 58.274' W

Canyon Jct.
33° 36.125' N
115° 57.936' W

Hike 16

Blockage

Pyramid

Box Canyon Rd.
(Ave. 66)

Slot

Pyramid
33° 36.396' N
115° 57.150' W

CP
Sign:
"Painted Canyon Rd."

CP 2.2 miles CP 2.5 miles

CP 3.4 miles

Hike 13

Slot

Canyon

Hikes 11 and 12
see page 41
for map details

CP 4.0 miles

Hike 20

Cairn

CP 7.8 miles

Meccacopia Trail Sign

CAR PARKING (CP) DISTANCES
ARE MEASURED FROM THE
"PAINTED CANYON RD." SIGN

Hike 18

Hike 17

Alt. Return Route
for Hike 17

Hike 24

Coachella Canal

CP 4.4 miles

CP 5.0 miles

Hike 19

Hike 16

Pumping Station

Sign
"Godwin Trail"

Alt. Return Rte.
for Hike 18

Sheep Hole
Oasis

CP 5.0 miles

Hike 22
See page 61
for map
details

CP 6.2 miles

S.R. 1181

Hike 25

Hike 26

Hidden Spring

CP for Hike 27
Haley Todd Ridge Sign
See page 69
for map details

Hike 23

Grottos

Overlook

Sign
"Godwin Trail 1809"

0.9   0   0.9   0.9   1.8   2.7 Miles

14 Big Colorful Canyon

(see map on page 45)

LENGTH: 6 miles

HIKING TIME: 3 hours

ELEVATION GAIN: 350 feet

DIFFICULTY: Easy

SEASON: October to April

INFORMATION:
No information available

This hike takes you into one of the largest canyons in the Mecca Hills Wilderness complex, comprising dozens of canyons. Of key interest is the colorful rock wall at the back of the canyon, accented by multi-layered and colorful rock strata. The wall is highlighted by a collection of boulders the size of automobiles, showing up as a bright red-orange burst of color embedded into equally colorful mauve, creamy coral, burnt sienna, and gray bedrock. The size of this canyon is large enough to include several large connecting canyons branching off the main canyon, each one inviting hikers to explore the intricacies of this colorful area.

DIRECTIONS

FOLLOW THE DIRECTIONS for Hike #13, Pyramid Canyon. Go 2.4 miles past the green Painted Canyon sign, staying on the paved Box Canyon Road. There is usually a flat break in the dirt border along the road where you can turn left (after 2.4 miles) and drive on the hard pack dirt 50 yards to the large row of boulders blocking vehicles from entering the canyon.

Begin hiking past the row of boulders, favoring the large canyon veering slightly left. The floods of the past several years have scoured the canyon floor almost free of loose sand, making this hike easy on the feet. After 0.25 mile you will see to your right the first canyon breaking off the main canyon. This is Pyramid Canyon, Hike #13. Continue hiking, however, into the wider canyon as it winds to the left past a relief of sharp uplifted strata. The canyon curves several times back and forth. After 0.8 mile you will see a narrow canyon break to your right off the main canyon. This is Slot Canyon Cave Trail. Stay in the main canyon as it narrows a bit past Slot Canyon, then quickly enlarges and turns left. A few hundred yards up-canyon to your right, look for a large collapsed hillside, spilling large sandy boulders onto the canyon floor. It is as if a large sand dune has broken apart, because if you examine the sand boulders, they crumble easily into fine, almost beach-like sand.

The canyon veers slightly to the left after the rockslide, narrowing for a while, then brings you back into a larger open space. Stay in the main canyon, although after 1.3 miles you'll see another breakaway canyon veering to the right. Continue in what actually is a somewhat northerly direction, and you will soon see, ahead in the distance, a high relief of first dark, colorful rock walls, then an almost bright creamy white mountain on the furthest horizon, more than a mile away. This hike is taking you towards those dark, colorful rock walls.

As the canyon narrows again you will spot a large green tamarisk tree along the left side wall of the canyon. Approach quietly, as I've observed up

to 10 large owls nesting in that tree. Indeed, this entire area seems to have drawn a large contingent of owls, more than anywhere else in the desert that I've hiked. If you're lucky, several owls might take flight, either from the tree on the left, or from the Palo Verde tree situated above the canyon, to your right.

Continue hiking along the left side of the canyon until the canyon "splits" with a rocky hill formation dividing the canyon. Stay on the left side, and note the first large canyon to your left, usually marked by a rock pile cairn just to the right of the canyon. This is Burnt Sienna Cutoff Ridge Loop. Continue past this canyon until after 0.2 mile the canyon again opens up. Favor the wash to your right, from which you can usually see a large dark, dead tree ahead, killed by desert mistletoe, a plant that sucks trees dry.

Crumbling cliff in Big Colorful Canyon

Hike past the dead tree and soon you will see far up ahead as you turn past a side canyon wall, the now very close colorful canyon walls of Big Colorful Canyon. Hike favoring the left side of the canyon, aiming for the now observable large red-orange rock formations. Once there you will be treated to a colorful rocky area you can explore and admire for the explosion of color it offers. Finish the hike by continuing up the left side of the canyon for another 0.25 mile, then turn around and trace your route back to your parked car. Notice the magnificent view of the blue Salton Sea as you head back. This hike is best done on clear, sunny days, early in the morning. On cloudy days the color is almost absent.

15 Burnt Sienna Cutoff Ridge Loop
(see map on page 45)

LENGTH: 6 miles

HIKING TIME: 3 hours

ELEVATION GAIN: 600 feet

DIFFICULTY: Moderate

SEASON: October to April

INFORMATION:
No information available

This hike offers you a sense of adventurous exploration and rock scrambling and pays off with stunning vistas of the Salton Sea, the Santa Rosa Mountains, and the Mecca Hills Wilderness. Not for the faint of heart, as a rock scramble off-trail is part of the challenge.

DIRECTIONS Follow the directions for Hike 14.

Do the hike for Big Colorful Canyon. Just past the tamarisk tree where owls are often sighted, you will soon come to the first large canyon to your left. A rock pile cairn is usually found just right of the canyon's entrance. Turn left into this canyon, which I call Burnt Sienna Cutoff, because it cuts off from Big Colorful Canyon and has a rock wall the color of burnt sienna; continue going straight into the canyon, do not take the canyon to the left that appears after a hundred yards. Burnt Sienna Canyon curves back and forth and takes on the feel of a narrow slot canyon. At the first major junction, take the canyon to your left. At the next major junction (a few hundred yards) take the larger

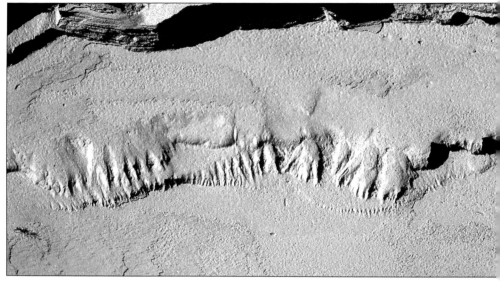

Miniature version of Mecca Hills!

canyon to the right (usually with boot prints in it), then at the next junction, veer left again. You will find that Burnt Sienna Canyon usually is the largest, flat-floored canyon at every turn. After 0.25 mile you will see the canyon narrow significantly, while climbing upwards in the process. Look for a pile of rocks (a cairn) just to the right of a small, fast rising draw that takes you up out of the canyon. Scramble up this slope to the top where another rock pile has been placed. Even if that cairn is gone, you will still arrive at the top after a hundred-yard steep hike up. You will find yourself on a little used trail atop the ridge, where magnificent views of the Salton Sea can be seen at once towards the south-east. Carefully follow the faint ridge trail as far as you are comfortable...it will be eroded in places and great care needs be exercised along the ridge. The best views of the Salton Sea basin can be had about 0.25 mile from where you accessed the ridge. Turn around and backtrack to where you first connected with the ridge, or head north along the ridge (the faint trail) until you come to the first ridge heading left and down into a large canyon. If you want to explore that canyon area, this is the safest and best route down; even then it's a challenge! Stay on the upper ridge trail for another 0.25 mile until arriving at a collection of three rock pile cairns, two to your left on the trail, and one to your right, down and on the trail to your right. Turn down and right at this juncture (but you can explore further north along the ridge to your heart's content). Before descending, look towards the southwest. You will see a great boulder-topped mountain and colorful rock formations. You are looking towards the area near which begins the famous Painted Canyon/ Ladder Canyon hike. Mt. San Jacinto can be seen on the western horizon.

Take the narrow trail down off the ridge to your right, heading back towards and into Big Colorful Canyon. After 0.25 mile you'll come to your first ridge heading right. Continue past this ridge and down towards your left to the next ridge, then hike along the ridge until you can see where a small canyon begins. Turn down and right, slowly making your way down and back into Burnt Sienna Canyon. Continue down and to your left until finally reaching the canyon floor. Even if you mistakenly take the wrong canyon down, you should eventually empty out into Big Colorful Canyon and back towards the trailhead.

This hike is for the adventurous willing to try a bushwhack off-trail experience that offers an exotic slot canyon and ridge vista payoff!

16 Slot Canyon Cave Trail

(see map on page 45)

LENGTH: 6.5 miles

HIKING TIME: 3 hours

ELEVATION GAIN: 100 feet

DIFFICULTY: Easy

SEASON: October to April

INFORMATION:
No information available

This hike offers both a slot canyon and a cave-like rock structure at trail's end where owls have been seen nesting. Slot canyon, cave and owls… Let's go!

DIRECTIONS   Follow the directions for Hike 14.

After 0.8 mile in Big Colorful Canyon, take the narrow canyon to your right. This is Slot Canyon Cave Trail (I name these trails, not the BLM, so don't look for them on any topo map!).

The trail quickly opens into a large Utah-like canyon and should be done on a clear day, in the early morning. Follow the canyon floor and note the scenic formations above you throughout the canyon. After 0.5 mile you'll come to a massive wall collapse, where a large section of canyon wall on your right

Colorful mesas near Pyramid Canyon, Mecca Hills

has fallen onto, and covers, the entire canyon floor. Negotiate this slide by veering to your left. Continue in the main canyon, passing another slide almost 0.5 mile past the first one. After hiking 1.8 miles from the canyon entrance, you'll come to a major split. Take the canyon to your right where large dark rocks accent and cover the canyon floor. Proceed up this canyon and enjoy narrowing curves and eventually a slot canyon that is quite fun for kids to meander through. As the slot canyon narrows it ends in a large cave-like chamber. You can scramble up the first rock ledge and once up and in, look back as the space opens up... you'll see a huge rock block that has broken off the canyon wall, as if a knife blade cut it off. Just up ahead is the last cave area, blocked by a 20-foot rock wall. No flashlights are needed, just a sense of adventure, as the "cave area" reminds one of what the home of a stone-age man might have looked like!

17 "Little Utah Canyon"

(see map on page 45)

LENGTH: 5 miles

HIKING TIME: 2 hours

ELEVATION GAIN: 600 feet

DIFFICULTY: Easy

SEASON: October to May

INFORMATION:
No information available

This colorful area is reminiscent of the low hills in southern Utah, which exhibit a similar reddish soil offset by layers of white and other lightly colored soil or rock strata.

> **DIRECTIONS**
>
> **FOLLOW THE DIRECTIONS** for Hike 1. Continue driving on Box Canyon Road 4 miles past the green Painted Canyon sign. Turn left off the road and park in front of the BLM sign that says Closed Area. The hike begins behind this sign.

Begin hiking into the large canyon in back of the sign, staying to the left and in the larger center canyon. After a mile, you will see colorful hills of burnt sienna, beige, and grayish rust, highlighted by well-defined white sandy strata. Turn left at the area of white strata and stay left at any canyon junction you come to.

After 2 miles the canyon narrows while taking the hiker higher up towards the surrounding ridge tops. Stay left in the larger canyon as it narrows until you reach

Hiking above Little Utah Canyon

what looks like a dead end. Scramble carefully up the left side of the hill to the top of the ridge, with views of the Salton Sea basin and the colorful reddish-beige canyons in this area of the Mecca Hills. Return to your vehicle via the same canyon you climbed up, or take the following, more challenging, alternative.

After walking at least 100 yards farther up the ridge, look to the southeast at the lower ridges where a faint jeep trail can still be seen. Hike down to this jeep trail and south along it for 50 yards until you can scramble down into the larger canyon looking east. This descent is not easy, and requires careful rock scrambling. You will enter a narrow canyon marked by brush and small dry falls. After hiking down for 0.25 mile, you will see a larger canyon that opens on the right. Another 0.75 mile of hiking down this larger canyon brings you to Box Canyon Road. Turn right and continue for 1.5 miles to your parked vehicle. A thru hike is possible by parking cars at both ends of this route, but the total distance of the hike without a shuttle is 5 miles.

18 "Utah Canyons" Overlook

(see map on page 45)

LENGTH: 4 miles

HIKING TIME: 2 hours

ELEVATION GAIN: 400 feet

DIFFICULTY: Easy

SEASON: October to May

INFORMATION:
No information available

DIRECTIONS

FOLLOW THE DIRECTIONS for Hike 1. Drive on Box Canyon Road 4.4 miles past the Painted Canyon sign, turn left for 20 yards, and park in front of the pair of thin wilderness signs.

Begin hiking into the canyon directly to the right and in back of the signs. This hike is similar to Little Utah Canyon but offers a more spectacular view and interesting return options. After nearly 0.5 mile, take the canyon to your left. In less than 0.25 mile it will split into several canyon routes. Take the far right canyon, which will continually narrow while climbing higher. At the very end of this canyon, climb carefully onto the ridge to the left. Continue hiking along the ridge as it rises higher to the left. The ridge must be carefully negotiated, as it is very narrow. After 0.25 mile, you will come to the high point of this ridge,

Colorful rock formations, Little Utah Canyon

overlooking many scenic and colorful reddish canyons and offering panoramas of the Salton Sea basin. You can return to your vehicle by backtracking the way you came, or take the following, more adventurous, return route.

Look to the east from the high point of the ridge for a white sandy soil outcropping. Carefully negotiate down toward this sandy area, staying in the basin to the right of it. After 50 yards, look over the left ridge for a safe descent into the large canyon in front of you. Once down in the canyon, continue downhill to the right. You will pass a deep red canyon wall on your left, made by rust-colored soil seeping down over the cliff wall after rainfalls. The canyon empties out onto Box Canyon Road, and by walking to the right along the road, you will reach your vehicle after 0.5 mile.

Little Utah Canyon rock strata, Mecca Hills

19 "Big Utah Canyon"

(see map on page 45)

LENGTH: 4.5 miles

HIKING TIME: 2 hours

ELEVATION GAIN: 400 feet

DIFFICULTY: Easy

SEASON: October to May

INFORMATION:
No information available

The name "Big Utah" emphasizes this canyon's size compared to the other Utah-like canyons nearby. The colors are rich, deep, and best viewed in early morning sunlight.

DIRECTIONS

FOLLOW THE DIRECTIONS for Hike 1. Drive on Box Canyon Road for 5 miles past the green Painted Canyon sign and park safely on the side of the road. This canyon hike begins on the left side of the road, a few hundred yards before the turnoff for Sheep Hole Oasis Trail.

Begin hiking in the wide wash that empties onto the road shoulder. Stay to the left, going behind the large trees at the canyon entrance. The canyon begins to narrow, but stays relatively wide during most of this hike. In less than 0.5 mile, the Utah-like feeling created by various shades of camel, rust, and creamy hues of white highlight the canyon walls. Areas of dark red wash down over lighter shades of cream near the bottom of the canyon.

Colorful rock strata, near the Grottos

Stay to the left, and eventually the canyon narrows considerably. Negotiate around any brush that grows on the canyon floor, enjoying the mystery of discovering what lies around each bend as the canyon winds ever higher. When you can go no farther, try rock scrambling up to a ridge to enjoy the scenic vistas of this colorful area in the Mecca Hills. Return the same way you came.

As with all these canyon hikes, I encourage an early morning departure to ensure a sky free from overcast or haze. The rich colors of the canyons merit this attention to aesthetics. The side canyons in this area are also worth exploring.

20   "Never Ending Canyon" Loop

(see map on page 45)

LENGTH: 4 miles

HIKING TIME: 2 hours

ELEVATION GAIN: 500 feet

DIFFICULTY: Easy

SEASON: October to May

INFORMATION:
No information available

This hike is a perfect combination of fun and scenic beauty. The kid in you will enjoy this loop hike while your own kids will love the adventure. A clear, early morning sky is the ideal accompaniment for this hike.

> ### DIRECTIONS
>
> **FOLLOW THE DIRECTIONS** for Hike 1. Drive on Box Canyon Road for 3.4 miles past the green Painted Canyon sign. Either turn off directly to the left where you can see a flat road shoulder and a faint road, or park safely off the side of the road.

This hike begins to the left of the road by crossing over the shoulder and following the faint dirt road to the north. This road goes for 30–40 yards then turns right, around a small ridge. Several-dozen large boulders block vehicles from driving into the canyon. Hike past these boulders and into the canyon, going just to the left and behind the small BLM sign in the canyon wash. Continue up canyon, favoring the left side. After about 15 minutes of walking, you will come to a canyon junction marked by a small, rusty icebox in the side canyon to your right. Continue hiking in the canyon to the left. You will pass a rusted old car wreck and, in a few minutes, arrive at another canyon divide. Here the canyon breaks into three canyons. Avoid the smaller right-hand canyon (I put a stone line across its entrance for clarity) but take the middle canyon that winds around

Desert canyon wash

to the right of a small hill feature in the middle of the canyon floor. Do not take the canyon to the far left around the hill.

As you continue your ascent, stay in the largest canyon that veers left at one juncture then right at another. The canyon walls become colorful, sometimes showing alternating soil and rock strata. This canyon winds ever higher in fantastic bends and turns, and requires you to negotiate small rockslides or dry falls. This giant but narrow slot canyon is like a maze, challenging you to keep hiking in order to both see what's still ahead and if you'll ever get out (trust me...you will)!

After 1.75 miles, the canyon narrows up to an easily ascended ridge. Enjoy the rewarding views from the ridge, and then hike up and to the left for a few more yards until you come to the saddle. From here, begin climbing down the gentle slope that marks the next canyon, to your left. This stair-step decent is relatively easy and is not marked by excessive steepness or thick brush.

As you come down the trail, you will notice the flat, sandy, somewhat rock-free canyon floor that makes the return part of this loop hike easier than most in the area. The canyon widens as it heads downward and keeps you guessing where and when you will come out. After 1.5 miles, this canyon joins the one you ascended at the hike's beginning. Note that the two canyons forming this loop are very different in feel, color, and geology, even though they are separated by just a few yards. Continue heading down, staying in the largest canyon, which mostly keeps to the left. You will soon reach your vehicle, completing this pleasant 4-mile outing.

21) The Meccacopia Trail to Salton Sea Overlook (see map on page 45)

LENGTH: 7 miles

HIKING TIME: 3 hours

ELEVATION GAIN: 200 feet

DIFFICULTY: Easy

SEASON: October to May

INFORMATION: BLM Office, Palm Springs, (760) 251-4800

DIRECTIONS

FOLLOW THE DIRECTIONS for Hike 1. Continue driving on Box Canyon Road for 7.8 miles past the Painted Canyon sign. You will see a sign with a large white map on your right. Pull off the road and park near this sign.

This hike, which leads to the western edge of the Orocopia Mountains north and east of the area known as The Grottos, begins on the dirt road to the left of the sign. It enters a sandy-bottomed canyon, marked at the entrance by a signpost designating the Meccacopia Trail SR1811. After 0.5 miles, the trail climbs onto a rocky plateau, turns south, and skirts the western edge of the mountains. Along the way, you will see some interesting rock formations and many outcroppings of white quartz.

After 1.9 miles, this trail junctions with Little Box Canyon Trail which veers off to the right and joins with Box Canyon Road south of the Meccacopia Trailhead. Continue on the Meccacopia Trail as it winds through the edge of these foothills, through canyon washes and eventually onto a plateau almost 3.5 miles from your start. From here, the trail offers you a lovely

Ocotillo in bloom

view of the Salton Sea and the mountains to the south and southwest, which house the cave structures known as The Grottos. Return by the same route.

This trail is best done early in the morning on a sunny day, when the sunlight plays off the rock formations and glistens on the Salton Sea. An easy hike with little elevation gain, you might choose to extend it by bushwhacking into the foothills to examine the white quartz deposits.

22 Meccacopia/Little Box Canyon Loop

(see map on page 61)

LENGTH: 7.5 miles

HIKING TIME: 3 hours

ELEVATION GAIN: 800 feet

DIFFICULTY: Moderate

SEASON: October to April

INFORMATION:
No information available

This is a great "wet winter" hike into the backcountry of the western Orocopia Wilderness, where you see great valley vistas, negotiate narrow canyons, and get a very personal feel for this section of wilderness hiking.

> **DIRECTIONS** Same as for the Meccacopia Trail to Salton Sea Overlook, Hike 21.

To make this a loop hike with two cars, drive 6.3 miles on Box Canyon Road past the green Painted Canyon sign, and park one car to the right in front of the white BLM map sign for the Orocopia Wilderness at Little Box Canyon trailhead. The other car can drive another 1.5 miles to the BLM sign on the right side of the road that begins the Meccacopia Trail.

If you don't have two cars, you'll have to walk on the road back to your car after the hike. Begin hiking past the Meccacopia Trailhead sign, following the wash trail as it turns right into the canyon ahead. The wash portion of this trail can be surprisingly lush in a wet winter or spring. After a mile the trail climbs out of the wash and offers views of the surrounding mountains. It soon turns east, taking you into a hidden valley, a place that is tranquil and off the beaten path.

After 2.2 miles this trail intersects the Little Box Canyon Trail heading right and west. Stay on the Meccacopia Trail for another 2 miles, being treated to beautiful vista views of the Salton Sea to the south. The trail will, at this point, become very rocky. At the brown Wilderness Access sign, turn right into the canyon wash heading away from the trail. This portion of the hike is an adventurous bushwack.

Stay in the wash as it gradually narrows and veers west and right, entering a canyon with rising walls. After 0.5 mile, take the first large canyon you come to that turns right away from the canyon you've been hiking in. This is a fun canyon, a little exotic in its presentation and rock formations. At the first junction after hiking not quite 0.5 mile, turn left into the canyon that veers left. Stay left for another 0.5 mile in this canyon, negotiating vegetation and brush and watching for a large owl that inhabits the vicinity. Gradually the canyon rises and loses its enclosed feeling, as low foothills begin to rise to your left and right. After 1.5 miles of hiking past and right of the brown Wilderness Access sign, look for the first jeep trails climbing out of the canyon up the steep hill to your left. Just past the first jeep trail, look for a jeep trail climbing out of the canyon on your right.

Take this trail up and out of the canyon, eventually reaching elevation points that give spectacular sweeping vistas of the Sea and the surrounding mountains, canyons, and valleys. Stay on this up and down trail as it negotiates the top of this plateau area, then drops steeply after 0.5 mile into Little Box Canyon. Once in the canyon, turn left (west), and you will arrive at the Little Box Canyon Trailhead, just off Box Canyon Road, after 1.7 miles.

This loop hike is fun and offers you the feeling of an exploratory adventure. From the top of the trail you'll see slashes of white quartz outcroppings that first drew prospectors to these parts over 100 years ago (Orocopia is Spanish for "much gold").

Califonia poppies in the Mecca Hills

Hike 22

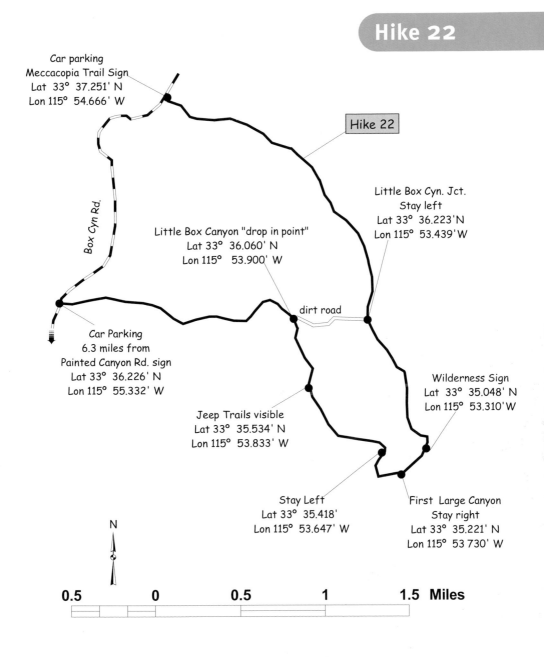

Car parking
Meccacopia Trail Sign
Lat 33° 37.251' N
Lon 115° 54.666' W

Hike 22

Little Box Cyn. Jct.
Stay left
Lat 33° 36.223'N
Lon 115° 53.439'W

Box Cyn Rd.

Little Box Canyon "drop in point"
Lat 33° 36.060' N
Lon 115° 53.900' W

dirt road

Car Parking
6.3 miles from
Painted Canyon Rd. sign
Lat 33° 36.226' N
Lon 115° 55.332' W

Wilderness Sign
Lat 33° 35.048' N
Lon 115° 53.310'W

Jeep Trails visible
Lat 33° 35.534' N
Lon 115° 53.833' W

Stay Left
Lat 33° 35.418'
Lon 115° 53.647' W

First Large Canyon
Stay right
Lat 33° 35.221' N
Lon 115° 53 730' W

N

0.5   0   0.5   1   1.5 Miles

23 The Meccacopia Trail to the Godwin Trail (see map on page 45)

LENGTH: 14.5 miles

HIKING TIME: 6 hours

ELEVATION GAIN: 300 feet

DIFFICULTY: Strenuous

SEASON: October to May

INFORMATION: BLM Office, Palm Springs, (760) 251-4800

DIRECTIONS   Follow the directions for Hike 21.

This hike gives you that out-in-the-wilderness, away-from-it-all feeling. Strenuous only because of the length, it offers hikers an opportunity to venture far without much elevation gain, and offers opportunities to explore interesting rock formations.

Begin hiking the Meccacopia Trail from the trailhead on Box Canyon Road. Roughly 3.5 miles past the Salton Sea overlook area, the trail drops down into a narrow canyon, winds south past colorful foothills to the right, and breaks out into the wide-open spaces north of the Salton Sea. You can see jeep trails to the east leading into foothill canyons, while hills border the trail to the west.

The trail continues winding into canyons and joins up with the Godwin Trail after 7.3 miles. (Look for the canyon rising to the right marked by a BLM trail post marked Godwin Trail 1809.) Return to your vehicle the same way you came.

Desert wash along the Godwin Trail

This route affords hikers a great "out-there" experience, good exercise, and interesting canyon and hill accents. Start early in the warmer months and bring plenty of water, as this trail warms up during the day and offers little or no shade.

24 The Godwin Trail

(see map on page 45)

LENGTH: 14 miles

HIKING TIME: 6 hours

ELEVATION GAIN: 200 feet

DIFFICULTY: Strenuous

SEASON: October to May

INFORMATION: BLM Office,
Palm Springs, (760) 251-4800

DIRECTIONS

FOLLOW THE DIRECTIONS for Hike 1. Drive down and past the canal, and park to the right at the first safe, convenient location on the roadside, several hundred yards before the Painted Canyon sign. Hike up to the Canal Road, built atop the dike just north of the canal. From here, turn left (or east) and begin hiking along the canal. This hike is best done in the early morning with clear skies.

The first stretch of this hike runs along the beautiful Coachella Canal, offering scenic views of the Salton Sea and wide expanses of verdant farmland. In less than a half mile, the agricultural lands become desert, but green fields can still be seen in the distance along with spectacular vistas of the Coachella Valley and the southern

Santa Rosa & San Jacinto Mountains National Monument Visitor Center

Santa Rosa Mountains. In winter months, the lacelike grapevines can be seen, and, by February and March, vibrant green leaves accent these vineyards.

Continue east along and above the canal. After 3 miles, turn left and head down the side road leading north and off the canal. (A pump facility and a split in the canal on the other side of the waterway mark this junction.) Hike on the dirt trail leading into the large canyon north of the canal. After 0.25 mile, you will see where this road meets the Godwin Trail coming in from your left. Continue north, up canyon (do not turn left at this junction or you end up right back at your vehicle), and turn right where the BLM sign post indicates the Godwin Trail is straight ahead. This stretch of Godwin Trail winds through the canyon, with interesting side canyons and colorful rock formations that invite you to explore. After 4 miles, you'll meet the Meccacopia Trail, the turn-around point for this hike. Return to your vehicle the same way you came.

This hike offers rich diversity of scenery and the opportunity to spend a long leisurely day in the desert.

25 Sheep Hole Oasis/Godwin Trail
Shuttle (see map on page 45)

LENGTH: 7 miles

HIKING TIME: 3 hours

ELEVATION GAIN: 100 feet

DIFFICULTY: Easy

SEASON: October to May

INFORMATION:
No information available

DIRECTIONS

FOLLOW THE DIRECTIONS for Hike 24. You will need to park one car just to the right of Box Canyon Road where that road drops down after crossing the Coachella Canal (see Hike 15). The other car(s) should continue on Box Canyon Road for 5 miles past the green Painted Canyon sign, and turn right at the sign for Sheep Hole Oasis. Follow the dirt road 100 yards to the parking area and a sign marking Sheep Hole Oasis Trail.

The hike begins just behind the sign and follows a small wash for 50 yards before climbing up a hill. When the trail first tops out, hikers are treated to spectacular views of the Salton Sea basin, the Santa Rosa Mountains, and the surrounding Mecca Hills and Orocopia Mountains. A second, more expansive, view comes after hiking another 100 yards up the hill to its final top. From here, hike down the trail, noticing the palm oasis in the wash to your left. The small hole at the base of the left palm tree is the water source known as Sheep Hole Oasis.

Turn right at the base of the hill, and proceed several hundred yards until this side canyon empties out into the larger Hidden Springs Canyon. Turn right into this canyon, and follow the gentle, down-slanting canyon bottom, always staying in the main canyon. The floor of this canyon has a fairly hard surface and makes for easy walking.

The canyon eventually opens into a wide wash area, joining the Godwin Trail, which heads to the left. Stay right

Hikers in 1st Grotto

in the large wash, and continue hiking down canyon all the way to the canal. Walk up the small dirt road that brings you to the top of the canal, and turn right (west). For the next 3 miles back to your car, you will be treated to expansive views of the Salton Sea and agricultural lands.

An alternate, more difficult, and less scenic return is done by turning right onto the Godwin Trail as you exit Hidden Springs Canyon. This section of trail is more friendly to jeeps than to hikers. If you do not set a vehicle shuttle, 5 miles are added to the hike back along Box Canyon Road to Sheep Hole Oasis.

26 Sheep Hole Oasis/The Grottos/ Meccacopia Trail Shuttle (see map on page 45)

LENGTH: 8 miles	SEASON: October to May
HIKING TIME: 4 hours	INFORMATION:
ELEVATION GAIN: 400 feet	No information available
DIFFICULTY: Moderate	

This fun and adventurous hike leads to the cave system known as The Grottos and above the Hidden Springs Oasis. Bear in mind that there are dark, confining spaces in The Grottos, and some of this hike requires crawling on hands and knees. Bring good flashlights!

DIRECTIONS

FOLLOW DIRECTIONS for Hike 1. Drive on Box Canyon Road for 7.8 miles past the green Painted Canyon sign. Park one vehicle on the right side of the road next to the map/sign for the Meccacopia Trail, then drive back 2.8 miles, turning left at the sign for Sheep Hole Oasis Trail. Park the other vehicle at this trailhead. Hiking from Sheep Hole Oasis to the Meccacopia Trailhead allows for a more leisurely hike with less uphill.

Begin hiking the trail behind the sign for Sheep Hole Oasis, follow it through a short narrow wash and up a hillside where two succeeding hilltops offer spectacular views of the Salton Sea basin and the Mecca Hills. Come down the trail and along the ridgetop, looking to your left at the canyon palm cluster known as Sheep Hole Oasis. At the bottom of the hill, head right for a few hundred yards, then turn left into the larger Hidden Springs Canyon. Proceed along the right side of this canyon next to the cliffs in order to see some of the interesting geology here.

The canyon narrows after about a mile, and takes you past sheer cliff walls. After hiking several hundred yards in this narrow stretch, look for the first small canyon to your left, highlighted by colorful rocks and soil. Carefully negotiate this small canyon, and after 50 yards you will come to Hidden Springs Oasis. Continue past the oasis for another 25 yards, veering into the

Hidden Springs Oasis

canyon ahead and to the right. Stay to the right as you turn into this canyon wash, and begin scrambling left up the hillside. You will most likely notice a makeshift trail leading to the top of the hill. Be very careful, as the hillside is composed of loose soil and rock. Once at the top, hike north along the ridge, away from the oasis, and be sure to look behind you as the spectacular vista opens.

After 0.75 mile, the trail turns to the right and heads down a very steep jeep road. After reaching the bottom of the hill, continue for another 50 yards or so and look for another narrow, steep jeep trail (gully is more like it) that heads down and right into another canyon. Turn right at the bottom of the hill to enter the caves (another 0.25 mile), from their north-facing backside. Be careful so you don't hit your head against protruding rocks on the low ceilings and narrow walls of the cave.

When you are finished exploring The Grottos, double back to where you entered the canyon at the bottom of the second steep jeep trail. Hike east by southeast in the narrow canyon, favoring the right side. After 0.5–0.75 mile, you will notice a wide wash going off in a northeast (left) direction. Follow this wash as it pulls away from the canyons and mountains, and in roughly 0.5 mile you will reach the obvious and well-traveled Meccacopia Trail (jeep road). Turn left onto this trail, and continue for 3-plus miles until the trail winds down and west towards Box Canyon Road and to your parked vehicle. You will be able to see the I-10 Freeway and all its traffic when you are less than a half-hour from the parking area.

27 Mystery Cairns Hike

(see map on page 69)

LENGTH: 4 miles

HIKING TIME: 2 – 3 hours

ELEVATION GAIN: 1,000 feet

DIFFICULTY: Moderate/Strenuous

SEASON: October to April

INFORMATION:
No information available

DIRECTIONS

4WD ONLY. This hike is in the very backcountry of the Orocopia Mountain Wilderness and the dirt roads necessitate 4wd vehicles only. I will give you two different sets of directions:

option 1: Coming from I-10, go almost 20 miles east past Indio to the Joshua Tree National Park/Mecca turn off. Turn right and drive towards Mecca for almost 7 miles. As you enter the Box Canyon area, look for a large white BLM map sign on your left, just off the road. Drive left off the paved road and continue past the sign and in 100 yards enter the small canyon on your right, marked by a post sign "Meccacopia Trail." Drive on this rough jeep road for almost 6 miles, then look for the sign post on your right indicating Haley Todd Ridge Trail. Park in this area. Note the steep jeep trail right and up the hill to a fence in front of the trail.

option 2: Another shorter drive is by following the driving directions for Hike #1, Painted Canyon/Ladder Canyon. Just before you reach the green Painted Canyon sign, drive right and off the road to the BLM sign post marker indicating the Godwin Trail. Drive over this rough dirt jeep trail for almost 2 miles, then right at the dirt road heading towards the Dike/Canal several hundred yards south, just past the large Power Lines. Drive up to the canal road on top, turn left and drive over 1 mile to the pumping station. Turn left down off the canal road and head north towards the large canyon/wash; you should see the BLM sign post for the Godwin Trail. Drive on this dirt jeep trail as it heads north/east then turns right into a large canyon. Continue for almost 1.3 miles until the canyon area begins to dramatically open up. Park just before the very steep down incline part of this jeep trail. Begin hiking down the steep drop and east for 0.75 mile until you reach another BLM sign post indicating the Haley Todd Ridge Trail to your left. Follow this canyon left and eventually up a very steep incline to a hilltop where a trail going steeply up the mountain to your left can be accessed by walking around the fence. This begins the trail.

This hike offers probably the most exotic, vista and color-filled canyon sights in this entire area. The trail leads steeply up to 5 "Mystery Cairns" because who made them and for what purpose? But it's a long hard drive to get there. Also the first 1.5 miles is straight up! The views of the Salton Sea Basin, the eastern Orocopia Mountains, and the "Badlands" canyons beneath you, as well as the "Rainbow Canyon" area near the 2nd Grotto makes it all worth it!

Begin hiking past the fence in front of the trail. Carefully negotiate this very one-after-another up hill adventure until arriving at the first of 5 "Mystery Cairns"—tall rock piles situated at the top of the mountain and along the trail. Note the explosion of colorful soil and canyon rock beneath you and to your right (regardless of what return route you choose, continue all the way to the last [5th] cairn in order to glimpse the spectacular color of the down slopes to your right). At the 2nd hilltop comprised of several cairns you can turn around and trace your steps back to your vehicles, depending where you parked/which approach you came in on. Or you can return a different way by heading west down the last steep incline (before reaching the last cairn). At the saddle, look for the very narrow faint trail to the right and heading down. Carefully take this trail down and right. It will first take you down a ways, then confront you with a large mountain top in front of you, heading north. Hike to the top, then at a 45-degree angle make a left for the down slope that drops you down a steep slope to a saddle. Turn right and down (east) and negotiate this gully until it bottoms into a canyon wash and eventually spills out onto the large Meccacopia Trail (dirt jeep trail). Turn right and after almost a mile you will reach your vehicle at the Haley Todd Trailhead. This hike offers great picture taking opportunities!

Box Canyon, dividing the Mecca Hills and the Orocopia Mountains

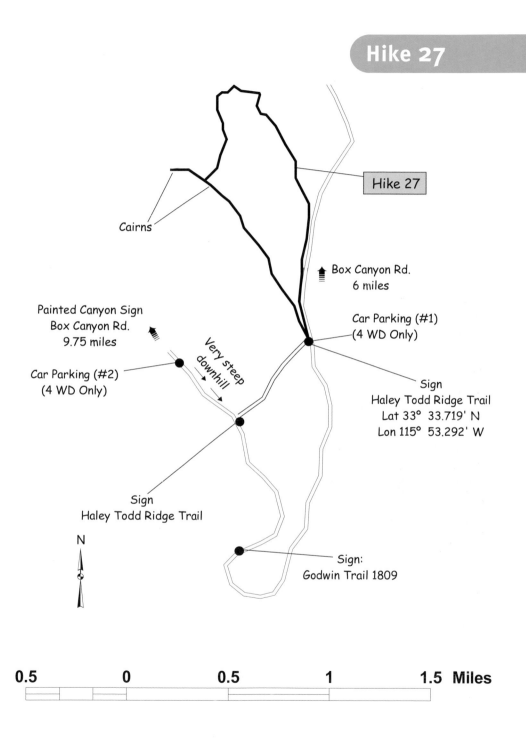

Hike 27

Cairns

Box Canyon Rd.
6 miles

Painted Canyon Sign
Box Canyon Rd.
9.75 miles

Car Parking (#1)
(4 WD Only)

Car Parking (#2)
(4 WD Only)

Very steep
downhill

Sign
Haley Todd Ridge Trail
Lat 33° 33.719' N
Lon 115° 53.292' W

Sign
Haley Todd Ridge Trail

N

Sign:
Godwin Trail 1809

0.5   0   0.5   1   1.5 Miles

28 "Coffee Bean Canyon"
(see map opposite)

LENGTH: 9 miles

HIKING TIME: 4 hours

ELEVATION GAIN: 300 feet

DIFFICULTY: Moderate

SEASON: October to May

INFORMATION:
No information available

DIRECTIONS

DRIVE EAST on I-10, just past Indio. Turn right onto 86s Expressway. After approximately 6 miles turn left onto Airport Blvd. and proceed 2 miles to the canal. Park at the canal. If you have a 4wd, continue up the road for 50 yards, over the canal, and past several sets of giant tires. Then turn right after the tires onto a small dirt road and follow it along the north side of the canal, heading east for approximately 2 miles. Turn left into the canyon where the dirt road goes into and park where convenient. Coffee Bean Canyon is the large canyon that the road continues into.

I named this hike to reflect the unique color and texture of the soil through and around the canyon. No topo map of the area will show a canyon named Coffee Bean, but after doing the hike you might agree with me! This hike should be done early in the morning on a bright sunny day for the maximum color effect.

Begin the hike by crossing over Airport Boulevard and the bridge over the canal, and walking up to the canal road. Turn right and continue along the canal road for 2 miles, enjoying magnificent vistas of rich farmland, the Santa Rosa Mountains, and the Salton Sea. A rock quarry and the beginnings of the Mecca Hills can be seen to the left.

After heading east by southeast for 2 miles, turn left down the dirt road coming off the canal road, and head into the large canyon. You will immediately see why this area is so named. Interesting soil and rock formations accent the canyon as it winds in a serpentine fashion before opening out into a fantastic vista of open space, canyons, and foothills. The massive 1,600-foot Mecca Hill lies directly to the north.

Continue on the dirt road, passing contorted, uplifted canyon foothills to your right forming a wall of canyons. If you head east, to the far end of this wall, you will be able to carefully scramble up the low hills and glimpse the stunning Salton Sea basin. Return to your vehicle the same way you came.

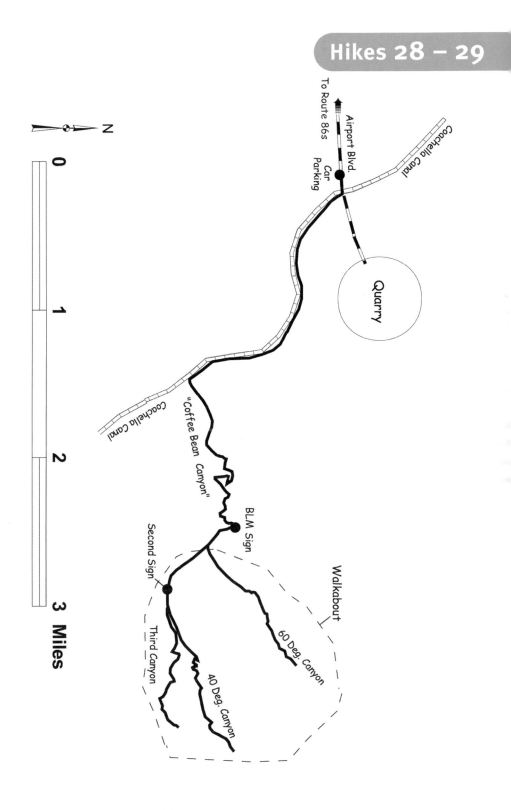

Hikes 28 – 29

29 "Coffee Bean Canyon"/Mecca Hill Canyons Walkabout (see map on page 71)

LENGTH: 13 miles

HIKING TIME: 6 hours

ELEVATION GAIN: 700 feet

DIFFICULTY: Strenuous

SEASON: October to May

INFORMATION:
No information available

This walkabout offers a lot of flexibility to wander wherever your interests lead you. Although the hike outlined here focuses on three main canyons that surround Mecca Hill, I encourage you to investigate any canyon, hill formation, or soil outcropping that draws your attention. A hike through these challenging, beautiful canyons—one of my favorite adventures—should be done on a clear sunny day.

DIRECTIONS
Follow the directions and hike description for Hike 28, "Coffee Bean Canyon."

After coming through Coffee Bean Canyon, the trail/dirt road veers to the right. You will shortly come to a BLM sign. Roughly 50–75 yards past the sign, note the canyon area to the north and left of the peak of Mecca Hill. This canyon lies at about a 60 degree compass bearing. Walk up the wash and into the canyon, and go as far as the canyon will allow you. Any side canyons of interest are yours to explore.

Return to the sign and the trail and continue walking east. You will see a second sign in less than 0.5 mile. Hike into the low wash to your left, just before this sign. After several hundred yards, you will come to a canyon. Continue past this canyon as the wash narrows. Your next canyon,

Dramatic dark coloration; Coffee Bean Canyon

to the left, is one you will want to explore. It lies at a 40 degree bearing and to the right of the peak of Mecca Hill. If you choose to continue through the narrowing wash, you will come to a third canyon that veers left and northeast. This canyon shouldn't be missed. When you are finished exploring, return to your vehicle the same way you came.

Coachella Valley Preserve HIKES 30 – 34

The 13,000-acre Coachella Valley Preserve is a lush concentration of California fan palms, rising miraculously in the alluvial gravel and sand deposits from the Little San Bernardino Mountains and Indio Hills. The San Andreas Fault encourages water to seep up to the surface. Here seeds of the fan palm, nourished by this once subterranean water, have grown into more than 1,200 palms. A trail system has been built to assist the visitor in seeing the wondrous effects of water and plant life surrounded by desert sands, low hills, and gentle canyons.

Coachella Valley Preserve Hikes 30 – 34

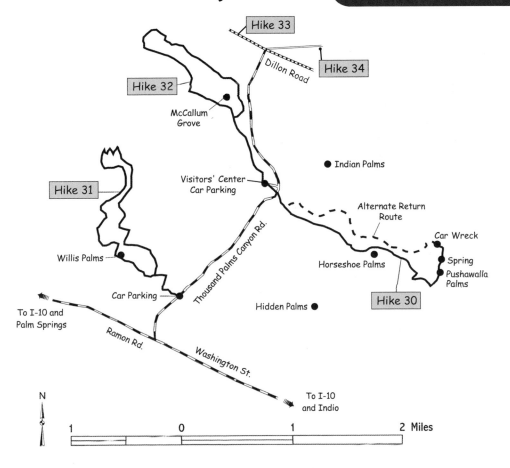

30 Pushawalla Palms and Canyon Trail

(see map on page 73)

LENGTH: 6 miles

HIKING TIME: 4 hours

ELEVATION GAIN: 300 feet

DIFFICULTY: Easy

SEASON: October to April

INFORMATION: Coachella Valley Preserve, Thousand Palms (760) 343-1234

DIRECTIONS

TO REACH THE PRESERVE, drive on I-10 to Washington Street exit, and drive left (north) for 5 miles, reaching Thousand Palms Canyon Road. Turn right and park in the preserve, located 2 miles after the turn.

From I-10, turn onto Ramon Road, left accross the overpass, and drive several miles until reaching 1000Palms Canyon Rd. Turn left and drive until reaching the CV Preserve Visitor's Center.

To begin the Pushawalla Palms Trail, head southeast from the parking lot toward the rocky bluff across the road.

Once up the hill you will be atop Bee-Rock Mesa. A trail heads to the left and takes you above Horseshoe Palms and then on into Pushawalla Palms Canyon. Or you can hike in a more southeast direction to arrive at the canyon before dropping down to explore the full length of the oasis. Pushawalla Palms represents a

long grove of palms growing in the narrow Pushawalla Canyon. There is a small stream running during the winter if rains have been plentiful. Unless it is done in early morning, anytime after March may be too hot for the unseasoned desert visitor to take this hike.

Palm oasis at the Coachella Valley Preserve Visitor Center

31 Willis Palms and West Mesa Trail

(see map on page 73)

LENGTH: 3 miles

HIKING TIME: 2 hours

ELEVATION GAIN: 300 feet

DIFFICULTY: Easy

SEASON: October to April

INFORMATION: Coachella Valley Preserve, Thousand Palms (760) 343-1234

This is another Coachella Valley Preserve hike that takes you to a grove of California fan palms situated on the San Andreas Fault and offers you expansive views of the western half of the Coachella Valley. While rated an easy hike, there is a climb up a short but steep cliff, and hikers new to the desert should be aware of warmer springtime temperatures.

DIRECTIONS

TO REACH THE TRAILHEAD, follow Washington Street north from I-10, as given in the directions for Hike 20. After turning right at Thousand Palms Canyon Road, look to your left at the low rise of hills. The trail begins after turning onto this road and is found to your left.

The trail starts west for 0.25 mile and then heads north up a sandy wash. Stay right in the wash, follow the trail for another mile, then up the side of the cliff. You will see some great views of the western Coachella Valley. Continue following the trail as it turns south and back to your starting position. Always take plenty of cool water even on a desert hike as short as this.

Sand dunes and palm oasis at Coachella Valley Preserve

32 Coachella Valley Preserve Trails

(see map on page 73)

LENGTH: 6 miles

HIKING TIME: 5 hours

ELEVATION GAIN: 100 feet

DIFFICULTY: Easy

SEASON: October to April

INFORMATION: Coachella Valley Preserve, Thousand Palms (760) 343-1234

The Coachella Valley Preserve is a great place to walk trails that are less demanding yet offer a real desert and oasis experience. The preserve is truly an island in the desert, with generous plant and bird life surrounded by small desert canyons, hills, washes, and mesas.

DIRECTIONS

THE PRESERVE IS REACHED by exiting from I-10 onto Washington Street, traveling north for 5 miles. Turn right at Thousand Palms Road for 2 miles until you see the lush vegetation on your left and the sign indicating the entrance.

There are several easy trails on the preserve, ranging from less than 0.25 mile to 1, 1.4, and 3 miles. The elevation gain is less than 100 feet but the hikes do cover sandy trails—especially the Wash Trail—and tend to slow the hike into a gentle walk.

The Coachella Valley Preserve is indeed a place to walk, enjoy scenes of rich plant and bird life, and capture the essence of a desert oasis. It is open from sunrise to sunset.

The ponds, Coachella Valley Preserve

33 East Deception Canyon

(see map below)

LENGTH: 10 miles

HIKING TIME: 5 hours

ELEVATION GAIN: 500 feet

DIFFICULTY: Moderate

SEASON: October to April

INFORMATION:
No information available

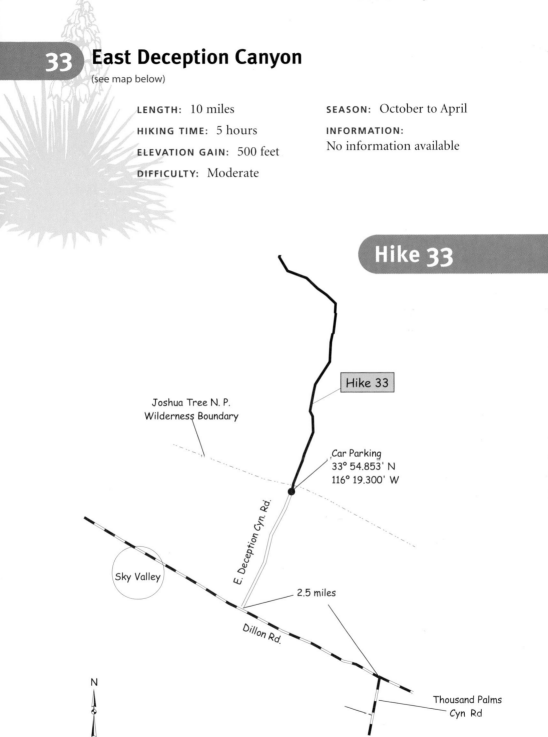

Hike 33

Joshua Tree N. P.
Wilderness Boundary

Hike 33

Car Parking
33° 54.853' N
116° 19.300' W

E. Deception Cyn. Rd.

Sky Valley

2.5 miles

Dillon Rd.

Thousand Palms
Cyn Rd

N

1   0   1   2   3 Miles

This hike is not on a trail but follows the wash bottom of East Deception Canyon. It makes for a good exploratory of how canyons erode via the action of water through a large wash. What the water brings down the wash from higher elevations can be most interesting...and curious!

DIRECTIONS

FROM I-10 take the Washington Street exit north (left if coming from the west; right, if coming from the east). Drive past Sun City, and after almost 4 miles you'll come to 1000 Palms Canyon Rd. Turn right and drive north for 4.7 miles until intersecting Dillon Road. Turn left at Dillon and drive 2.2 miles until reaching East Deception Road. Turn right and drive on the paved road for another 2 miles, staying always on the right fork of the road. After 2 miles you cross a large wash. Park where convenient.

The wash "is" the trail. Head north towards the mountains, hiking carefully on the wash bottom. Past floods have scoured this canyon so thoroughly that hardpack sand makes this wash like walking on a sidewalk! Make your way through the wash, looking for pinecones and other "treasures" that have washed down from above. After several miles the wash enters between two low mountain ranges and turns left.

You can explore as far as you like. As you leave the views of the Coachella Valley to the south, this hike takes on the feel of a wilderness exploratory. The nice thing is that you are free to climb whatever hill strikes your fancy, or continue in the wash for many miles.

34 Hidden Gold Mine Exploratory

(see map on page 79)

LENGTH: 10 miles

HIKING TIME: 4 – 6 hours

ELEVATION GAIN: 1,400 feet

DIFFICULTY: Moderate/Strenuous

SEASON: October to April

INFORMATION:
No information available

This hike follows an old mining road into the Little San Bernardino Mountains north of Indio, and gives you a sense of isolation and a feel for the "Old West" as you leave civilization behind.

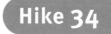

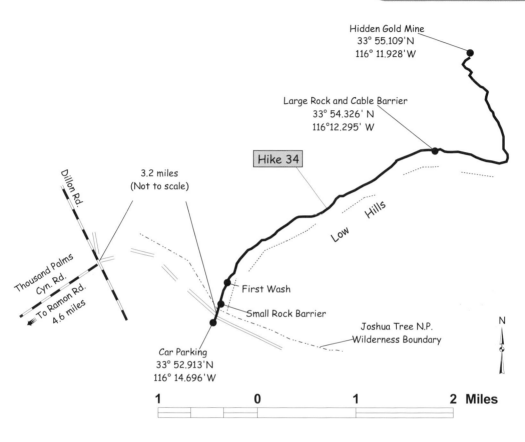

Hidden Gold Mine
33° 55.109'N
116° 11.928'W

Large Rock and Cable Barrier
33° 54.326' N
116°12.295' W

Hike 34

3.2 miles
(Not to scale)

Dillon Rd.

Thousand Palms
Cyn. Rd.

To Ramon Rd.
4.6 miles

Low   Hills

First Wash

Small Rock Barrier

Joshua Tree N.P.
Wilderness Boundary

Car Parking
33° 52.913'N
116° 14.696'W

N

1   0   1   2 **Miles**

DIRECTIONS

SAME AS FOR EAST DECEPTION CANYON. However, as soon as you arrive at Dillon Road, cross Dillon and access the broken-down paved road north of the Dillon/1000 Palms Canyon Rd. intersection. This road takes a sharp 45 degree turn to the north, a one lane affair that seems to be going nowhere except away from civilization! As it heads north, always stay on the obvious larger, better-maintained road, as several lesser roads break off to the left. After 3 miles you'll see the large protruding hill to your right, Fan Hill. From Dillon Rd. drive exactly 3.9 miles. Ahead you'll see the road split. Park anywhere convenient. Notice the large boulder to your left forming part of the road border at 3.9 miles.

The faint "rocky road" trail begins just behind this boulder. You can see several tall markers/metal stakes just north of the road. Hike to them, noting the wilderness boundary marker. Continue on this old rock road trail as it crosses through a wash, then turns right and continues towards the low mountains off to your right.

After over a mile the trail turns right along the mountain and into a wash. Follow the trail as if the wash and it were the same. Eventually, the trail veers right nearer the mountains, leaving the wash and heading northeast towards a narrowing canyon. After 4 miles a row of large boulders with a metal rope affixed atop them tries to block the road. It doesn't...just walk over the rope! You'll begin to see signs of past human work. Follow the road/canyon wash as far as you're comfortable with, looking out for the old hidden gold mine. Note the colorful rock formations in the canyon.

This hike feels off the beaten path...and it is. The early morning or late afternoon shadows along the mountain valley are especially beautiful.

Palm Oasis, Coachella Valley Preserve

Desert Cities
HIKES 35 – 47

Trailhead Locations in Desert Cities

Hikes 35 – 47

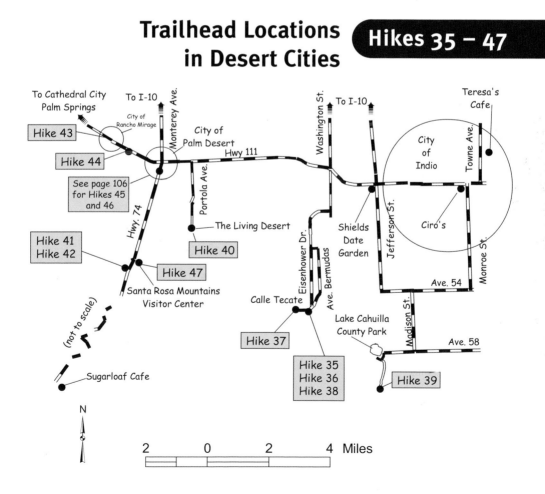

To Cathedral City Palm Springs

To I-10

Monterey Ave.

City of Rancho Mirage

City of Palm Desert

Washington St.

To I-10

Teresa's Cafe

Hike 43

Hwy 111

City of Indio

Towne Ave.

Hike 44

Portola Ave.

See page 106 for Hikes 45 and 46

Jefferson St.

Ciro's

Hwy. 74

Monroe St.

The Living Desert

Shields Date Garden

Hike 41
Hike 42

Hike 40

Eisenhower Dr.

Ave. Bermudas

Hike 47

Ave. 54

Santa Rosa Mountains Visitor Center

Calle Tecate

Lake Cahuilla County Park

Madison St.

Ave. 58

(not to scale)

Hike 37

Hike 35
Hike 36
Hike 38

Hike 39

Sugarloaf Cafe

N

2   0   2   4 Miles

35 Guadalupe Trail to Sugarloaf Cafe
(see map opposite)

LENGTH: 15 miles	**SEASON:** October to April
HIKING TIME: 8 hours	**INFORMATION:** BLM Office, Palm Springs, (760) 251-4800
ELEVATION GAIN: 5,000 feet	
DIFFICULTY: Very strenuous	

While not commonly found on most hiking maps, the Guadalupe Trail to Sugarloaf Cafe is one of the premier strenuous wilderness hikes in the Santa Rosa Mountains. This hike requires a shuttle, with cars parked at Sugarloaf Cafe on Hwy. 74, 14 miles up the road from Palm Desert, and at the Boo Hoff/La Quinta trailhead. The climb up the northeast flank of Martinez Mountain—or at least it's close enough to be considered Martinez Mountain—gives hikers incredible vistas of the entire lower Coachella Valley and Salton Sea Basin. Eventually the trail penetrates the upper reaches of the Santa Rosa Wilderness and joins with the Cactus Spring Trail for the trek back through Horsethief Creek.

Hikers negotiating a creek in the lower Santa Rosa Mountains

DIRECTIONS **TO REACH THE TRAILHEAD,** take Hwy. 111 to La Quinta at Washington Street. Turn south onto Washington Street (right, if you are going east on Hwy. 111 from Palm Desert). After several miles, turn right onto Eisenhower Street (stoplight) and continue several more miles until Eisenhower dead-ends at Avenida Bermudas. Turn right and go for 0.3 mile until you see Avenida Ramirez on your right. Turn left off the road and into the dirt parking lot.

Start the hike by heading south by southeast across the open dirt flatlands, following the dirt path. After 0.25 mile you will reach the drop-off from the flat area, going down and around some metal posts and into a wash. Follow the trail and wash, first going right and then left (south), heading past some junky remains of trash. This dirt path heads south toward the opening between two low hills. After 0.5 mile the trail climbs right and up onto a small ridge above the canyon you've been hiking in. Follow the trail above the ridge, as it soon veers down and

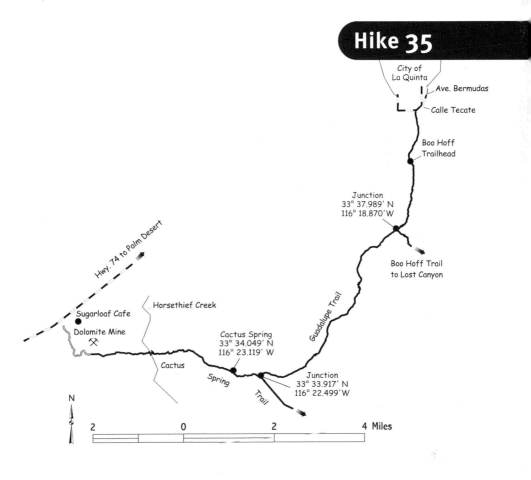

Hike 35

into the small canyon to your right. Stay right for another 0.25 mile and you will soon come to a metal sign which reads "Boo Hoff Trail."

From here, the hike is part of the Boo Hoff Trail, as it climbs steeply up the mountainside. About 3 miles up on your right is a small rock cairn, the "official" start of the Guadalupe Trail. This is actually an old Indian trail, which travels through the Guadalupe Canyon and along the rim of Devil's Canyon. The trail looks onto steep, granite sanctuaries for bighorn sheep. Ahead of you as you climb south up this steep, rocky, and sometimes faint trail, will be a tepee-type peak.

Farther up the trail, 4 miles from the parked vehicles, is an Indian flat area (tepee-type peak is now 50 feet east), where pottery pieces might be found. As the trail winds relentlessly up the mountains, you will reach a top area where pine and juniper begin to accent the slopes. As you enter the level mountainous area, you will come upon an old cowboy camp, where the remains of stoves, iron implements, tin cans, etc., can be found strewn over a wide area. The trail pushes back from here into a dense canyon thicket, where a stream sometimes flows during wet winters. Eventually the trail breaks out into a widening wash, which you will favor as it veers slowly to the right. In a short time you will come to your first signpost, indicating that your trail is joining with the Cactus Spring Trail. Follow this trail right (west) for 2 miles to Horsethief Creek and another 2.5 miles to the Cactus Spring Trailhead. From here you can follow the jeep road to Sugarloaf Cafe just up the hill, along Hwy. 74. As demanding as this trail is, it is worth all the effort, but it is most safely done with someone knowing the way.

36 The Boo Hoff Trail to La Quinta
(see map on page 86)

LENGTH: 12 miles

HIKING TIME: 6 – 7 hours

ELEVATION GAIN: 2,000 feet

DIFFICULTY: Strenuous

SEASON: October to April

INFORMATION: BLM Office, Palm Springs, (760) 251-4800

The Boo Hoff Trail takes the hiker deep into the Santa Rosa Mountains along the north drainage of Martinez Mountain, with wide, impressive vistas of the Salton Sea Basin. This interior trail leads into the wilderness areas where hikers find it difficult to believe that just over the hill is the sprawling Coachella Valley and the city of La Quinta. Along the way the trail treats you to wild desert mountains, solitude and, if you are lucky, some of the bighorn sheep, which live in the Santa Rosa Wilderness.

DIRECTIONS

FOLLOW THE DIRECTIONS for Hike 39, until you reach the trail sign for the Boo Hoff Trail.

Continue up the Boo Hoff Trail for the better part of 2 miles until the canyon drops down into the wash just past the sprawl of cholla cacti. Continue up the trail, as it climbs up and out of the wash. You will gradually climb 2 more miles. Along the way are numerous side canyons, dry falls, and washes that are typical of the Santa Rosa Wilderness. Following a wet winter, sometime between mid-March and mid-April, you will see rivers of flowers flowing from the canyon sides along the trail. These can be spectacular but must have enough water to really grow profusely. (Be sure to start early on the trail, as it gets hot this time of year.)

At the western end of the Boo Hoff Trail, you will find yourself above La Quinta. From here you can turn around and head east, retracing the same route. Some hikers make a shuttle hike out of the Boo Hoff Trail by following the wash/jeep road down to the street. This way, the hike is about 8-9 miles one way. The trail was affectionately named for Mr. Boo Hoff, a leading figure with the equestrian group, The Desert Trail Riders.

Hikers negotiating a creek in the lower Santa Rosa Mountains

37 Bear Creek Canyon Ridge

(see map below)

LENGTH: 8 miles

HIKING TIME: 5 hours

ELEVATION GAIN: 2,000 feet

DIFFICULTY: Strenuous

SEASON: October to April

INFORMATION: BLM Office, Palm Springs, (760) 251-4800

This hike is one of the many canyon hikes found along the foothills of the Santa Rosa Mountains. These mountains form the southern boundary of the Coachella Valley, with Martinez Mountain dominating the southeast portion of this range. Bear Creek Canyon flows north as a major drainage from Martinez Mountain, towards the city of La Quinta. The ridge affords expansive views of not only the city, but also, in a single sweep of the eyes, both the Salton Sea and the distant, often snowcapped San Jacinto and San Gorgonio peaks.

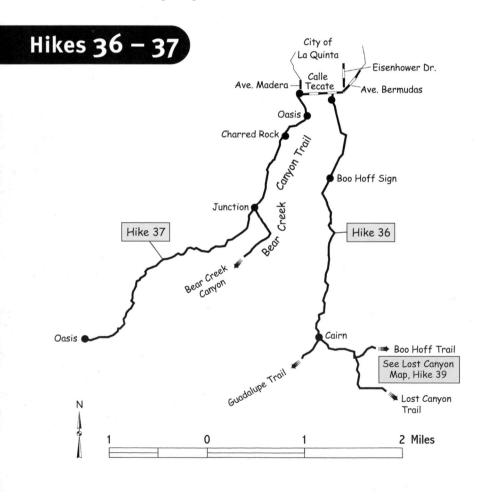

Hikes 36 – 37

City of La Quinta

Eisenhower Dr.

Ave. Madera — Calle Tecate

Ave. Bermudas

Oasis

Charred Rock

Bear Creek Canyon Trail

Boo Hoff Sign

Junction

Hike 37

Hike 36

Bear Creek Canyon

Bear Creek

Oasis

Cairn

Boo Hoff Trail

See Lost Canyon Map, Hike 39

Guadalupe Trail

Lost Canyon Trail

N

1   0   1   2 Miles

DIRECTIONS

TO REACH THE TRAILHEAD, take Hwy. 111 to La Quinta and turn right (south) at Washington Street into La Quinta. Continue to Eisenhower Drive, turn right, and follow Eisenhower until it ends at the end of town at Avenida Bermudas. Turn right, noting that Avenida Bermudas becomes Calle Tecate. Park where Calle Tecate meets Avenida Madero. Looking to the south you will see broad, sandy flatlands bordered by low foothills to the right.

Begin walking south on the dirt path that makes its way between a low ridge of foothills and a palm oasis left of the trail. The trail then veers to the right before being blocked by some boulders, and then drops into a wide wash.

Once you're in the wash, turn south (left) and favor the left for about a 20-minute walk. Chuparosa, with its colorful red and orange blossoms, is abundant, especially from February to April. As the canyon narrows, look for the small, sharply defined canyon to your right that shows charred rock from campers' use. Just past this canyon, at the palo verde tree, is the beginning of Bear Creek Canyon Ridge Trail.

For the first 0.5 mile, stay on the established trail, being careful of false side trails, which are often blocked by rocks. As you climb back into the massive canyon network, you can feel a wild, distant land, void of any human influence.

Rock scrambling through the Santa Rosa Mountains

After 1.5 miles you will begin to rapidly ascend the ridge, surrounded by ocotillo that dominate the landscape. Down to your left is the massive rocky canyon of Bear Creek, offering a good water flow during bountiful, wet winters.

After 2 miles, hikers will find themselves on a plateau from which they can see the mountain ranges surrounding the Coachella Valley, and the Salton Sea to the east. A lacework of canyons flowing from the Santa Rosas surround the trail in all directions. As you continue up the trail, the views to the north allow you to peek into Joshua Tree National Park. Still farther up, the hiker is treated to hidden valleys deep in the interior mountains and the culmination of a massive verdant oasis tucked into the fold of a canyon. Here you are over 4 miles from the trailhead. You can choose to lunch here or continue exploring to see what lies over the next ridge. There are no trails beyond the oasis, but any wash will lead you into either dry or flowing waterfalls, depending on how wet the winter has been.

38 Bear Creek Urban Trail, La Quinta
(see map opposite)

LENGTH: 6 miles

HIKING TIME: 3 hours

ELEVATION GAIN: 150 feet

DIFFICULTY: Easy

SEASON: September to May

INFORMATION: City of La Quinta, (760) 777-7000

A lovely urban walk along the western edge of the city of La Quinta, this outing offers sweeping vistas of Martinez Mountain, dominating the southern horizon, as well as the Santa Rosa Mountains and foothills. A hike in the early morning or just before sunset offers colorful sun-accented mountain vistas and is considered the best time of day for this trail. The great restaurants in La Quinta make for another adventure afterwards!

DIRECTIONS

FOLLOW THE DIRECTIONS for Hike 35. You may park on the street or in the dirt/gravel parking lot just south of the road. You might also try parking on a street near the north end of the trail and walking uphill, so that your return walk will be on a downhill bias. For this option, take Eisenhower Drive, turn right on Montezuma, just past Tampico, then right again on Velasco, and pick up the trail (sidewalk) at the north end of the street.

egin your walk on the sidewalk south of the road, and head west toward the mountains. As the walkway begins to turn north and downhill, you will see a small bench, plaque, and water fountain, as well as the trailhead for the Bear Creek Ridge Trail. Vistas of the desert valley outside of La Quinta unfold to the north. The cove, as this area is called, is somewhat protected from wind and sandstorm conditions. To the left of the trail is a water runoff channel that protects La Quinta from flash floods. As you continue downhill, notice the colorful adobe homes to the right of the trail.

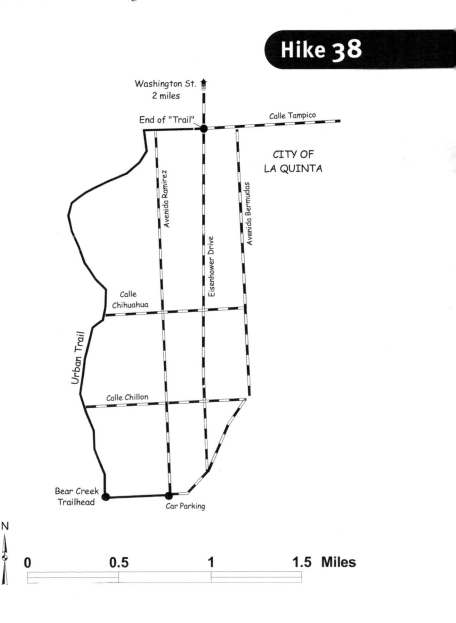

Hike 38

After 2.5 miles, the walkway turns northeast. As you pass alongside the neighborhoods, you might want to wander the streets and examine some interesting architecture. The trail signs will eventually take you to the intersection that meets Eisenhower Drive. You can turn around here, or continue north for 0.5 mile before returning the same way you came.

View north from Bear Creek Urban Trail

39 Lost Canyon via the Boo Hoff Trail

(see map on page 92)

LENGTH: 8 miles

HIKING TIME: 5 hours

ELEVATION GAIN: 1,500 feet

DIFFICULTY: Strenuous

SEASON: October to April

INFORMATION: BLM Office, Palm Springs, (760) 251-4800

Of the many canyon hikes found in the foothills of the Santa Rosa Mountains, the Lost Canyon hike offers some of the most diversified terrain and breath-taking views. For the entire hike the massive, imposing form of Martinez Mountain looms above the hiker's southern view. During a rainy winter, the north face of the mountain is streaked with many rivulet-type waterfalls. These serve to accent the canyons emerging from the mountainside and feed the vegetation trapped in washes. Although plant life is sparse, cholla, barrel cacti, and ocotillo are abundantly dispersed throughout the length of the hike.

DIRECTIONS

DRIVE ON HWY. 111 EAST past the city of La Quinta several miles until reaching Jefferson Street. Turn right at Jefferson and drive south until reaching the PGA West Golf Club. Turn left at PGA West (Ave. 54), right at the next stop sign (Madison) and right again at Avenue 58, following the signs to Lake Cahuilla County Park. As you approach the park, the road rises then dips just before reaching the Quarry Golf Club. Note the dirt road dipping down and left, just before the Quarry. As you drive down this car-approved road, note the "trail" marker indicating that the dirt jeep road will take you to the Boo Hoff Trail. Follow the dirt road first east towards the mountains, then south for a mile until reaching the built up dike. 4wd vehicles can continue (cars need to park just before the dike and hikers hike the rest of the way), up over the dike and continue following the dirt road for a mile to where a row of signs marks the furthest you can drive. Walk past the Boo Hoof Trail map sign for about 10 minutes, staying in the main sandy wash as it veers right. As the wash closes towards a narrowing canyon, and large granite and red-desert varnish colored boulders build up to your right, look for the black metal sign saying "Boo Hoff Trail" on your right. This marks the beginning of the trail.

Take the Boo Hoff Trail into the high foothills. As the wilderness canyons of the Santa Rosa Mountains impress you with dry and sometimes wet waterfalls along the north face of Martinez Mountain, you'll feel truly away from it all.

As you ascend, look south. You will be following a large canyon, which at this point in the hike begins to draw closer. After 1.5 miles on the Boo Hoff Trail you will begin to drop down into a thickly vegetated wash, after passing through an extensive stand of cholla cacti. Although the trail continues on the hillside past the wash, turn left into the wash and begin traveling down canyon. Stay to the right as you climb down several dry waterfalls until you come to the spectacular canyon drop that spills into Lost Canyon. Most hikers can negotiate this 150-foot drop without a rope. Stay

Hikers find the breathtaking views at Lost Canyon well worth the effort

to the left as you crawl down the rockfalls and onto the trail. Keep bearing left and descend down into the canyon. Be especially careful of loose gravel and rock. With its view of the Salton Sea framed by the slopes of Lost Canyon, this section looks awesome and might appear impassable. But children—with careful adults there to help—have done this section without incident, so it's as safe as the hiker is.

Take the canyon left for 0.5 mile until you reach another large dry falls. The trail can be found 15 to 20 yards before you reach the falls, and up on the hillside to your right. Here you will drop down into your final canyon. To the right, at 200

Hike 39

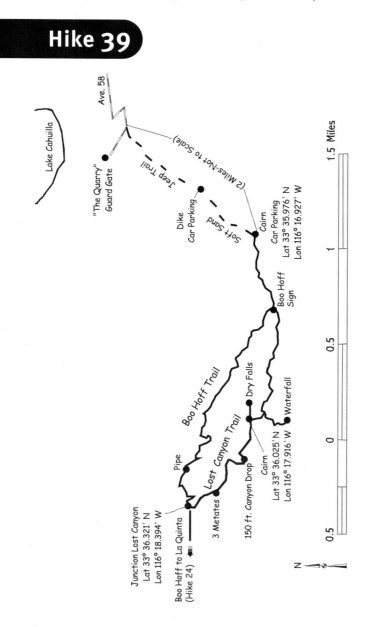

yards, is a waterfall, generously flowing after a good rainfall. After seeing this last waterfall, turn back and continue down canyon for 0.5 mile until you see the Boo Hoff Trail marker to your left. From here it's a simple matter of following the wash back to your vehicle.

The Lost Canyon hike is impressive to desert visitors for its cacti, soaring canyons, impressive views, and most of all that unforgettable descent down the large dry falls that upon first glance leaves some hikers with a feeling of "no way!"

40 Eisenhower Peak Loop

(see map on page 94)

LENGTH: 6 miles

HIKING TIME: 4 hours

ELEVATION GAIN: 700 feet

DIFFICULTY: Moderate

SEASON: October to April

INFORMATION: The Living Desert, Palm Desert
(760) 346-5694

The Living Desert is a visitor's mecca for those wishing to learn more about the flora and fauna of the Coachella Valley. This preserve has grown to include its own wildlife zoo. You will find walking paths that highlight varieties of plant and animal life found in the local desert. As you would expect, there is also a major hiking trail within the grounds that takes you up toward Eisenhower Peak, whose 1,952-foot elevation corresponds perfectly to his election year! The trail is a good representation of desert terrain and makes a perfect beginning to your Living Desert tour.

DIRECTIONS

TO REACH THE TRAILHEAD, turn south onto Portola Avenue from Hwy. 111 in Palm Desert. After 2 miles you will see the entrance to the Living Desert on your left. From the main entrance, turn right and follow the sidewalk and signs to the wilderness loop. Many docents are available to help direct you. Pick up a plant and tree guide as you leave the main building, as the plant life is well marked along the trail.

After you've walked 0.75 mile to the end of the inner loop, then 0.75 mile to the Quail Guzzler, the canyon leg starts. This is very rugged terrain, necessitating wash-walking and boulder-hopping. At the 0.75-mile marker post, you will begin to climb a very defined trail heading first east and then north to the picnic tables. Eisenhower Mountain is directly on the right but you must bushwhack to the top, as there is no defined trail. The view from the top gives you a fabulous look at the whole of the Coachella Valley. After leaving the tables and heading down the ridge leg, you are treated to stunning glimpses of the estate homes of Eldorado and Vintage Country Clubs. Signs along the way highlight the history of both the palm trees and the trail itself. This section is an easy 1.5-mile meander back to the patio, the bookstore, and a well-deserved snack in the main buildings. In warmer months be sure to bring 2 quarts of a cool drink to quench the desert thirst.

Hike 40

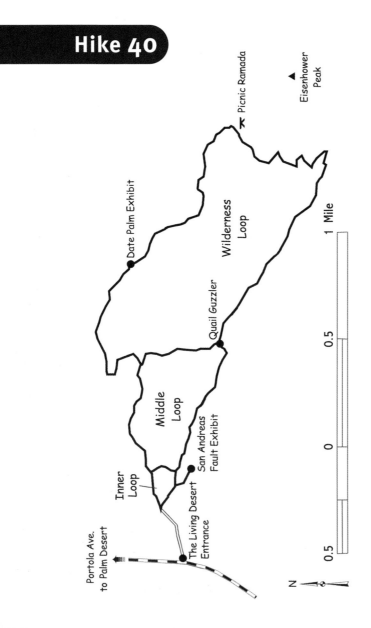

41 Carrizo Canyon   This trail is open October 1-Dec 31 only

(see map on page 96)

LENGTH: 4 – 6 miles

HIKING TIME: 3 – 4 hours

ELEVATION GAIN: 500 feet

DIFFICULTY: Moderate

SEASON: October to April

INFORMATION: BLM Office, Palm Springs, (760) 251-4800

This is another Santa Rosa Mountain trail that exposes the hiker to canyon hiking. Most of this hike takes place in the canyon and is highlighted by a series of dry or wet waterfalls, depending on the amount of rainfall. In a wet season the hiker is treated to lush vegetation that hardly suggests the presence of the surrounding harsh desert, minutes from the narrow confines of the canyon interior.

DIRECTIONS

TO GET TO CARRIZO CANYON, turn south from Hwy. 111 in Palm Desert onto Hwy. 74. After about 4 miles the highway begins to turn up the mountains just past the Bighorn Development to your right. You can park in the parking lot on the right side of the road designated Art Smith Trailhead, 0.25 mile past the Santa Rosa Wilderness Area sign.

Drop down into the wash, or south of where you park, and hike up the wash as it veers to the left and on into Carrizo Canyon. It can be pleasantly cool here, even in the warmer spring months, but it is always wise to carry at least 2 quarts of a cool drink—no matter how cool the canyon is.

Continue along the canyon floor until you reach the first large falls, and climb above it by scrambling up the right side. Be careful of wet rock or algae, and make sure your footholds are secure. You can continue up this canyon's many falls, but be aware that this can be tiring. This is a great short hike that gives the hiker a sense of adventure, being "on the

Indian paintbrush along a desert trail.

edge" enough to keep your attention, while showing the rocky innards of a typical desert canyon. As the trail continues up the side of the mountain it becomes more of a rock scramble and should be attempted only by hikers comfortable with this kind of combination hiking/scrambling.

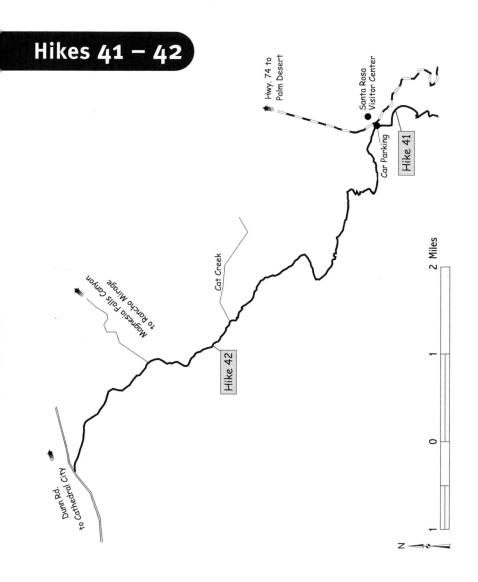

42 Art Smith Trail
(see map opposite)

LENGTH: 16 miles

HIKING TIME: 8 hours

ELEVATION GAIN: 1,200 feet

DIFFICULTY: Strenuous

SEASON: October to April

INFORMATION: BLM Office, Palm Springs, (760) 251-4800

This hike is a real treat for the hiker who enjoys a full day's journey without excessive elevation gains. The Art Smith Trail serves as a major link between the Palm Desert portion of the Santa Rosa Mountains and Palm Canyon's network of trails, including the Murray Peak area south of Cathedral City. This day hike allows you to penetrate the mountains while resting along the way in the several palm oases that accent the trail.

DIRECTIONS

TO REACH THE TRAILHEAD, turn south from Hwy. 111 in Palm Desert onto Hwy. 74. After 4 miles, park at the Santa Rosa Mountains Visitor's Center or across the street at the paved Art Smith Trailhead parking lot.

Begin hiking after the Art Smith sign to the west of the parking lot. After several hundred yards the trail will cut across the wash and pick up on the other side, climbing steeply up the mountain-side. As the trail continues, stay left on the main trail, disregarding the several side trails that veer off to the right. Beneath you is the Big Horn Golf Club & Development. After over 1.5 miles you will finally reach the top portion of the Art Smith Trail.

The trail takes you through several palm oases for the next 2 miles. During March and April, this section of the trail is abundant with plant life, barrel cacti, and other colorful wildflowers and cacti in bloom . . . a real contrast to the stark look in autumn.

By the third mile you are hiking beneath the flat-topped Haystack Mountain facing due south. As you continue, the cities of the valley floor look up from the north, but at times the trail takes you into sheltered areas where no civilization is apparent. After almost 5 miles, the trail crosses the upper reaches of Magnesia Canyon, a palm-filled canyon that makes a sheltered lunch stop. Feel free to explore down the canyon before continuing to the western end of the trail at Dunn Road.

"I thought I saw a lizard," Dakota says.

43 Magnesia Springs Canyon
(see map on page 101)

LENGTH: 10 miles

HIKING TIME: 5 – 7 hours

ELEVATION GAIN: 1,250 feet

DIFFICULTY: Strenuous

SEASON: October to April

INFORMATION:
No information available

This hike takes you to one of the desert's largest and impressive "Dry Falls" within a long canyon that eventually connects to the Art Smith Trail in the higher elevation foothills of the Santa Rosa Mountains. The "Dry Falls" is steep and should be done by confident rock scramblers. A long strong rope would be a plus, but is not required. A series of rock scrambles, dry falls, and dense underbrush makes this "hike" quite an adventure. I strongly advise that only confident, strong hikers do this hike, and only in a group or with at least one other hiker; never alone. This is not a hike for anyone uneasy about off-trail rock scrambling or bushwhacking off-trail.

DIRECTIONS

FROM FRED WARRING DRIVE in Palm Desert turn right towards Rancho Mirage /Palm Springs onto Hwy. 111 for 1.7 miles, then turn left on Mirage Rd. Coming from Palm Springs, once entering Rancho Mirage on Hwy. 111, turn right at Mirage Rd. almost a half mile past Thunderbird Country Club (on your left). Proceed to the rock sign indicating Blixeth Mountain Park (parking). Park in this convenient parking area.

The hike begins by first crossing over the small bridge and gate near the parking area. Follow the trail as it keeps to the right of the storm channel. Several "false trails" meander off the main trail, but by staying on the most developed trail you will, in about 0.5 mile, find the trail taking you alongside the mountain. To your left is the Porcupine Creek Golf Club. When you reach the cement dike, scramble up and over it, then down the large cement structure, across the dirt holding area and up the other side to the trail. Once at the top veer left until you reach the road/trail near the left side of the mountains. Continue towards the now looming canyon in front of you. The trail hugs the left side of the wash near the mountain and brings you quickly into the canyon area to the left and a stone ledge about 10 feet high. Climb over the ledge, and continue for a hundred yards as the canyon swings right and into the base of a high, wide dry falls. Carefully negotiate the dry falls; staying left seems to work best (it can be wet in winter or after a heavy rain; a 50-70 foot rope would help, but is not necessary). Once at the top continue up-canyon, exploring the various branches, but basically staying right in the largest canyon. You will be confronted with several dry falls and rock ledges. Stay in the right section of the canyon, and when climbing up the rock falls, staying to the left side of each falls gets you above them.

You eventually reach a split in the canyon at a small palm oasis. Several rock cairns at another dry falls on your left are the indicator to take this left fork into the upper canyon. Once above the dry falls and after less than 0.5 mile, you will come to a cairn 100 yards just before a very high dry falls. Scramble up the right side of the canyon wall, following along a steep scree ledge until you gain the saddle at the top. Hike over the saddle and to your left and down into the canyon behind the high dry falls. Continue for another mile through dense underbrush and rock falls.

You will now encounter another tall dry falls. Scramble up the steep boulder slope to the left, a difficult, steep ascent. Once at the top make for the flat area, noting the steep canyon to your right. Hike on the top plateau for a hundred yards or so until you can drop back down into the canyon to your right.

Here, another series of dense trees, bush, and weeds must be negotiated. Within 0.5 mile the canyon splits; stay right. Very shortly the canyon again splits, but note that the left branch is now a more flat sandy wash. If you take the left branch you will connect with the Art Smith Trail in 0.5 mile, as it comes down a small hill to your left, crosses the wash, then continues up the hill to your right. If you take the right branch, considered by many to be easier, you will encounter a wide, sloping dry waterfall. Climb up to the right and within 100 yards you will also reach the Art Smith Trail where a sign indicates your connection.

By parking at the Art Smith Trailhead in Palm Desert, you can make a 13-mile shuttle hike out of this one. Once reaching the Art Smith Trail, just turn left and in 8 miles you will reach its eastern terminus at Hwy. 74, across the street from the Santa Rosa, San Jacinto Mountains National Monument.

Lupine and desert flowers

Hike 43

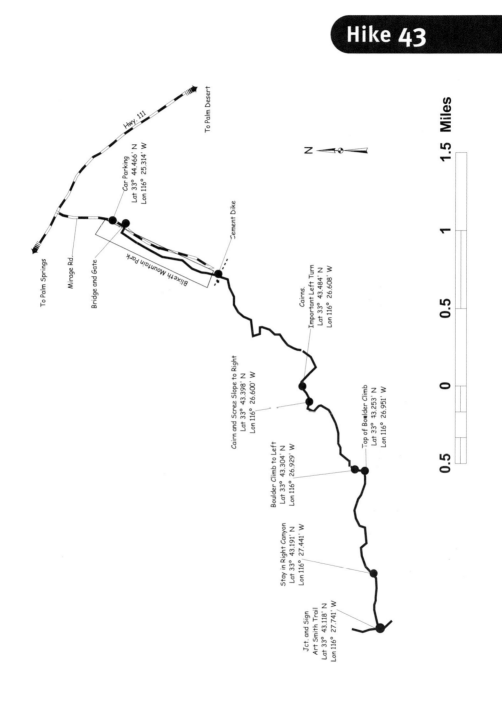

To Palm Springs

Hwy. 111

Mirage Rd.

To Palm Desert

Car Parking
Lat 33° 44.466' N
Lon 116° 25.314' W

Bridge and Gate

Blixerth Mountain Park

Cement Dike

N

Cairns
Important Left Turn
Lat 33° 43.484' N
Lon 116° 26.608' W

Cairn and Scree Slope to Right
Lat 33° 43.398' N
Lon 116° 26.600' W

Top of Boulder Climb
Lat 33° 13.253' N
Lon 116° 26.951' W

Boulder Climb to Left
Lat 33° 43.304' N
Lon 116° 26.929' W

Stay in Right Canyon
Lat 33° 43.191' N
Lon 116° 27.441' W

Jct. and Sign
Art Smith Trail
Lat 33° 43.118' N
Lon 116° 27.741' W

0.5   0   0.5   1   1.5   Miles

44 Mirage Trail (aka "Bump and Grind")

(see map page 103)

LENGTH: 2 miles

HIKING TIME: 1 – 2 hours

ELEVATION GAIN: 800 feet

DIFFICULTY: Easy/Moderate

SEASON: October to April

INFORMATION: Rancho Mirage, (760) 324-4511

This is a "short 'n sweet" exercise hike above Rancho Mirage, popular with locals because of its closeness and its steep grade that affords a good work-out. Be advised, that some of this trail is being considered for closures or re-routes and parking is an issue.

DIRECTIONS

FROM HWY. 111 IN PALM DESERT, where Fred Warring connects, drive north towards Palm Springs/Rancho Mirage for almost a mile to Magnesia Falls Drive. Turn left and travel five blocks to where Magnesia Falls almost meets Estellita Rd. The trail sign to your left and atop the dike is a good starting point. From Palm Springs, drive into Rancho Mirage on Hwy. 111 and take the first street to your right (Magnesia Falls Dr.), just after passing Bob Hope Drive on your left. You might also park in Roy's Restaurant on your right or at Provident Bank. Walk down Magnesia Falls Drive to the trail sign. At press time, you are still permitted to park along Magnesia Falls Drive between 10am and 3pm, and after 6pm. Check with Rancho Mirage if trailhead parking has changed. You can also access the trail by turning west off Hwy. 111 onto Fred Warring Rd., then turning left onto Painter's path. Continue 100 yards to the trailhead.

Desert palm oasis near the San Andreas Fault

Hike east past the trail sign on the dirt road above Magnesia Falls Drive. It turns south after 0.25 mile and meets up with an iron white gate. You'll see the trail heading uphill to your right. Follow the trail as it climbs steeply and winds above the desert floor, offering great views of the "urban" environment of Rancho Mirage and Palm Desert beneath you. The trail (road) cuts through a small hill notch, allowing you to see south towards the Santa Rosa Mountains. From here it again rises steeply until it ends high above you on a flat mountainous area. A connector trail, the Hopalong Cassidy Trail, will connect somewhere near the top, and take you above Palm Desert all the way to the Art Smith Trailhead at the southernmost end of Palm Desert.

Hike 44

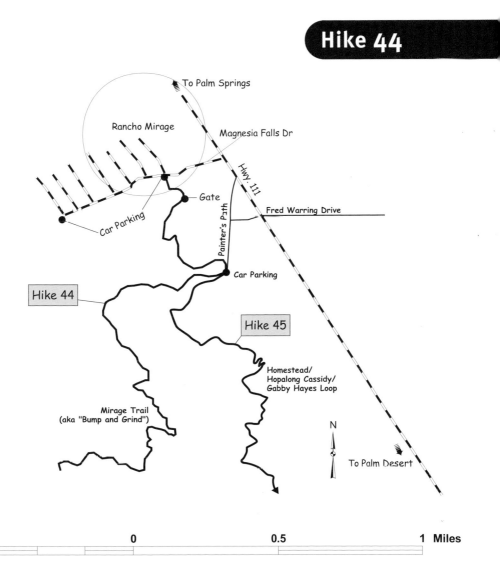

To Palm Springs

Rancho Mirage

Magnesia Falls Dr

Hwy. 111

Gate

Painter's Path

Fred Warring Drive

Car Parking

Car Parking

Hike 44

Hike 45

Homestead/
Hopalong Cassidy/
Gabby Hayes Loop

Mirage Trail
(aka "Bump and Grind")

N

To Palm Desert

0.5   0   0.5   1 Miles

45 Homestead/Hopalong Cassidy/ Gabby Hayes Loop (see maps pages 105 and 106)

LENGTH: 2.5 miles

HIKING TIME: 1 – 2 hours

ELEVATION GAIN: 375 feet

DIFFICULTY: Easy

SEASON: October to April

INFORMATION: Palm Desert (760) 568-1441

A quick trail above Palm Desert, short with great views. Good exercise, as the trail is steep and offers some good uphill/down hill sections.

DIRECTIONS

FROM HWY. 111 IN PALM DESERT, turn south onto Hwy. 74 and drive 1 mile, turning right onto Thrush, just before Palm Desert Community Church. Drive 0.25 mile and cross the bridge where Cap Homme-Ralph Adams Park is marked by a large stone marker. Turn right and proceed for several hundred yards to the trail parking area.

Riders near the Hopalong Cassidy Trail

The trail begins at the oasis and kiosk, where several trails start up the mountain. The connector trail to the top is called the Homestead Trail. At the top is a small shaded rest stop from which views of Palm Desert spreading out east, south, and north can be had. Continue up the mountain on the section that is the first part of the Hopalong Cassidy Trail. After a short but steep climb of 0.5 mile, take the trail heading down to the right, known as the Gabby Hayes Trail. This trail drops quickly, winding downhill in a playful fashion, a section kids would enjoy for the sheerness of the trail. As you come down towards the bottom, several trails join, each going right. Each eventually leads back to the tennis courts at Cahuilla Hills Park. Stay on the trail past several of these right exit trails to see the maximum sights available. Eventually the trail climbs a hill near the tennis courts, and you can get down by either of the routes that travel down, or by going across the low ridge. Once down, make for the road bordering right of the storm channel and walk the last 0.5 mile back to the parking area.

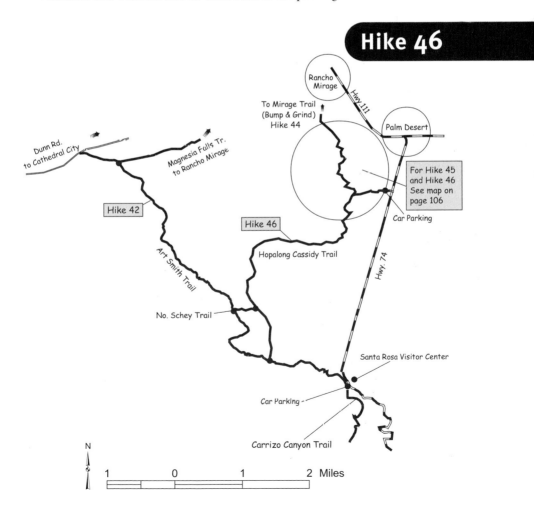

Hikes 45 – 46

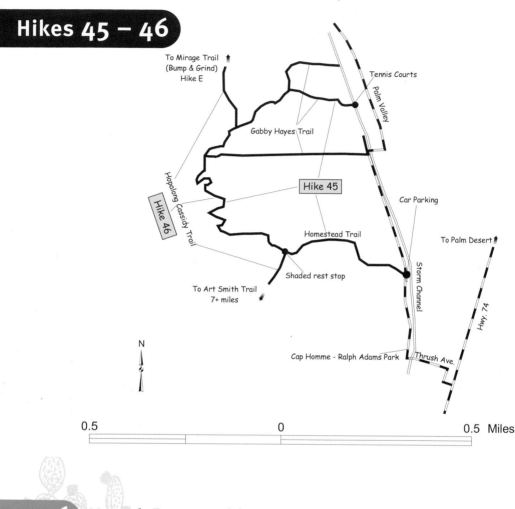

0.5   **0**   **0.5 Miles**

46 Hopalong Cassidy Trail

(see map above)

LENGTH: 12 miles

HIKING TIME: 5 – 6 hours

ELEVATION GAIN: 1,000 feet

DIFFICULTY: Moderate/Strenuous

SEASON: October to April

INFORMATION: Palm Desert
(760) 568-1441

This trail runs above Palm Desert's western hills, affording great vista views of the city and the Coachella Valley. The trail links the Mirage Trail in Rancho Mirage to the Art Smith Trail in south Palm Desert. Check the visitor's center for trail information.

DIRECTIONS   Same as Homestead/Hopalong Cassidy/Gabby Hayes Loop, Hike 45.

The trail first begins as the Homestead Trail (a connector trail) just west of the parking area and steeply climbs to the top of the first hill where it soon becomes the Hopalong Cassidy (a 1950's cowboy movie star) Trail. The route heads south, climbing to give great views of Palm Desert to hikers. At the junction with the Gabby Hayes Trail, you can turn right and take that trail north for over 1 mile until the Hopalong Cassidy Trail branches off and heads further north to connect with the Mirage Trail (Bump & Grind). By not turning right onto the Gabby Hayes connector section thereby staying on the southern portion, you begin to eventu-

ally head south. The views along the way are expansive vistas of Palm Desert beneath you to the east. After more than seven miles you link up with the Art Smith Trail that heads west to Palm Springs, or south/east to the trailhead parking lot along Hwy. 74, across from the Santa Rosa/San Jacinto Mountains National Monument Visitor's Center.

"Wilshire Peak" from Bogart Park

47 Randall Henderson Trail
(see map page 108)

LENGTH: 2.5 miles

HIKING TIME: 1.5 hours

ELEVATION GAIN: 350 feet

DIFFICULTY: Easy

SEASON: October to April

INFORMATION:
(760) 862-9984

DIRECTIONS   **FOLLOW DIRECTIONS** for the Art Smith Trail, but park on the left side of Hwy. 74, at the Santa Rosa/San Jacinto Mountains National Monument Visitor's Center.

This short trail begins as you drive into the Visitor's Center, to your right, at the first large sign. Park in the parking lot and walk back to the trailhead.

The trail winds through the low foothills of the Santa Rosa Mountains, and is best done in a wet spring/winter to see whatever desert plants might be in bloom.

The trail has several aspects to it. One travels along a small ridge, the other stays in the wash and hugs the foothills. After this hike, see the magnificent visitor's center, where displays of local flora and fauna, photographs, prints, posters, and hiking books might be seen. Also make sure to walk around the building's plant garden, where many of the local desert plants have been identified.

Hike 47

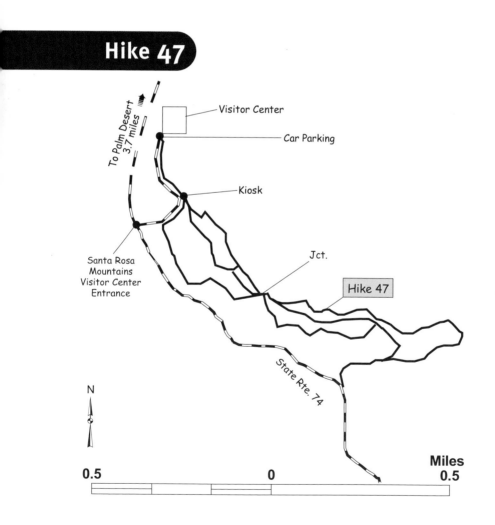

Palm Springs and Indian Canyons

HIKES 48 – 64

OPEN: October 1–July, 8am-5pm.
July to October open Friday-Sunday.

INFORMATION: (760) 323-6018

Trailhead Locations in Palm Springs and Indian Canyons

Hikes 48 – 64

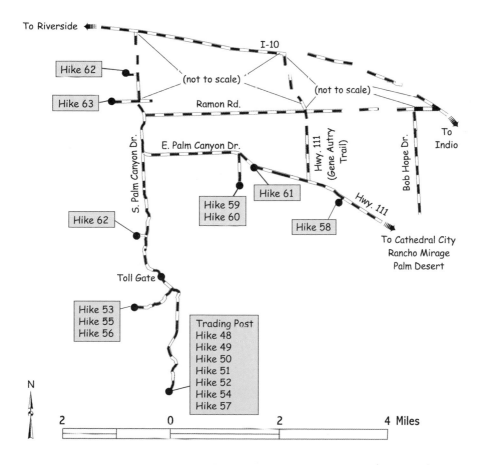

To Riverside

I-10

Hike 62

(not to scale)

Hike 63

Ramon Rd.

(not to scale)

To Indio

S. Palm Canyon Dr.

E. Palm Canyon Dr.

Hwy. 111 (Gene Autry Trail)

Bob Hope Dr.

Hike 59
Hike 60

Hike 61

Hike 58

Hwy. 111

Hike 62

To Cathedral City
Rancho Mirage
Palm Desert

Toll Gate

Hike 53
Hike 55
Hike 56

Trading Post
Hike 48
Hike 49
Hike 50
Hike 51
Hike 52
Hike 54
Hike 57

N

2   0   2   4 Miles

48 Fern Canyon
(see map opposite and on page 109)

LENGTH: 3.5 miles

HIKING TIME: 2 hours

ELEVATION GAIN: 400 feet

DIFFICULTY: Easy

SEASON: October to April

INFORMATION:
(760) 323-6018

Fern Canyon offers the hiker the surprise find of a generous outgrowth of ferns growing in a cactus-filled desert! The hike allows you great views of the South Palm Canyon near Hermit's Bench (the Indian Trading Post) and good vistas of Palm Springs and the nearby San Jacinto Mountains and canyons.

DIRECTIONS

DRIVE THROUGH PALM SPRINGS on Hwy. 111 until reaching the juncture with South Palm Canyon Drive. Turn onto South Palm Canyon Drive, following the signs to the Indian Canyons for 2 miles. From the Tollgate, proceed 2.5 miles to the Palm Canyon parking lot where the trading post is. Head east down the road/trail at the east end of the parking lot (the Additional Parking Lot). Fern Canyon trail begins at the north end of the Parking Lot.

Palm Canyon Trail rewards hikers with lush palm oasis.

Follow the trail just west of Palm Canyon Creek. The trail turns right and crosses over Palm Canyon Creek and into Fern Canyon. After 1 mile plus you will reach the area where ferns grow in abundance, especially in a wet winter. However, in drought seasons, this often spectacular display of ferns can be sparse. With a trail map from the Tollgate you will see that you can access both the Vandeventer Trail and the Hahn Buena Vista Trail from the Fern Canyon Trail if you want to make this short but scenic hike into something longer.

Hikes 48 – 52, 57

Hikes 48 and 57 continue on page 126

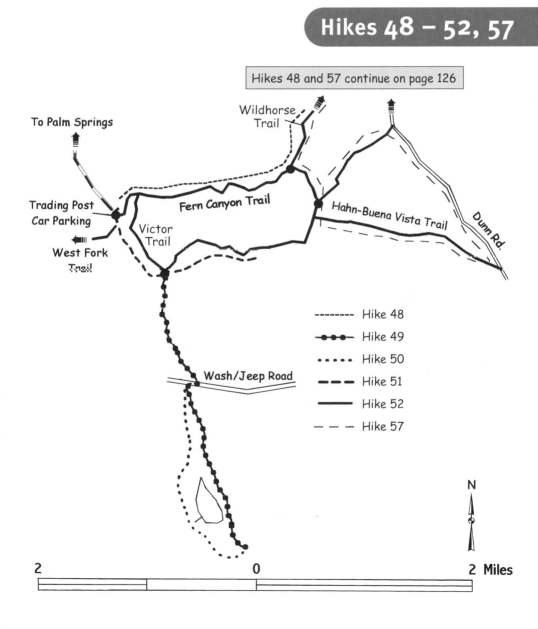

49 Palm Canyon Trail to the Stone Pools

(see map on page 111)

LENGTH: 6 miles

HIKING TIME: 3 hours

ELEVATION GAIN: 880 feet

DIFFICULTY: Moderate

SEASON: October to May

INFORMATION:
(760) 323-6018

This trail takes you through the lush junglelike river bottom of Palm Canyon, out onto backcountry high desert plateaus where the entire horizon seems to open up. Looking 14 miles south toward the distant Santa Rosa Mountains, the trail is surrounded by the soaring San Jacintos, which thrust up dramatically from the canyon floor. Stunning views of the desert and Palm Springs will appear to your rear, followed by a series of magnificent plunging cliffs, waterfalls, and exotic pools fed by clear, shimmering ribbons of water racing through the rock gorges. What are we waiting for? Let's go!

DIRECTIONS

BEGIN THIS HIKE by reaching Palm Canyon in the Agua Caliente Indian Canyons south of Palm Springs, as described in Hike 48.

Above Palm Canyon

Drop down into Palm Canyon from the trading post and continue for almost 0.5 mile until you cross the Palm Canyon Creek to your left. As you pass the right fork of Palm Canyon, veer left and follow the streambed and trail for another 0.5 mile until you reach the marker indicating that the trail crosses the stream and climbs up the south bank and the ridge above. Head south along this trail. Very soon the climb takes you out into the open country where the full, magnificent beauty of these canyons can be appreciated. The trail stays on a high plateau, with some occasional glimpses into small adjacent canyons. After 2 miles of hiking you will reach a wide dirt wash/jeep road. Take the trail straight ahead, rather than fol-

lowing the wash to the left. You will eventually arrive at a place where the trail melts away into the sandy rock, but is still faintly visible on the slowly climbing rise above the canyon to your right.

Turn right and down towards the canyon when it is obvious that the canyon bottom is less than 30 feet from the trail, and when a small trail comes off the main trail to take you to the area known as the Stone Pools along Palm Canyon Creek. In a wet year water flows freely and deep, often creating a series of small pools (hence the stone pools name), but in a dry year only sporadic water can be seen. Feel free to explore both up and down the canyon bottom before returning to the main trail and back to the trading post. A great spot to enjoy lunch!

Stone Pools area, Palm Canyon

50　Palm Canyon Trail to Indian Potrero

(see map on page 111)

LENGTH: 9 miles

HIKING TIME: 4 hours

ELEVATION GAIN: 950 feet

DIFFICULTY: Moderate

SEASON: October to April

INFORMATION:
(760) 323-6018

For centuries, the Agua Caliente Indians inhabited the magnificent canyon lands south of Palm Springs and Palm Canyon. You may expect to find some artifacts and signs of human habitation somewhere in or near Palm Canyon, and on this hike you do. The main draw, however, continues to be the stunning and expansive scenery, as Palm Canyon is ringed by dozens of adjacent canyons and looks up toward the high-country mountains of Desert Divide and San Jacinto Mountain. A stream flows beneath its towering mass and encourages the lush, junglelike growth found in this section of upper Palm Canyon. A fire in 1994 severely burned this area, so vegetation is only now making a comeback.

DIRECTIONS　Follow the directions for Hike 48.

Palm Canyon Gorge

From the Trading Post, hike down into Palm Canyon and head south (through the large grove of Palms and picnic tables). Follow Palm Canyon Creek from the trail above for .5 miles then cross over and walk alongside the canyon bottom as it turns east. In another almost 0.5 mile the trail junction/sign indicates the Indian Potrero Trail to be south of the creek. Cross over and begin a climb out of Palm Canyon. Soon the majestic San Jacinto Mountain/valley vistas reward you with stunning scenery. As you continue south you are east and just a few yards away from Palm Canyon, now hidden to the west by a rocky ridge.

After 2.25 miles from the Trading Post you intersect the dry wash and trail sign indicating Indian Potrero Trail still heading south. Continue for .75 miles until the trail leads you down into Palm Canyon. In a wet winter there is a generous stream and pools to enjoy.

Once on the canyon bottom turn left and follow the signs across the canyon and up the steep trail on the west side of the creek bed. As the trail climbs you will continue heading south but now on the west side of Palm Canyon. The wide-open mountain valley is a "real west" experience, beautiful in its rugged uplifted escarpments and expansive views. After 2 miles the trail meets up with the Palm Canyon Trail. You can return via the same way you came, or turn left (north) onto the Palm Canyon Trail, more like a road here, as it heads back to the trading post. Stay to the right whenever the trail leaves the canyon bottom for even a few yards, as it sometimes climbs just a few feet above the canyon below. Eventually you will intersect the Palm Canyon Trail where it meets the dry wash at the major sign/intersection. Continue right and up as you backtrack to the Trading Post, now just 2.25 miles away.

51 Lower Palm Canyon Trail

(see map on page 111)

LENGTH: 3–4 miles

HIKING TIME: 2 hours

ELEVATION GAIN: 100 feet

DIFFICULTY: Easy

SEASON: September to June

INFORMATION:
(760) 323-6018

This is a wild canyon scramble through twisted rock formations, along and sometimes in a rushing stream, with lush groves of massive Washingtonia palms providing a junglelike setting. Palm Canyon is the jewel of the many canyon hikes found in the sprawling Agua Caliente Indian Canyons south of Palm Springs. It is not as easy a hike as it looks. The rocks are very slippery, and the current can be surprisingly strong during peak snowmelt and runoff.

DIRECTIONS

TO REACH THE TRAILHEAD, drive through Palm Springs on Hwy. 111 until reaching the juncture with South Palm Canyon Drive. Turn onto South Palm Canyon Drive and proceed 2 miles to the Indian Canyons tollgate, then continue 2.5 miles to Palm Canyon and the trading post. The trail begins down the walkway from the trading post and to the right.

San Jacinto Mountains from Palm Canyon Trail

For the first 0.75 mile you are treated to a pathway above the stream; contorted rock formations which act as the riverbed; assorted pools (and often sunbathers); and a truly incredible concentration of palm trees, vines, cottonwoods, and desert plants, made possible by the abundant water supply.

The trail then drops down to Palm Canyon Creek and crosses over to the left side. In a very wet year, this crossing can be iffy, due to high water. The trail continues through the magnificent palm groves and eventually connects with the Victor and Palm Canyon Trail that heads south towards Hwy 74. Hike, however, on the Palm Canyon Trail that stays in the canyon and heads east. This segment becomes the East Fork Trail. Continue for another .5 to 1 mile before turning around and heading back to the trading post. The canyon bottom, cool in warm weather, makes for a perfect picnic spot.

52 The Victor Trail / Fern Canyon

(see map on page 111)

LENGTH: 2.5-5 miles

HIKING TIME: 2-3 hours

ELEVATION GAIN: 250-400 feet

DIFFICULTY: Easy

SEASON: September to June

INFORMATION:
(760) 323-6018

The world-famous Palm Springs Indian Canyons are fun to explore. I describe two routes here that can be easily combined, as one trail practically adjoins the other. The best time of day for this hike is early morning, as the canyons in fall and spring can get very warm very quickly.

DIRECTIONS

Follow the directions for Hike 51.

Begin the 2.5-mile route by heading down into Palm Canyon, just south of the trading post. Head along the lower Palm Canyon Trail, which follows alongside and then above the stream to the left of the trail. In 0.5 mile, you will cross the stream on your right and pass through a palm jungle. In another 0.5 mile, you will see a sign for the Victor Trail. Hike up the hill to your left, and you'll soon be treated to magnificent views of Palm Canyon below and mountains in the distance. Be careful of the cactus and other desert plants found in great abundance along the trail!

After more than a mile, you will drop back down into Palm Canyon. You can turn left, following the stream back to the trading post, or continue north for a matter of yards until you reach the sign for the Fern Canyon Trail.

Palm groves in Palm Canyon

If you choose to explore Fern Canyon, this hike becomes a 5-mile adventure. The walk to Fern Canyon is best done when the water is flowing, for giant ferns inhabit the main section of their namesake canyon when moisture is present. Once you've reached these unlikely desert dwellers, you can turn around and head back to the trading post.

53 Murray Canyon Trail
(see map opposite)

LENGTH: 6 miles

HIKING TIME: 4 hours

ELEVATION GAIN: 500 feet

DIFFICULTY: Moderate

SEASON: September to June

INFORMATION:
(760) 323-6018

Murray Canyon Trail takes you deep into the lower reaches of the San Jacinto Mountains via a palm-enclosed canyon stream found on the Agua Caliente Indian Reservation in south Palm Springs. This canyon differs somewhat from its close neighbor, Andreas Canyon, by offering the hiker many more miles of trail on which

to explore higher canyon elevations. The California fan palm is quite abundant in Murray, giving another lush escape from the surrounding desert heat. This hike requires more caution during high spring runoff, as the streambeds tend to challenge the trail at several crossings. You can hike farther up Murray Canyon in bushwhacking style, depending on the thickness of the undergrowth, the strength of the rushing waters, and your own adventurous spirit.

Yucca in the Palm Canyon area

DIRECTIONS

REACH THIS TRAIL by following directions for Andreas Canyon (Hike 56), found at the south end of Palm Springs in the Agua Caliente Indian Canyons, 2 miles south of Hwy. 111 on South Palm Canyon Drive.

When you reach Andreas Canyon, cross the stream and follow the signs south of the river. The trail meanders a while through the underbrush and along the stream before beginning to break away from its sister canyon and head in a more southwest direction. Desert willow, assorted cacti, and a scattering of cottonwood are found along the river. Take extra care along this waterway during strong and high runoff; hikers have been injured on the slippery rocks and in the deep water. This hike makes a great picnic adventure and treats you to the vistas of high canyon country and soaring cliffs.

Hikes 53 – 56

S. Palm Canyon Dr.
to Palm Springs

Toll Gate

Andreas Canyon

Car Parking

Maynard Mine

Murray Canyon

· · · · · Hike 53

- - - - - - Hike 54

– – – Hike 55

··—··— Hike 56

Trading Post
Car Parking

Lower Palm
Canyon Trail

West Fork Trail

● Indian Spring

Dos Palmas Spring
Jo Pond Trail to Cedar Spring

N

1   0   1   2 Miles

54 The West Fork Trail to Andreas Canyon
(see map on page 119)

LENGTH: 10 miles

HIKING TIME: 6 hours

ELEVATION GAIN: 2,500 feet

DIFFICULTY: Strenuous

SEASON: October to April

INFORMATION:
(760) 323-6018

The West Fork/Jo Pond Trail climbs dramatically and steeply upward out of Palm Canyon, eventually reaching the Pacific Crest Trail and Desert Divide, 6,000 feet above the valley floor. After 2 miles, the trail joins with another section heading north and climbs to reach a maximum elevation gain of 2,500 feet. By taking this right fork the hiker can make his or her way back to Andreas Canyon, thereby requiring a shuttle or car to be parked there and at the Indian Trading Post in Palm Canyon. You are treated to the most magnificent vistas of the high country above Palm Springs, as well as the long, palm-filled canyons below.

DIRECTIONS

To begin, head to the Agua Caliente Indian Canyons south of town described in Hike 51.

Just after several hundred yards down the Palm Canyon Trail, look to the right for a signpost which marks the beginning of the West Fork Trail.

You will climb through a wonderland of rocks and mountain vegetation—note as you ascend how quickly the scenery opens up below you. This trail is steep and strenuous. It can be demanding in warm weather. Hikers should take plenty of water and be careful of overextending themselves on a hot day.

After 2 miles take the trail to the right (northwest). The trail takes you to a rushing stream, surrounded by lush greenery. This could be the halfway point for hikers not wishing to do the total 10 miles or who have not made provisions for a shuttle.

From here the trail picks up across the stream and begins another rapid ascent up the mountain. The views will continue to amaze you. During late winter the slopes are ablaze with flowers and by spring the cacti follow suit. You will continue on this trail until it begins to emerge overlooking Murray Canyon to the north. The trail then descends to the lower slopes and crosses several streams, notably Murray Canyon. You might find the crossing difficult in wet winters, but continue downstream until you connect with a good crossing point. The trail picks up on the other side and eventually joins with the Murray Canyon Trail, taking you back to the parking lot in Andreas Canyon.

"Dakota—where did that mouse go?"

55 Maynard Mine Trail

(see map on page 119)

LENGTH: 7 miles

HIKING TIME: 3 hours

ELEVATION GAIN: 2,000 feet

DIFFICULTY: Strenuous

SEASON: October to April

INFORMATION:
(760) 323-6018

Alongside the mountainous ridge which rises above Murray Canyon on the western side of Agua Caliente Indian Canyons is a rugged trail leading up to the remains of an old tungsten mine, worked during World War II and known as the Maynard Mine after its developer, Jim Maynard. This hike not only takes you to the scattered remains of the mine, but also gives you great views of the canyon slopes across Palm Canyon Valley as well as the snowy ridgeline of Desert Divide. This is a great winter hike, taking you close to the Pacific Crest Trail above the valley, while showing you the swirling clouds and storms associated with the upper ridge.

DIRECTIONS

TO REACH THIS TRAIL, follow the directions for entering the Agua Caliente Indian Canyons given in Hike 56. Park at the Andreas Canyon parking area, cross the stream at the road walkway, and look for signs to Murray Canyon.

Begin on the Murray Canyon Trail as it makes its way quickly up the mountain. In short order you will come to a rock marker indicating a trail rising from the Murray Canyon Trail and heading in a steep fashion up another ridge. This is the Maynard Mine Trail.

The climb up the slope is relentless—nothing gradual about it. No shade covering is offered so hikers doing this trail in October or on a warm March day must be prepared for warm weather hiking. Essentially, you will be hiking

on slopes where the heat is reflected back by the rocks. After 5 miles you will reach your objective, the Maynard Mine.

All that remains is a 10-foot-deep hole for you to examine, and an old gas-powered engine, rather large, suggesting the strenuous work it took to haul it up the same slope you just hiked. Return by the same trail, treated to the many beautiful vistas of the valley and the distant peaks to the south.

"Where did you say we are?"

56 Andreas Canyon

(see map on page 119)

LENGTH: 2 miles

HIKING TIME: 2 hours

ELEVATION GAIN: 50 feet

DIFFICULTY: Easy

SEASON: September to June

INFORMATION:
(760) 323-6018

Tucked away in the southwestern corner of Palm Springs is a hiker's paradise, known locally as the Indian Canyons and situated on several thousand acres of the Agua Caliente Indian Reservation. The canyons join with the foothills of the soaring San Jacinto Mountains rising from the canyon floor and culminating in the 10,801-foot San Jacinto Peak. The Pacific Crest Trail looks down into these canyons from Desert Divide, the south by southwest mountain ridge which borders the reservation, and, during the winter, torrents of water wash through the canyons below. Many spectacular hikes begin or end in these canyons. One of the shorter but still quite lovely hikes is the Andreas Canyon hike, found less than a mile from the tollgate. This trail follows a stream (sometimes a river during peak mountain runoff) while winding through hundreds of native California fan palms. The towering snow-capped mountains above suggest to the hiker that countless hiking adventures await at higher elevations.

DIRECTIONS

TO REACH ANDREAS CANYON, drive south onto South Palm Canyon Drive where it meets Hwy. 111 in the south end of Palm Springs. Follow the signs to the Agua Caliente Indian Canyons, and after paying the toll, take the road to the right 0.75 mile to the picnic tables.

The trail follows the right side of the stream and crosses over several times before bringing you to a wire fence exactly 1 mile from the start. This stream can be quite high after heavy rainfall or when the snows melt in the mountains above the desert, usually in late February. The

Dakota alert to approaching wildlife

lush palms, vines, and bushes along the stream suggest a more tropical setting and contrast sharply with the desert below. Be careful of slippery rocks and hard-to-negotiate places. Andreas makes a great picnic or romantic get-away hike . . . but even the kids will find high adventure as they make their way under towering cliffs and through the rushing stream. March, early April, and late October are especially fine times to hike this and other trails found in the Indian Canyons.

57 The Hahn–Buena Vista Loop

(see maps on pages 111 and 126)

LENGTH: 16 miles

HIKING TIME: 8 hours

ELEVATION GAIN: 2,000 feet

DIFFICULTY: Strenuous

SEASON: October to May

INFORMATION:
No information

The Hahn–Buena Vista Loop was named after Jean Hahn, a member of the Desert Riders and an ardent equestrian. Buena Vista translates into "good view," and the 360 degree vistas afforded by this trail validate this choice of names. The trail itself is an isolated segment of the much larger network of trails surrounding the Murray Hill area east of Palm Canyon, and on the westernmost reaches of the Santa Rosa Mountains.

DIRECTIONS
To reach this beautiful section of trail, follow the directions for Hike 48.

Hike Fern Canyon until it joins the Wild Horse Trail. Turn right towards the Hahn-Buena Vista Trail. At the "Y" intersection, go left, making what appears to be a northwest jaunt to Dunn Road.

At Dunn Road turn right (south) and continue to where the Art Smith Trail joins it. You will find some much appreciated picnic tables where you can rest. Turn right off Dunn Road and begin following the Hahn–Buena Vista Loop back to the Wildhorse Trail and your eventual starting point. The views here are spectacular, and in a wet spring, wildflowers and blooming cacti accent the area.

This section of trail, as well as all the Murray Hill trail network, tends to warm up quite a bit on most fall or spring afternoons, so come prepared with adequate water and food.

Hikers should expect to traverse seasonal waterfalls in this section of the Santa Rosas.

Hikes 57 – 61

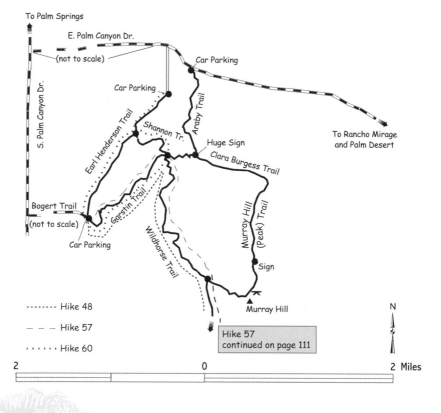

To Palm Springs

E. Palm Canyon Dr.

(not to scale)

Car Parking

Car Parking

Araby Trail

To Rancho Mirage
and Palm Desert

S. Palm Canyon Dr.

Earl Henderson Trail

Shannon Tr.

Huge Sign

Clara Burgess Trail

Garstin Trail

Bogert Trail

(not to scale)

Car Parking

Wildhorse Trail

Murray Hill (Peak) Trail

Sign

Murray Hill

------- Hike 48

– – – Hike 57

· · · · · Hike 60

Hike 57
continued on page 111

N

2   0   2 Miles

58 Murray Hill (Peak)

(see map above)

LENGTH: 9 miles

HIKING TIME: 5 hours

ELEVATION GAIN: 2,100 feet

DIFFICULTY: Strenuous

SEASON: October to April

INFORMATION:
No information

It's difficult to call Murray Hill anything but a "peak," yet officially it's a hill on all the maps. Unofficially, after climbing the 2,100 feet to the top, you'll think of it more like a PEAK! The views are magnificent, showing the region around Palm Springs, Cathedral City, and Palm Canyon, while offering you the nearby San Jacinto Mountains to the west.

DIRECTIONS   See directions for Hike 59, next page.

Murray Hill or "Peak" can be done using several combinations of trail. With this route you begin by following the directions for Hike 59 Earl Henderson Trail. Proceed up the mountain until reaching the junction for the Shannon Trail. From the Shannon Trail you have several options. Where the Shannon Trail connects to the Wild Horse Trail, take the Wild Horse Trail to the left and up until after 3 plus miles you access the picnic tables at Murray Hill. You can return the way you came or loop back on the Clara Burgess Trail until you again arrive at the Shannon Trail. You can also do this in reverse on the way up and proceed back via the Wild Horse Trail.

The landscape in a wet year can be quite green and bushy, with wildflowers scattered about. However this is an exposed trail with no shade and can be quite hot. In dry years the desolate landscape is countered by the magnificient vista views of the surrounding mountains, especially the San Jacinto Mountains to the west.

Vegetation along a desert creek bed in a wet year.

59 Earl Henderson Trail

(SEE MAP ON PAGE 126)

LENGTH: 4 miles

HIKING TIME: 3 hours

ELEVATION GAIN: 400 feet

DIFFICULTY: Easy

SEASON: October to May

INFORMATION:
No information

This trail is one of the many interconnecting trails found on the ridges and plateaus surrounding Murray Hill, east of Palm Canyon. The trail is named after Earl Henderson, past president of the equestrian group the Desert Riders. At the top of this trail, you are rewarded with scenic views of Canyon Country Club, South Palm Springs, and the San Jacinto Mountains thrusting up from the west side of Palm Canyon.

DIRECTIONS

FROM PALM DESERT, go west to Palm Springs via Hwy. 111 and Palm Canyon. Turn left (south) onto Araby Drive, proceed through Palm Canyon Wash, and park on the left-hand side of the road.

Head west up the wash for about 0.25 mile to the Palm Springs Trail sign. Turn left and follow the trail up to the Henderson and Shannon Trail signs. Continue southwest on the Earl Henderson Trail. After 2 miles, the trail ends at the Garstin Trail sign. From here, you are treated to a vista of Palm Springs, Palm Canyon, and Canyon Country Club. This makes a great early morning or evening hike—short, but with just enough elevation gain and good views to make the effort worthwhile.

Hikers sometimes encounter cattle along the trail above Palm Canyon.

60 Shannon Trail Loop
(see map on page 126)

LENGTH: 7 miles

HIKING TIME: 4 hours

ELEVATION GAIN: 1,000 feet

DIFFICULTY: Moderate

SEASON: October to May

INFORMATION:
No information

The Shannon Trail Loop is one of several beautiful variations of hiking loops offered by the unique interconnections of crisscrossing trails found in and around Murray Hill, on the eastern side of Palm Canyon. This loop gives you good views of the Palm Springs area and the nearby San Jacinto Mountains. The trail was named after Shannon Corliss, daughter of the equestrian Desert Riders' past president, Ray Corliss.

DIRECTIONS

TO REACH THE TRAILHEAD, drive east on Hwy. 111 toward Palm Springs and turn south (left) onto Araby Drive. Proceed through Palm Canyon Wash and park on the left or south side of the wash.

Lupine and desert wildflowers

Head west up the wash for 0.25 mile to the trailhead sign, Palm Springs Trail. Turn left and hike up the switchbacks until reaching the signs for the Earl Henderson and Shannon Trails. From here, view Canyon Country Club and Palm Springs.

To make the loop, continue along the Earl Henderson Trail until reaching the signpost for the Garstin Trail. Follow the Garstin Trail up to the overlooks of South Palm Canyon and the signpost for Wildhorse/Berns/Shannon/Garstin and Palm Canyon. Continue straight ahead in a northerly direction for a short distance to the next signpost, Garstin/Shannon/Henderson. From here, proceed left down the trail, quite steep in places, and take the Shannon/Henderson Trail back down to your starting point. This trail loop makes a wonderful early morning hike in spring, but take care to avoid hot desert afternoons, and always take a good supply of water.

61 The Araby Trail
(see map on page 126)

LENGTH: 6 miles

HIKING TIME: 3 hours

ELEVATION GAIN: 800 feet

DIFFICULTY: Moderate

SEASON: October to May

INFORMATION:
No information

Colorful rock outcropping, Mission Creek Area

The Araby Trail could also be dubbed the "trail to the stars," as it climbs above the Bob Hope Estate and the home of the late Steve McQueen. The view of these magnificent homes is readily available on this trail, along with that of Palm Springs. The Araby Trail is another great short but sweet "exercise" trail, allowing you to make the up-and-back trip in under 6 miles.

DIRECTIONS

FROM PALM DESERT, drive west to Palm Springs on Hwy. 111. Turn left (south) at the Rimcrest/Southridge Road and development. The trail can be found on the left (east) side of the road, shortly after turning.

As you hike up the Araby Trail, you are in for 3 miles of spectacular scenery and homes. The trail skirts the home of Bob Hope as it makes its way to the top of the ridge, before connecting with Berns/Garstin/Henderson Trail. At the signpost for these trails, one can return to the trailhead or continue and eventually interconnect with the many other trails found in these foothills. Take plenty of cool water if you do this hike in late spring or early fall—afternoon temperatures can approach 100 degrees.

62 North and South Lykken Trail
(see map on page 132)

LENGTH: 9 miles

HIKING TIME: 5 hours

ELEVATION GAIN: 800 feet

DIFFICULTY: Moderate

SEASON: October to March

INFORMATION:
No information

In 1972 the Skyline Trail was renamed the Lykken Trail in honor of Carl Lykken, a Palm Springs pioneer and the town's first postmaster. This magnificent desert view trail travels along the San Jacinto Mountains above Palm Springs, roughly following Palm Canyon Drive. The views of Palm Springs and the valley, which stretch toward the eastern horizon, will be awesome as you negotiate through the rocky terrain, accented in the spring with yellow blooming brittlebush and flowering cacti. En route to the end of the South Lykken Trail, you are treated to fabulous views of Palm Springs and of Tahquitz Canyon, held sacred by the Cahuilla Indians and abounding in vegetation and waterfalls.

TO BEGIN HIKING the South Lykken Trail, drive into Palm Springs via Hwy. 111, which becomes Palm Canyon Drive, and turn south onto South Palm Canyon Drive. Proceed south to Canyon Heights Road; 250 feet farther along on the west side of the road is a trail sign. As this is a shuttle hike, cars need to be parked here. The shuttle spot for the Lykken Trail is Cielo Drive off Panorama Road in Palm Springs.

Head west up the trail; before the switchbacks begin, you will come to the trailhead sign. The trail continues for 3 miles before it goes down to street level at Tahquitz Creek. Go north through Tahquitz Creek, following the trail signs (if there has been heavy rainfall or snowmelt, go over the creek by using the cement water dike). Meander over and down La Mirada Street until it meets Ramon Road. This marks the beginning of the North Lykken Trail.

Hikes 62 – 63

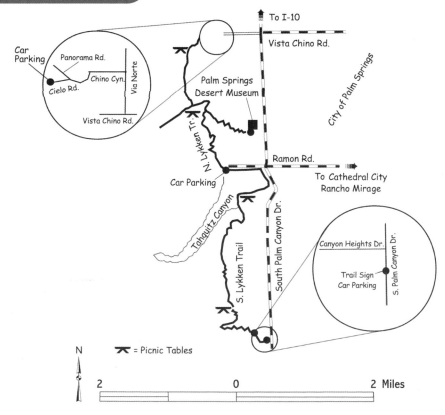

N

2   0   2 Miles

☩ = Picnic Tables

The trail becomes a switchback as it heads northwesterly toward Chino Canyon. After several miles you will reach the picnic tables overlooking the Palm Springs Desert Museum. Continue to take the trail north, as if heading around the corner of the mountain. The trail meanders down through a wash full of large rock and desert growth. On the other side of the wash you will have a gradual climb toward Chino Canyon, where the trail ends in a subdivision by descending the faint trail on the north side of the picnic table.

Hedgehog cactus

There is no shade on this trail so be sure to take plenty of cool water.

63 The Palm Springs Desert Museum Trail (see map opposite)

LENGTH: 2 miles

HIKING TIME: 2 hours

ELEVATION GAIN: 1,000 feet

DIFFICULTY: Moderate

SEASON: October to May

INFORMATION: Palm Springs Desert Museum, (760) 325-0189

DIRECTIONS

TO REACH THE TRAILHEAD, drive into Palm Springs on Hwy. 111 until reaching the downtown area. Turn west on Tahquitz Way, then right on Museum Drive. The museum is found directly in back of the Desert Fashion Plaza Mall. The trail begins in the north parking lot of the museum.

The Palm Springs Desert Museum is a cultural landmark in Palm Springs for all valley residents and visitors . . . an oasis offering the finest in art and cultural entertainment. So what better way to immediately involve yourself in the desert hiking scene than by walking out of the Desert Museum and onto the challenging Museum Trail found just outside its front door? The view from the top gives you a great look into the sprawling city of Palm Springs and the desert beyond. Although it's a steep hike of over 1,000 feet in just a mile, if the pace is kept slow and steady, most hikers can reach the picnic tables found at the trail's end with little trouble. After steeply ascending the mountain, the trail connects with the Carl Lykken Trail.

Desert wildflowers displayed along the trail

64 Tahquitz Canyon

(see map below)

LENGTH: 2.5 miles

HIKING TIME: 2 hours

ELEVATION GAIN: slight

DIFFICULTY: Easy

SEASON: September to May

INFORMATION: Tahquitz Visitor Center, (760) 416-7044

DIRECTIONS

FROM DOWNTOWN PALM SPRINGS, head south on Hwy.111/Palm Canyon Drive, looking for Ramon Road. Just south of Ramon is Mesquite Ave. Turn right here, and proceed to the end at the Tahquitz Visitor Center (500 West Mesquite). Hours are from 8a.m.–5p.m., with the last guided hike at 2p.m. Call for current admission fees.

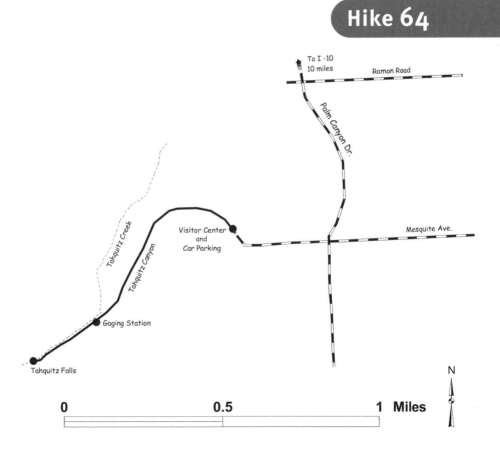

Hike 64

The South Lykken Trail leads above Tahquitz Canyon.

Staff from the Tahquitz Visitor Center will guide you on this 2.5-mile hike, accented by beautiful palms, native plants, wildlife, and spectacular rock formations. The visitor center itself maintains educational and cultural exhibits, an observation deck, a garden, a picnic area, and a theater room with a video about the legend of Tahquitz.

The Tahquitz Canyon area is one of the most beautiful of the famous Indian Canyons and is certain to provide hikers of all ages with a fun-filled adventure. While you're here, inquire about the other hiking trails in the Agua Caliente Reservation, just south of Tahquitz Canyon. The best time of year to visit this area from February through early April, when plants are greener due to winter rains, and the temperature is more moderate.

San Jacinto Mountains

HIKES 65 – 95

Trailhead Locations in the San Jacinto Mountains

Hikes 65 – 95

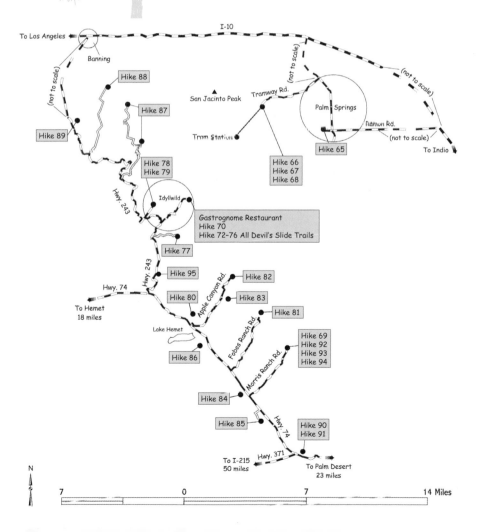

To Los Angeles

I-10

Banning

Hike 88

San Jacinto Peak

Tramway Rd.

Palm Springs

(not to scale)

Ramon Rd.

(not to scale)

To Indio

Hike 87

Hike 89

Tram Station

Hike 65

Hike 78
Hike 79

Hwy. 243

Idyllwild

Gastrognome Restaurant
Hike 70
Hike 72–76 All Devil's Slide Trails

Hike 66
Hike 67
Hike 68

Hike 77

Hwy. 243

Hike 95

Apple Canyon Rd.

Hike 82

Hwy. 74

Hike 80

Hike 83

To Hemet
18 miles

Lake Hemet

Fobes Ranch Rd.

Hike 81

Hike 69
Hike 92
Hike 93
Hike 94

Hike 86

Morris Ranch Rd.

Hike 84

Hike 85

Hwy. 74

Hike 90
Hike 91

To I-215
50 miles

Hwy. 371

To Palm Desert
23 miles

N

7   0   7   14 Miles

65 Cactus to Clouds Hike

(see map opposite)

LENGTH: 22 miles

HIKING TIME: 13 hours

ELEVATION GAIN: 10,400 feet

DIFFICULTY: Very strenuous

SEASON: May to October

INFORMATION: BLM Office, Palm Springs, (760) 251-4800

You crossed the Sahara Desert lately? Swam the Amazon River recently? Ran the Boston Marathon last week? Have we got a challenge for you! In all of the continental United States there is perhaps no higher elevation gain in one day than the Cactus to Clouds hike. From the beginning of the trailhead, this hike takes you up, and up, and up, 10,400 feet to the top of San Jacinto Peak . . . all in one day, all 22 miles of it!

The views of the Coachella Valley and surrounding mountain ranges are spectacular. The views of the seemingly impossible top are, too! But be in the best shape of your life to handle this one. One consolation: You get to ride the tram down to Palm Springs, instead of descending those 10,400 feet!

DIRECTIONS

DRIVE INTO PALM SPRINGS on Ramon Road from I-10 and park at the road's end. Park a second car at the Palm Springs Aerial Tramway.

Take the Lykken Trail up the switchbacks for about 1.5 miles until you reach a coffee-table size boulder on the left side of the trail. Painted on this boulder is a sign, "Long Valley 8 miles" (Long Valley is the valley adjacent to the Mountain Tram Station at 8,600 elevation).

This section of the trail looks down into Tacheva Canyon to the right (north) for about 2.5 miles. Although this early section of the trail is somewhat easy to find, the remainder of the trail to the top of Long Valley is sometimes faint and poorly marked and should be done only with someone who has previously hiked this section. This entire trail is virtually an unending succession of upward-reaching switchbacks—perhaps a respectable "hiking cousin" to the famed 97 switchbacks to Mt. Whitney.

There is no water available on this trail until you reach Long Valley. Up to the ranger station in Long Valley is almost 11 miles (about 8 hours hard hiking). From this point exhausted hikers may opt to make the short walk to the tram station and catch the next tram down to Palm Springs. (Don't feel too bad; many who have attempted the "Cactus to Clouds" saga have done just that.)

If you decide to continue, you will need a wilderness permit from the ranger station. The trail from here is clearly marked and well used. From the ranger station, proceed to Round Valley, then up to Wellman Divide. Here, the last section of the trail takes you almost directly to San Jacinto Peak. One-third mile from the peak is the side trail that will take you to your final destination. Several hundred yards from the peak is a stone cabin that serves as necessary shelter in poor weather conditions.

Once on the peak, you will enjoy a 360 degree view—of what seems like the whole world.

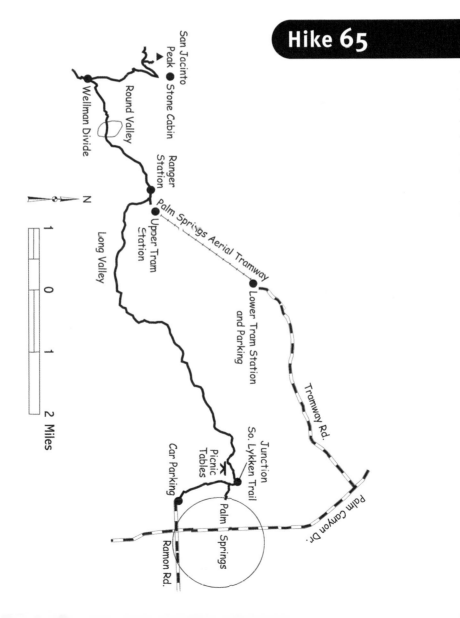

66 Palm Springs Aerial Tramway to San Jacinto Peak (see map opposite)

LENGTH: 11 miles

HIKING TIME: 6 hours

ELEVATION GAIN: 2,300 feet

DIFFICULTY: Strenuous

SEASON: May to November

INFORMATION: USDA Forest Service, Idyllwild, (909) 382-2922 or (951) 659-2117

Famous naturalist John Muir, after climbing to the top of San Jacinto Peak, exclaimed that the view was one of the most sublime spectacles seen anywhere on earth. This kind of endorsement is enough to get any serious hiker up the slope to the top! The peaks in the San Jacinto Mountains are huge granite massifs that remind the well-traveled hiker of the High Sierras, especially the chain of peaks from Lone Pine to Bishop. The 360 degree view from the top gives you a complete reference for all of southern California's mountain and desert landmarks, and on a very clear day you can actually peer into Nevada! The San Jacinto Mountains are relatively young, geologically speaking—perhaps 20 million years young. But the rocks in these mountains have been upthrust from deep within the earth and are perhaps 500 million years old! The hike to the top is varied, with the lower elevations offering sylvan meadows and streams before bringing you to the more demanding final climb up the alpine slopes near the peak.

DIRECTIONS

TO BEGIN THIS ADVENTURE, take the Hwy. 111 exit from I-10 into Palm Springs, or take Hwy. 111 from Palm Desert to Palm Springs. From the interstate exit, drive 9 miles to Tramway Road, then turn right and drive until you reach the parking area. Shuttle trams will take you to the tram station on crowded days. After paying the fee, ride the tram to the top, exit at the mountain station, and head toward the ranger station located 0.25 mile to the west. Obtain your day hiking permit, sign in, and take the trail leading to Round Valley.

During the early summer you will cross many streams or travel alongside them, but by early fall most have dried up. The trail winds up through the pine thickets until coming to beautiful Round Valley. Here the grass is deep green, tall, and richly watered—look for deer munching tender plants.

Continue toward the peak by taking the trail to Wellman Divide. This is a short, steep climb that gives you teases of views to come as you look back to the north and east into the desert below. At Wellman Divide the views are spectacular, both of the Tahquitz Peak area and the farther Santa Rosa Mountains. From this point you are only 2.7 miles from the peak. Follow the trail to the top, up steep switchbacks. The views will continue to amaze, as vistas grow ever more expansive and breathtaking. Near the top there is another trail junction: Take the one for San Jacinto Peak. In a short time you will come to and then pass a stone shelter for those caught in stormy weather. Just up from there is the peak.

Geographers claim that the angle of descent—the steepness of San Jacinto Mountain from top to base—is the sheerest in the United States. From the top looking down, most tend to agree. It can be quite cool at the top, even cold and very windy. Take a windbreaker, a pair of binoculars . . . and enjoy the view!

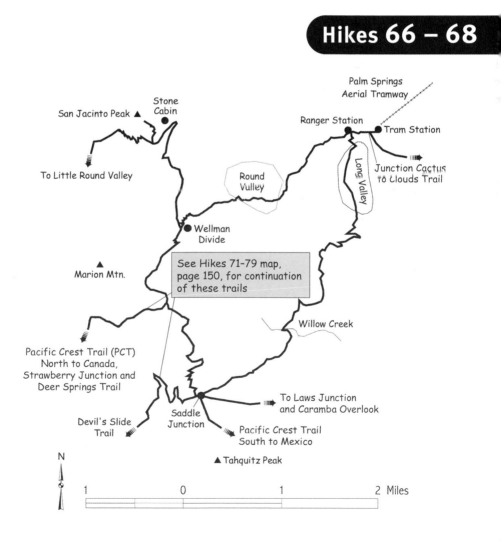

Hikes 66 – 68

Palm Springs
Aerial Tramway

Stone
Cabin

San Jacinto Peak ▲

Ranger Station

Tram Station

To Little Round Valley

Round
Valley

Long Valley

Junction Cactus
to Clouds Trail

Wellman
Divide

See Hikes 71-79 map,
page 150, for continuation
of these trails

▲
Marion Mtn.

Willow Creek

Pacific Crest Trail (PCT)
North to Canada,
Strawberry Junction and
Deer Springs Trail

To Laws Junction
and Caramba Overlook

Devil's Slide
Trail

Saddle
Junction

Pacific Crest Trail
South to Mexico

N

▲ Tahquitz Peak

1   0   1   2 Miles

67 Palm Springs Aerial Tramway to Saddle Junction Loop (see map on page 141)

LENGTH: 12 miles

HIKING TIME: 7 hours

ELEVATION GAIN: 3,000 feet

DIFFICULTY: Strenuous

SEASON: May to November

INFORMATION: USDA Forest Service, Idyllwild, (909) 382-2922 or (951) 659-2117

The top of San Jacinto Mountain and Wilderness Area is shaped in the form of a bowl, with the western side considerably higher than the eastern. This geographical feature allows hikers to do a magnificent loop hike from the Mountain Tram Station toward Saddle Junction above Idyllwild. The route follows a gradual descent from the high point of the "bowl" at Wellman Divide down to the bottom at Saddle Junction, along the bottom of the valley floor, and then finally up to the northern top ridges near the starting point. Hikers are treated to wide vistas that reinforce the notion of San Jacinto Mountain as being an "island in the sky."

DIRECTIONS

TO REACH THE TRAILHEAD, follow directions for Hike 66. Take Hwy. 111 into Palm Springs, turn up Tramway Road, and park. After riding up to the top of the mountain, head for the ranger station 0.25 mile west of the mountain station. Sign in and pick up your wilderness permit for your day hike to Saddle Junction.

Follow the trail up to Wellman Divide. This first 3-mile leg takes you up 1,200 feet through pine forests, along mountain streams that are quite full in early summer, and alongside the lush green grasslands of Round Valley. At Wellman Divide you first glimpse the expansive horizon vistas that will fill your vision for the better part of the next 2.5 miles. The towering granite massif of Tahquitz Peak dominates your view to the southeast.

As you head down the trail you will pass a series of small but delightful springs that flow from the mountainside and encourage a proliferation of ferns, flowers, and grasses. Descending farther, you will pass the junction with the Pacific Crest Trail, then head rapidly down to the pine groves surrounding Saddle

Junction. You will usually find a number of hikers gathered here, as this is the main crossroads for the hikes above Idyllwild.

Continue back to the tram by taking the trail from Saddle Junction north and west of Skunk Cabbage Meadows. This section of trail is populated by huge ponderosa pines, some say the largest in California. You will soon come to the cool waters of Willow Creek. Take a good rest here; for the next 2 miles the trail winds steadily up the mountain, but offers you good views of the Desert Divide and Santa Rosa Mountains to the southeast. You will finally reach the top of the "bowl" and can soon see the tram station in the near distance. Take at least 3 quarts of water, since this hike begins cool but ends warm.

View of the Coachella Valley from the tram to Saddle Junction

68 Palm Springs Aerial Tramway to Idyllwild (see map on page 141)

LENGTH: 8/9/11 miles

HIKING TIME: 4/5/6 hours

ELEVATION GAIN: 500/1,000 feet

DIFFICULTY: Moderate/Strenuous

SEASON: May to November

INFORMATION: USDA Forest Service, Idyllwild, (909) 382-2922 or (951) 659-2117

DIRECTIONS Follow the directions for Hike 66.

This hike description highlights three routes that will take you to Idyllwild from the Tram. They all begin after filling out your day-hiking permit at the ranger station, 0.25 mile west of the Tram.

Route 1: Willow Creek Crossing

Follow the trail west from the ranger station, then turn left at the first junction. A sign points to Idyllwild and Saddle Junction/Humber Park. After a mile of steady climbing, you'll begin topping out near Hidden Divide, and, shortly after, the trail will reach the edge of the mountain and start heading down. Spectacular views of the Coachella Valley to the east and north, the ridge of mountains heading southeast from San Jacinto Mountain, and Tahquitz Peak due south are visible as you begin down the south side of the mountain towards Saddle Junction.

In about 2.6 miles, you will reach Willow Creek Crossing—a fine spot for lunch in the spring and early summer when the creek is generously flowing. Roughly 2 more miles take you to Saddle Junction. Along the way, you will see the

remains of a recent forest fire, and, in early summer, a thicket of ferns and Skunk Cabbage. The trail continues south at Saddle Junction, then begins a 2.5-mile, 1,700-foot decent to the trailhead at Humber Park. Expansive views of the Santa Ana Mountains, to the west, and the Palomar Mountains, to the south, are visible for much of the descent.

View of the San Jacinto Mountains near the tram

Since this is a one-way hike to Idyllwild, your car or pick-up person must be waiting for you at the Humber Park Trailhead. This is the shortest, easiest route to Idyllwild.

Route 2: Wellman Divide

This route is only slightly longer than the Willow Creek hike, but it adds an additional 500 feet of elevation gain. After leaving the ranger station, continue 2.1 miles to Round Valley, a delightful forest-and-meadow combination. If the snowfall was adequate during the winter, you will follow a creek for much of the way. Another mile of hiking uphill takes you to the spectacular vistas from Wellman Divide, featuring Tahquitz Peak due south.

From here, the trail heads down for about 3 miles to Saddle Junction. This section was built on what looks like the high point of a large bowl-like ridge, and offers

Tahquitz Peak from Wellman Divide

great views east and down into the valley below. The trail continues heading down from Saddle Junction to Humber Park, as described in Route 1.

Route 3: Strawberry Junction/Deer Springs Trail

This is the longest route to Idyllwild and ends at the Deer Springs Trailhead, described in Hike 78. Begin by following the Wellman Divide as in Route 2. Head south towards Saddle Junction for 1 mile past Wellman Divide, then take the trail to the right to Strawberry Junction. This section offers very scenic and expansive vistas as you come over the western side of San Jacinto Mountain. This is a very stunning high-country environment. Turn left (south) at Strawberry Junction, and head down the mountain for 4.1 miles to the Deer Springs Trailhead. I feel that this route is a bit longer than the 11-plus miles shown on maps, and it can be quite warm on the Deer Springs side of the mountain in the summer. But the scenery and the feel of coming down off the mountain excites the senses, making this strenuous hike one of my favorites on San Jacinto Mountain.

69 Jo Pond/Cedar Spring Trail to Palm Canyon Trading Post (see map opposite)

LENGTH: 13 miles

HIKING TIME: 8 hours

ELEVATION GAIN: 1,300 feet

ELEVATION LOSS: 5,850 feet

DIFFICULTY: Strenuous

SEASON: October to April

INFORMATION: USDA Forest Service, Idyllwild, (909) 382-2922 or (951) 659-2117

For sheer, majestic vistas and spectacular spring flora, few trails in or near the Coachella Valley match the Jo Pond/Cedar Spring Trail, with its entire length stretching from atop the Desert Divide Ridge/Pacific Crest Trail (PCT) to the Indian Trading Post in Palm Canyon. This is a shuttle hike. Someone must drop you off at the Cedar Spring Trailhead in Garner Valley and pick you up at the Indian Trading Post in Palm Canyon. The best time for this adventurous hike, in regard to temperature, flora, and river runoff, is March to mid-April. The views are inspiring and beautiful as you hike up and over the Desert Divide Ridge, make your way along West Fork Canyon, and finally emerge over the sprawl of Palm Canyon before reaching the trading post at the canyon's head. Take your camera, hope that the snow is still blanketing the higher peaks, and be prepared for the rigors of an almost 6,000-foot drop in elevation— protect those knees and toes!

DIRECTIONS

TO REACH THE TRAILHEAD, drive 28 miles south on Hwy. 74 from Palm Desert and Hwy. 111, or almost 11 miles east of Mountain Center on Hwy. 74 if you come from Hemet. Turn north onto Morris Ranch Road at the CDF Fire Station, and proceed 3 miles to the sign that reads "Park Off Pavement." After parking, pick up the trail for Cedar Spring just a few hundred yards up the road.

You spend the first 0.5 mile walking through beautiful oak woods, along a rushing stream and over a stunning meadow before beginning the ascent up the slope to the PCT and Desert Divide Ridge. At the trail's beginning, a large sign marking the southern terminus of the newly built Jo Pond Trail indicates 3 miles to Cedar Spring, 7 to the picnic tables above West Fork Canyon, and 12.5 to the Indian Trading Post (it says 15 miles to the tollgate, which is 2.5 miles beyond the trading post).

As you climb toward the PCT, looking south you can see the Palomar Mountain Observatory atop Palomar Mountain and sections of Garner Valley. Once you're at the crest, and as you begin your descent over the ridge, the entire Coachella Valley spreads out before you, with Palm Canyon's 16-mile length snaking its way far below to the east. After a mile you will reach the cool incense cedar grove and camping area of Cedar Spring. From here the trail should be signed, indicating a climb left from the campground, along a stream/gully, and eventually climbing up and over to the burned mountainous area northwest of Cedar Spring, consumed by the July 1994 fire.

Once over this section, you will be hiking along the Garnet Ridge for 3 to 4 miles, with awesome high-country views of the entire length of the San Jacinto

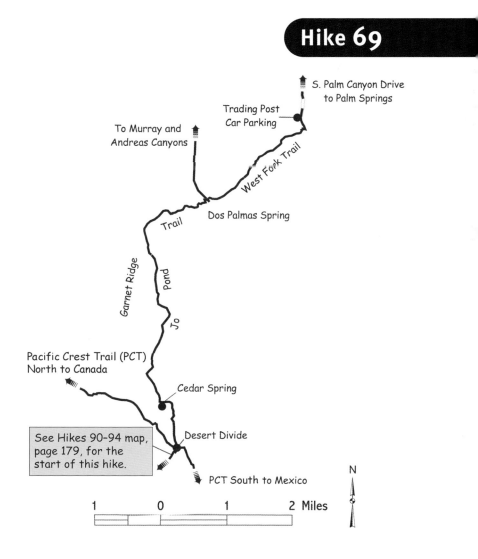

Hike 69

S. Palm Canyon Drive
to Palm Springs

Trading Post
Car Parking

To Murray and
Andreas Canyons

West Fork Trail

Dos Palmas Spring

Trail

Garnet Ridge

Pond

Jo

Pacific Crest Trail (PCT)
North to Canada

Cedar Spring

See Hikes 90–94 map,
page 179, for the
start of this hike.

Desert Divide

PCT South to Mexico

N

1   0   1   2 Miles

*The trees of
Cedar Spring
Grove provide a
shady resting spot
for fatigued hikers*

Mountains to the west, made especially scenic by a thick winter snow cover. Palm Canyon will continue to amaze you as you look east, with noticeable green patches, tree-filled canyons, and the obvious meandering trail along its bottom.

After the trail steeply drops for 7 miles down the ridge, with dozens of switchbacks, you will reach a trail junction where you turn right. From here the scenery really captures your aesthetic senses, as the trail comes down along the West Fork Canyon and offers you green valleys, waterfalls, grass-covered slopes, oases, stunning verdant canyons, flowers, and flowering cacti. This part of the hike is more like a trip through a nature preserve than through desert canyons!

After almost 12 miles, you will finally come over the ridge and look into verdant Palm Canyon. The trail quickly takes you to the canyon's bottom along a short section of raging stream and up to the Indian Trading Post for a richly deserved cool drink. This hike does test your ability to come down a steep trail . . . strong knees are a must!

70 The Ernie Maxwell Scenic Trail

(see map on page 150)

LENGTH: 5 miles

HIKING TIME: 3 hours

ELEVATION GAIN: 300 feet

DIFFICULTY: Easy

SEASON: May to November

INFORMATION: USDA Forest Service, Idyllwild, (909) 382-2922 or (951) 659-2117

The Ernie Maxwell Scenic Trail is the perfect leisurely hike, especially for families. This trail is marked by gentle contours, an occasional stream, and a generous mix of Jeffrey, ponderosa, and Coulter pines, with some incense cedar and fir. The trail bears the name of a local Idyllwild resident, Ernie Maxwell, to honor his pioneering conservation efforts and his love of the surrounding mountains.

DIRECTIONS

TO HIKE THIS TRAIL, follow the directions for Hike 72, taking Fern Valley Road out of Idyllwild. Just before reaching the topmost parking area, you will see the sign marking the entrance to the Ernie Maxwell Trail. No permit is needed for this trail.

Enjoy the gentle, quiet trail as it works its way through the forest thickets; September and October are especially nice months for walking this scenic route. The trail ends at a dirt road, where you simply return to the trailhead.

Thomas Mountain from Deer Springs Trail

71 Humber Park – Devil's Slide Trail to Caramba Overlook (see map below)

LENGTH: 14 miles

HIKING TIME: 8 hours

ELEVATION GAIN: 3,400 feet

DIFFICULTY: Strenuous

SEASON: June to November

INFORMATION: USDA Forest Service, Idyllwild, (909) 382-2922 or (951) 659-2117

San Jacinto Mountain stands like a cool sentinel rising from the hot desert floor of the Coachella Valley. From late spring to early fall, hikers refresh themselves in the forests 8,000 feet above the valley floor, and after hiking to one of the most spectacular desert overlooks at Caramba, they gaze with relief into the searing deserts below. The view stretches eastward all the way to the Salton Sea, while encompassing the Santa Rosa Mountains to the south.

Hikes 70 – 79

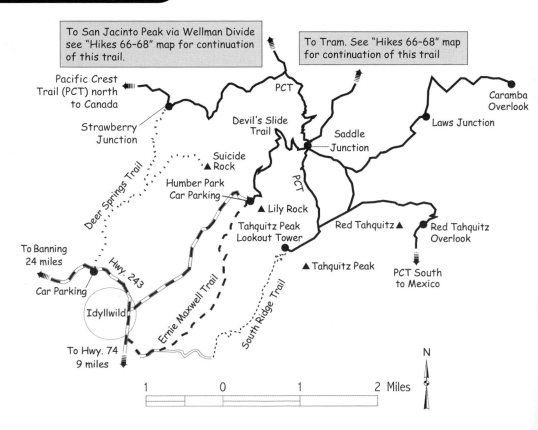

To San Jacinto Peak via Wellman Divide see "Hikes 66–68" map for continuation of this trail.

To Tram. See "Hikes 66–68" map for continuation of this trail

Pacific Crest Trail (PCT) north to Canada

PCT

Caramba Overlook

Strawberry Junction

Devil's Slide Trail

Laws Junction

Saddle Junction

Suicide ▲ Rock

Deer Springs Trail

Humber Park Car Parking

PCT

▲ Lily Rock

Tahquitz Peak Lookout Tower

Red Tahquitz ▲

Red Tahquitz Overlook

To Banning 24 miles

Hwy. 243

▲ Tahquitz Peak

PCT South to Mexico

Car Parking

Ernie Maxwell Trail

South Ridge Trail

Idyllwild

To Hwy. 74 9 miles

N

1   0   1   2 Miles

DIRECTIONS

TO MAKE THIS SPECTACULAR HIKE to the overlook, follow the trail directions for Hike 72. This hike requires a wilderness permit, which can be picked up at the ranger station in downtown Idyllwild.

After 2.5 miles you will come to the Saddle Junction intersection. Head for Laws Junction through and past the lovely Tahquitz Creek Valley, with its running streams and lush emerald grasses. After 4.7 miles you will reach Laws Junction, which makes a perfect lunch spot, highlighted by the beautiful sylvan water setting of Willow Creek.

The trail to Caramba Overlook leaves from Laws Junction and is a 2-mile descent through thinning forests to the rock formations known as Caramba. If the winter has been wet, you can find good water in nearby Tahquitz Creek, and even a running waterfall found by scrambling down from Caramba. This can be a very hot trail at the height of summer, so come prepared with an ample supply of water.

From Caramba, view the quiet desert below and the distant mountain ranges surrounding the Coachella Valley before starting the long climb back to Idyllwild.

Skitts near Saddle Junction above Idyllwild

72 Devil's Slide Trail to Saddle Junction

(see map on page 150)

LENGTH: 5 miles

HIKING TIME: 3 hours

ELEVATION GAIN: 1,700 feet

DIFFICULTY: Moderate

SEASON: May to November

INFORMATION: USDA Forest Service, Idyllwild, (909) 382-2922 or (951) 659-2117

Devil's Slide Trail is the most frequently used access trail to the glorious hiking and sylvan beauty found in the San Jacinto Wilderness area and along the many miles of trail which crisscross San Jacinto Mountain. Along this trail, the hiker gets to enjoy wonderful views of Marion Mountain and Suicide and Lily rocks, as well as great exercise in the short distance of 2.5 miles. By reaching Saddle Junction you will be at the main focal point of several key trails heading off in all directions, including the Pacific Crest Trail. Because this trail is very well used, especially during summer, day permits for the Devil's Slide Trail are limited on weekends and holidays between Memorial Day and Labor Day and need to be picked up at the Forest Service Office in Idyllwild.

DIRECTIONS

TO REACH THIS TRAILHEAD, drive into Idyllwild from Hwy. 243 from Banning and I-10, or take Hwy. 74 and 243 from Palm Desert. In Idyllwild, turn east on North Circle Drive (at The Fort Retail Shopping Center). Proceed north for over a mile until you reach South Circle Drive. Turn right, and then take your first left onto Fern Valley Road. Take the Fern Valley Road to Humber Park (about 2 miles from downtown). Park as the road begins to turn around at the trailhead and loop back on itself. Be advised that on busy weekends you need to get there early.

The trail starts right up the mountain along a series of steep switchbacks. You can see Suicide Rock to your left and the huge granite monolith of Lily Rock to your right rear . . . both popular for serious rock climbers.

The trail crosses six or seven small streams flowing down the mountainside, some of which will flow all summer if the snowfall was heavy. The views are breathtaking as you look back down into Idyllwild and to the south. It may be only 2.5 miles to the top, but if you explore around Saddle Junction in the morning and descend late afternoon during the summer, it can be quite hot, so carry a good supply of water.

Suicide Rock as viewed from Devil's Slide Trail

For years, Devil's Slide and the generous trail system found at the top have offered a cool respite for the desert dwellers of nearby Coachella Valley. The perfect ending to the perfect day is a well-deserved late lunch at one of the many fine restaurants in Idyllwild.

73 Devil's Slide Trail to Tahquitz Peak Lookout Loop (see map on page 150)

LENGTH: 13 miles

HIKING TIME: 7 hours

ELEVATION GAIN: 2,500 feet

DIFFICULTY: Strenuous

SEASON: May to November

INFORMATION: USDA Forest Service, Idyllwild, (909) 382-2922 or (951) 659-2117

This loop hike gives the hiker a chance to see the full range of peaks and valley views from the southern portion of San Jacinto Mountain and Wilderness Area. It is a strenuous full day of exploring the ridges and vistas found above Idyllwild and can be either a shuttle from the Devil's Slide Trailhead to Tahquitz Peak Lookout and down to South Ridge Road, where cars can be parked at both trailheads, or a full loop made by returning to Humber Park via the Ernie Maxwell Scenic Trail.

DIRECTIONS

TO BEGIN THIS DEMANDING YET SPECTACULAR LOOP, follow the directions for Hike 72. This hike requires a permit from the Forest Service Office in Idyllwild and a maximum of 15 is allowed in any one party.

After reaching Saddle Junction, take the trail to the right for Tahquitz Peak. During the next mile-plus, you will gradually ascend along a ridge that affords you dramatic views of the desert to the north and the flanking eastern slopes of San Jacinto Mountain. You reach a crossroads of several trails after hiking 1.4 miles. From there take the trail to the south as it makes its way up to the Tahquitz Peak Lookout. This section of the hike is dominated by granite mountains and steep slopes, less forested than at lower elevations. After reaching the lookout tower, head down the trail to South Ridge Trailhead. If you made this a full loop and not a shuttle, then once down South Ridge Road to where it meets Tahquitz View Drive, turn right up the road for about a mile until it meets the south end of the Ernie Maxwell Trail. This is the trail that will take you back to your vehicle at Humber Park.

This loop hike offers views of a full range of peaks and valleys, including South Ridge and Lily Rock.

74 Devil's Slide Trail to Laws Junction

(see map on page 150)

LENGTH: 10 miles

HIKING TIME: 5 hours

ELEVATION GAIN: 2,000 feet

DIFFICULTY: Strenuous

SEASON: May to November

INFORMATION: USDA Forest Service, Idyllwild, (909) 382-2922 or (951) 659-2117

The lush green meadows and scented pine forests of Tahquitz Valley invite the hiker to escape the warm summer lowlands of Southern California and the blistering desert of the Coachella Valley. Once at the top, you are treated to soft green and celery-colored grasses and a scattering of ferns and skunk cabbage, all watered by the cool mountain streams of Tahquitz and Willow Creek.

DIRECTIONS To reach this sylvan paradise, follow the directions for Hike 72.

Take the Devil's Slide Trail to Saddle Junction. There, the trail divides into several routes. Take the middle route to Laws Junction. In about a mile you will reach the cool, green meadows of Tahquitz Valley and Tahquitz Creek. As you head north toward Laws Junction, you will see a grassy field to your right surrounding a small rocky outcropping. Make for the rocks and enjoy a quiet snack next to Tahquitz Creek; deer often are seen drinking at the water's edge.

Continue down the trail through great stands of ponderosa pine until you reach Laws Junction. Lunch alongside beautiful Willow Creek. This is a spot of rare

Tahquitz Mountain from Hurkey Creek area

beauty—cool, serene, and a welcome halfway spot during a warm summer's day.

The route back is best made by following the trail left, avoiding the trail to Caramba Overlook. After a peaceful lunch you might find this section tiring, as it rapidly and unrelentingly climbs from the valley floor back to the trail heading south to Saddle Junction. You are rewarded, however, by several stream crossings and a picturesque look into the desert below. Be sure to take adequate cool water, since these mountain trails can be very hot in summer. A day permit is required for this and every hike that begins with the Devil's Slide Trail.

75 Devil's Slide Trail to Red Tahquitz Overlook (see map on page 150)

LENGTH: 11 miles

HIKING TIME: 6 hours

ELEVATION GAIN: 2,000 feet

DIFFICULTY: Strenuous

SEASON: May to November

INFORMATION: USDA Forest Service, Idyllwild, (909) 382-2922 or (951) 659-2117

This series of trails leads to an overlook near Red Tahquitz Mountain and gives the hiker great views of the Desert Divide Ridge, the Santa Rosa Mountains, and Tahquitz Valley. The trail takes you into the backcountry, onto the Pacific Crest Trail (PCT), and finally down through the cool, green watershed of Tahquitz Valley and Tahquitz Creek. This day hike allows you to feel and experience the wide diversity of all the various mountain ecosystems found along the southern and eastern flanks of the San Jacinto Mountain Wilderness.

Flowers found in the San Jacinto Mountains

DIRECTIONS   Begin this wonderful hike by following the directions for Hike 72.

Make your way up to Saddle Junction, and take the far right trail toward Tahquitz Peak for 1.4 miles until you reach the junction. Head down and east toward the trail for Red Tahquitz and Little Tahquitz Valley. The views here are wide and magnificent as you head into the valley. At the first junction turn right, up along the PCT. After one mile you will come to a large fallen dead tree along the right side of the trail. Look up and to your right, and begin bushwhacking up the 50 feet of slope, down a small gully, and up again until the high ground is reached. This is the lookout over the entire Desert Ridge Trail. You don't actually reach Red Tahquitz Peak, but this lunch spot offers stunning views to reward your scramble.

When returning, follow the trail down into Tahquitz Valley, then go left where the sign indicates a return back to Saddle Junction. The lush green here offers a stark contrast to the rocky overlook near Red Tahquitz Peak.

76 Devil's Slide Trail to San Jacinto Peak

(see map on page 150)

LENGTH: 16 miles

HIKING TIME: 7 – 8 hours

ELEVATION GAIN: 4,400 feet

DIFFICULTY: Strenuous

SEASON: June to October

INFORMATION: USDA Forest Service, Idyllwild, (909) 382-2922 or (951) 659-2117

DIRECTIONS   Follow the directions for Hike 72.

After parking at Humber Park, begin this adventure hike by taking the Devil's Slide Trail 1,700 feet and 2.5 miles up to Saddle Junction. From there, turn left toward San Jacinto Peak, making your way through white fir and Jeffrey pine, with spectacular views of Lily Rock and Tahquitz Peak. In 2 miles you will reach the trail going left to Strawberry Cienaga, but continue past this side trail toward Wellman Divide.

As you approach the divide, droplets of water often flow from above, over the thick moss to the left of the trail. At Wellman Divide the trail continues up and left toward San Jacinto Peak while another right branch drops down toward Round Valley and the tram station. On the way up the trail you will continue to get great views of the surrounding peaks and the San Jacinto Mountain high

country, until coming to the last section of trail, a short "peak" trail that passes a stone cabin, which is 0.2 mile to the peak.

From there the views are magnificent, especially on clear days when no marine layer of clouds is present to the west.

For a different return, you can have someone wait for you in the Palm Springs Lower Tram Station, and take the left fork trail down to the

Colorful floral display in Garner Valley

tram at Wellman Divide. This "short version" saves you almost 3 miles versus the same-way return to Humber Park and Idyllwild.

77   South Ridge Trail to Tahquitz Peak Overlook (see map on page 150)

LENGTH: 7 miles

HIKING TIME: 4 hours

ELEVATION GAIN: 2,000 feet

DIFFICULTY: Strenuous

SEASON: May to November

INFORMATION: USDA Forest Service, Idyllwild, (909) 382-2922 or (951) 659-2117

The South Ridge Trail offers the hiker access to the higher southerly elevations of the great granite massif of San Jacinto Mountain. This steep trail takes you quickly through Jeffrey pine, live oak, and white fir to the more numerous lodgepole pine around Tahquitz Peak. The views, however, are the real treat. Along the way, the entire vista of the Desert Divide and Pacific Crest Trail, which form the eastern flank of the San Jacinto Mountains, can be seen. To the north, the hiker sees Marion Mountain surrounded by its granite crags. This trail is steep in places and demands that the hiker be in good aerobic condition.

DIRECTIONS

THIS TRAIL requires a wilderness permit from the Forest Service Office in Idyllwild and is reached by driving on Hwy. 74 south from Hwy. 111 in Palm Desert, turning right on Hwy. 243 at Mountain Center and proceeding about 4 miles to Saunders Meadow Road. From I-10 in Banning, take Hwy. 243 to Idyllwild and proceed south out of town until you come to this same road. Turn onto Saunders Meadow Road, then left on Pine Street for 0.25 mile, then right on Tahquitz View Drive for about 0.75 mile. You will then come to the base of South Ridge Road to the right. If you have a 4WD vehicle, proceed up the road for 1.5 miles to the trailhead; otherwise walk up to avoid the deep potholes and washouts if the winter has been severe.

Once at the trailhead, you will begin a steep climb that quickly offers you those great views. After a mile you'll be able to see Garner Valley, Thomas Mountain, and Lake Hemet to the south. A little farther up, the full glory of the Desert Divide Ridge is revealed to the east. Many hikers photograph themselves at a unique "window rock" found 1.5 miles up the trail which frames the wild granite crags to the north. The trail steeply switchbacks up to Tahquitz Peak Lookout Tower, offering you a 360-degree sweep of all the mountains in this area.

San Jacinto Mountains from Keenwild Trail, May Valley Road

78 Deer Springs Trail to Saddle Junction/ Humber Park (see map on page 150)

LENGTH: 12 miles	SEASON: May to November
HIKING TIME: 7 hours	INFORMATION: USDA Forest
ELEVATION GAIN: 3,300 feet	Service, Idyllwild, (909) 382-2922
DIFFICULTY: Strenuous	or (951) 659-2117

The Deer Springs Trail offers a vista-filled hike up San Jacinto Mountain's southwest flank, connecting to the Pacific Crest Trail (PCT) before descending along a lengthy ridge to Saddle Junction and finally to Humber Park Trailhead. The views from the ridge above Idyllwild are memorable, with the massive granite Tahquitz Ridge and Lily Rock filling the southeast horizon. This is a shuttle hike requiring hikers to park cars at both the Humber Park Trailhead (Devil's Slide Trail) and Deer Springs. The late summer weather can be tricky. The last time I did this hike we began in 80 degree temperatures and ended with a torrential downpour accompanied by hail.

DIRECTIONS

TO REACH THE DEER SPRINGS TRAIL, take Hwy. 243 west of Idyllwild for 1 mile, and park on the left at the Idyllwild County Park Visitor's Center. The trail begins across the street at the wooden sign.

For the first 4.1 miles, you will climb through Jeffrey pine, oak, and manzanita. Looking west you will see the Hemet Valley and Santa Ana Mountains . . . on a smog-free day, that is! You will then intersect the PCT, which you'll take up to the

ridge. Along the way you are treated to beautiful views, an occasional running spring, and an excellent chance to see wildflowers, especially Indian paintbrush.

After 8.3 miles you will arrive at Saddle Junction for your 2.5-mile descent to Humber Park. If you are shuttling, remember that on summer weekends and holidays, the Humber Park area can be filled with cars by mid morning; also, a day-hike permit is required.

Lily Rock beneath Tahquitz Peak

79 Deer Springs Trail to Suicide Rock

(see map on page 150)

LENGTH: 7 miles

HIKING TIME: 3 – 4 hours

ELEVATION GAIN: 1,400 feet

DIFFICULTY: Moderate

SEASON: May to November

INFORMATION: USDA Forest Service, Idyllwild, (909) 382-2922 or (951) 659-2117

This hike is especially beautiful when winter snows have melted enough to allow a clear trail to the summit of Suicide Rock, or there are 6 inches or less on the trail at the base of Suicide Rock.

DIRECTIONS

Follow the directions for Hike 78.

After parking at the trailhead, walk across Hwy. 243 to access the beginning of the hike. Deer Springs Trail leads through chaparral of manzanita and ribbonwood, pine, and low brush. In a wet winter this trail is best done in May-June, as several good streams cross or run alongside the trail and thick moss sometimes can blanket rocks where the runoff is generous. The trail climbs quickly toward the junction with the side trail that leads to Suicide Rock after 2.3 miles. At this point the ponderosa pine are large and dominant. At

Flowers found in the San Jacinto Mountains

the junction turn right, noting Tahquitz Peak as the tallest mountain to the east across the valley, and Lily Rock—a rock formation that lures many climbers on any summer weekend—as a prominent granite formation down and to the left of Tahquitz Peak.

After turning right onto the trail to Suicide Rock, you are treated to vistas of Garner Valley and Thomas Mountain to the southeast and open horizons of the Santa Ana Mountains to the west. The trail encounters a fast-running stream, which drops down across the trail, and large scattered pines near Suicide Rock.

The last 0.25 mile climbs to Suicide Rock, where you must negotiate large boulders to gain the "summit." You will enjoy 360 degree views of the lands south and west of Idyllwild.

Hikes 80 – 83

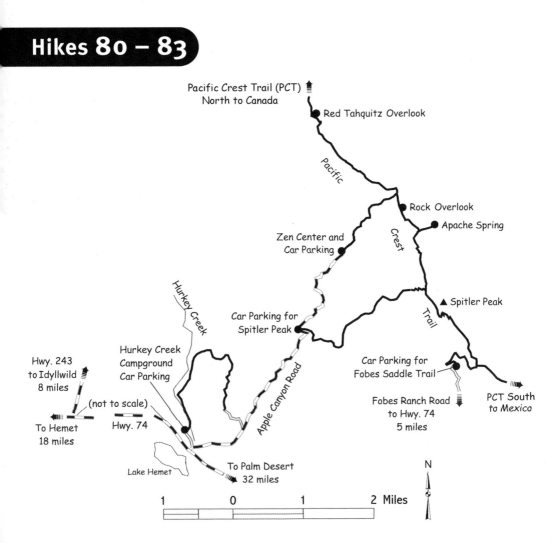

80 Hurkey Creek Trail

(see map opposite)

LENGTH: 3 miles

HIKING TIME: 2 hours

ELEVATION GAIN: 300 feet

DIFFICULTY: Easy

SEASON: May to November

INFORMATION: Hurkey Creek Campground, Hurkey Creek (909) 659-2050

San Jacinto Mountains from Hurkey Creek Trail

South of the Desert Divide Ridge and the Pacific Crest Trail in Apple Canyon, the mountains slope down and across a valley to reach over to Thomas Mountain. Hurkey Creek drains this area, and a county-run campground can be accessed for reservations from April 1 to October 21. The area around Hurkey Creek is quiet and scenic and offers a convenient campsite for those coming from either the Coachella Valley or metropolitan Los Angeles. A short but very scenic trail winds its way out of the campground and into the surrounding higher elevations. For day hikers wanting an easy hike, this trail fits the bill. From May to early June, flowers are in bloom along its path, and gentle vistas of the surrounding mountains complement the simplicity of this trail.

DIRECTIONS

TO REACH THE TRAIL and campground, drive on Hwy. 74 out of Hemet, to almost 4 miles past the junction of Mountain Center and Hwy. 243, or drive south on Hwy. 74, 32 miles from Hwy. 111 in Palm Desert. At Apple Canyon Road, across from Lake Hemet, turn north and then take a sharp left into the campground. The trail begins at the far west/southwest part of the campground.

In early spring, be prepared for water and runoff spilling across and alongside the trail. The hike follows a wide dirt trail, climbs onto a nearby plateau and, if the brush has been cleared, leads back into the campground. Most hikers prefer to walk to the scenic open spaces, admire the view, and smell the flowers before turning back.

81 Fobes Saddle to Spitler Peak and Apache Spring (see map on page 162)

LENGTH: 9 miles

HIKING TIME: 4 hours

ELEVATION GAIN: 1,800 feet

DIFFICULTY: Strenuous

SEASON: March to December

INFORMATION: USDA Forest Service, Idyllwild, (909) 382-2922 or (951) 659-2117

The advantage of the Fobes Saddle Trail is the quick access it gives the hiker to the Pacific Crest Trail (PCT). This section of the PCT/Desert Divide is known for its ruggedness, chaparral, and scrub brush and continues to take the hiker closer to the large mass of San Jacinto Mountain.

DIRECTIONS

TO GET TO THE TRAILHEAD, take Hwy. 74 south from Palm Desert for almost 30 miles. After passing Morris Ranch Road, begin looking to the right for the large sign indicating Fobes Saddle Trail. The entry past the sign is through a metal gate left open during the day. This road to Fobes Saddle Trailhead is not paved and is more safely done by a 4WD vehicle.

The trail begins after a 4-mile drive down the dirt road. There is a very fast switchback of 1.5 miles up to the ridge and the PCT. Turn left and up the mountain through brush and forest thickets. If the trail has not been well maintained, you will find the going slow. The views of the Coachella Valley are beautiful but the vegetation is more wilderness scrub. Continue for almost 2.5 miles to Spitler Peak, which rises above you to the south. After the peak, continue west until you see the sign for Apache Spring, a 500-foot descent down the mountain. If the winter snow has been heavy, this section might have several feet of snow for you to contend with.

82 The Zen Center to Red Tahquitz Overlook (see map on page 162)

LENGTH: 12 miles	**SEASON:** May to November
HIKING TIME: 7 hours	**INFORMATION:** USDA Forest
ELEVATION GAIN: 2,500 feet	Service, Idyllwild, (909) 382-2922
DIFFICULTY: Strenuous	or (951) 659-2117

There are vista hikes all along the Pacific Crest Trail (PCT) ridge of the San Jacinto Mountains. However, this section of trail has many a hiker's vote for being the most scenic and spectacular. It is one of the favorite hikes of the Coachella Valley Hiking Club and offers a stunning variety of vistas and terrain. The trail is not on many maps because the first section of the trail begins on private property at the Zen Center east of Idyllwild. The Zen Master in residence allows hikers to use this trail but with several cautions. Bring as few vehicles as possible. Hike quietly for the first 0.5 mile, to avoid disturbing the meditation and tranquility of those staying at the Center. Keep groups small, and no dogs are allowed.

DIRECTIONS

TO REACH THE TRAILHEAD, drive 3.5 miles east of the Hwy. 74/Mountain Center junction, or approximately 33 miles south of Palm Desert on Hwy. 74. Turn onto Apple Canyon Road and continue almost 4 miles until you reach the large Retreat Center, which looks like a hotel. Drive down the dirt road—found to the right of where the paved road ends and next to a small fence—until you reach the Zen Center. Park in the small dirt area just before entering the grounds.

The trail begins north of the parking area and meanders through the center's scattering of cottages and trailers. Cairns mark the trail. You continue this way for almost 0.5 mile until the trail appears to end in a grove of beautiful incense cedar, converging along a quiet stream. Look up and to the left to find the trail marked as it begins climbing the hillside through thickets of bush, pine, yucca, and manzanita. Keep a sharp eye out for the trail, as it seems to sometimes merge into other side trails.

The ascent up the mountain is a steep 1,200-foot gain in just over a mile. Be careful of the cacti and slippery trail conditions. Once at the top, to the right you will find a log resting place for a well-deserved break. The trail intersects the PCT a few feet north of the logs. Although the day's hike is to the west, take the trail to the right (east) for 0.5 mile up and alongside the mountain. This section is highlighted by awesome sheer drops into steep rocky canyons and colorful rock formations. You will finally turn a corner and see a 200-yard rock overlook to your left. Hike out to the end for the most awesome views of this entire desert and mountain region. Return to where the trail heads west from the log rest stop. You are treated along the way to splendid canyon views of West Fork and Murray canyons, rising steeply out of Palm Canyon below.

The trail is an adventurous hike beneath the ridge of the mountain and sometimes actually reaches the crest from which you can see toward San Diego and the Pacific Ocean. The magnificence of the views along this hike cannot be overstated. They will make you feel happy to be alive and glad you took up hiking! There is an exhilarating feeling of openness all during the hike. As you head ever closer to the view of Red Tahquitz and massive San Jacinto Mountain, you can look down the entire length of the Salton Sea, accented by the equally exciting view of the mountain ranges which extend to the Anza-Borrego Desert.

The hike ends when you come to a granite saddle from which Red Tahquitz Peak looks so very close but is still several miles of strenuous hiking away. If you have the stamina you can continue to Red Tahquitz. The return hike gives you miles of great vistas all the way from where the trail starts down to the Zen Center. Here, be very careful. The trail is steep and the footing is slippery. Remember to observe silence or at least quiet conversation as you approach the Zen Center.

The connector trail up to the PCT is not maintained by the Forest Service and can be quite difficult to negotiate. Also, there is no trail sign indicating the PCT where the connector trail meets at the top of the ridge. Take extra care to note this trail juncture for your return. Because of the rough trail conditions, this hike should be done in a group or with someone who has done the trail previously.

Santa Rosa Mountain from Garner Valley

83 Spitler Peak Trail

(see map on page 162)

LENGTH: 10 miles

HIKING TIME: 6 hours

ELEVATION GAIN: 2,000 feet

DIFFICULTY: Strenuous

SEASON: Year-round

INFORMATION: USDA Forest Service, Idyllwild, (909) 382-2922 or (951) 659-2117

This trail to Spitler Peak is the most direct route up the mountain, allowing the hiker to avoid lengthy sections of the Pacific Crest Trail (PCT) in an attempt to reach the peak. The views at the top show the panorama of the Santa Rosa and San Jacinto mountains with glimpses of the Palomar Range to the south. The first 3–4 miles of this hike are especially scenic, offering great views of Lake Hemet to the south. You may choose to do only the first 3 miles of this hike for an easy, but very scenic, experience.

DIRECTIONS

REACH THE TRAILHEAD by following the directions for Hike 65. Drive 33 miles south of Palm Desert on Hwy. 74. Turn right on Apple Canyon Road (3.5 miles east of Mountain Center). At nearly 3 miles you will see the sign for the Spitler Peak Trail on the road's right shoulder. Park here and begin the climb to the peak.

The trail winds steeply up through manzanita and other chaparral brush. If the trail has been properly maintained, as it usually is, the ascent up the slope is relatively unimpeded. Once at the top, you can choose to head either east toward Fobes Saddle and down to the trailhead, or west to where the PCT meets the Zen Center Trail. Either way, you must arrange a shuttle. Each of these hikes is close to 8 miles long and is also described elsewhere in this book. The trail to Spitler Peak is a short 0.5 mile from where the PCT meets the trail coming up from the trailhead.

Dakota scouting among rocks along Spitler Peak Trail

Hikes **84 – 86**

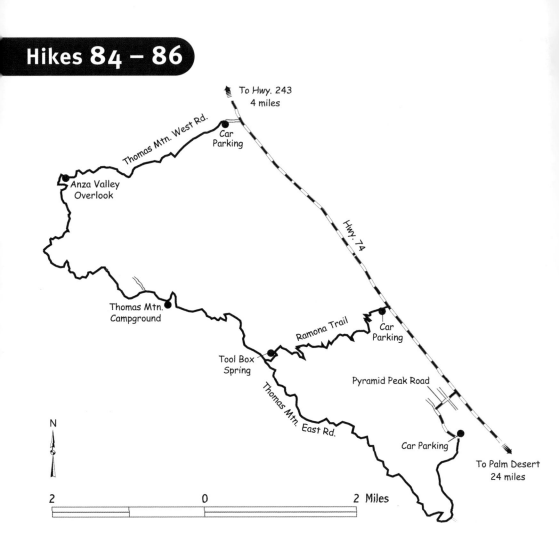

To Hwy. 243
4 miles

Thomas Mtn. West Rd.

Car
Parking

Anza Valley
Overlook

Hwy. 74

Thomas Mtn.
Campground

Ramona Trail

Car
Parking

Tool Box
Spring

Pyramid Peak Road

Thomas Mtn. East Rd.

Car Parking

To Palm Desert
24 miles

N

2   0   2 Miles

84 Ramona Trail to Tool Box Spring

(see map opposite)

LENGTH: 10 miles

HIKING TIME: 6 hours

ELEVATION GAIN: 2,000 feet

DIFFICULTY: Strenuous

SEASON: Year-round

INFORMATION: USDA Forest Service, Idyllwild, (909) 382-2922 or (951) 659-2117

South of the San Jacinto Mountains rises the much smaller Thomas Mountain. This mountain forms the southern border for the intervening Garner Valley. There are few trails on this mountain, the San Jacintos having captured the lion's share with the Pacific Crest Trail and Desert Divide Ridge. Still, the beautiful trail to the top of Thomas Mountain via Tool Box Spring is worth the effort.

DIRECTIONS

TO REACH THIS TRAILHEAD, travel 8 miles east from the junction of Hwy. 243 and 74, staying on Hwy. 74 until you see the trailhead sign to your right. From Palm Desert, take Hwy. 74 south almost 28 miles and look for the trail sign to your left indicating Thomas Mountain.

Access the trail by walking along the trail south of the fence and parking area, then taking the trail behind the trail sign as it begins its switchback up the mountain. As is common to these mountains, you will hike through thick outgrowths of manzanita, ribbonwood, and sage. Manzanita is the smooth bush with dark red bark that is often mistaken for ribbonwood, which has ribbonlike bark hanging as streamers. The valley and mountain views are panoramic!

After almost 3 miles you will arrive at Tool Box Spring, where a dirt road joins with the trail. Continue for another 1.5 miles west along the mountain ridge to a junction where you can turn left for the 0.5-mile ascent of Thomas Mountain.

The views at the top are of Anza Valley to the south and the San Jacinto Mountains to the north, with Garner Valley in between. This trail can be hot in the summer, depending on whether cool ocean breezes are blowing onshore from the Pacific.

Cattle round-up, Garner Valley Ranch

85 Thomas Mountain East Road to Summit (see map on page 168)

LENGTH: 10 – 12 miles

HIKING TIME: 6 hours

ELEVATION GAIN: 2,000 feet

DIFFICULTY: Moderate/strenuous

SEASON: Year-round

INFORMATION: USDA Forest Service, Idyllwild, (909) 382-2922 or (951) 659-2117

This hike offers spectacular views of the Anza Valley to the south and the San Jacinto Mountains/Desert Divide Ridge—along which the Pacific Crest Trail follows—to the north. The top of Thomas Mountain is well forested with ponderosa pine and gives cool relief to desert hikers from late spring through early fall. Restrooms and picnic tables complete the amenities, but the real reward is a scenic, gently graded trail that is more moderate than strenuous.

DIRECTIONS

FROM HWY. 111 in Palm Desert, turn south onto Hwy. 74 and proceed for 24 miles until you pass Hwy. 371 to San Diego. Stay on Hwy. 74 for 3 miles past the 371 cutoff. Look to the left for Pyramid Peak Road with a brown sign indicating Thomas Mountain (6s13). Turn left down Pyramid Peak Road until it dead-ends at the stop sign. Then turn left at Hop Patch Springs Road and continue for another mile until the road changes from paved to dirt. Park where convenient. A National Forest Adventure Pass (NFAP) is required for parking. If you arecoming from Hemet, Pyramid Peak Road is almost 9 miles from Mountain Center on the right.

After parking, begin the gentle hike up this dirt road, being watchful for any vehicles coming down the mountain. The drivers often do not expect hikers, so give them ample road space. The first 0.5 mile features ponderosa pine, but soon the vegetation thins out into high chaparral, with a bias toward ribbonwood. If the winter rains have been generous, this trail will yield a rich array of wild-flowers and flowering bushes in late March through May. It's best to do this hike in the early morning to smell the sage and other flowering plants while the air is still cool and moist.

The first section of the hike reminds me of the Hill Country near Austin, Texas, and offers pastoral views of the valley to the south. After almost 3 miles the views begin to favor the San Jacinto Mountains to the north. If winter snow is abundant on this range, the view in early spring can be stunning. The hike continues past a cow grating where cows may be grazing. Quickly and quietly pass by, and continue up the mountain, turning back often to see the Anza-Borrego Desert far to the southeast.

After almost 5 miles you will enter the thickly forested area at the top of Thomas Mountain. Restrooms soon come into view, along with picnic tables. You can continue on this trail and see beautiful pine forests, turning back and returning down the same trail whenever you feel that you've gone far enough. This trail is delightful in any season, offering great vistas to the north and south, as well as Garner Valley lying between Thomas Mountain and the San Jacinto Mountains to the north.

High chaparral near Thomas Mountain East Road

86 Thomas Mountain West Road to Anza Valley Overlook (see map on page 168)

LENGTH: 10 miles

HIKING TIME: 4 – 5 hours

ELEVATION GAIN: 2,000 feet

DIFFICULTY: Moderate/strenuous

SEASON: Year-round

INFORMATION: USDA Forest Service, Idyllwild, (909) 382-2922 or (951) 659-2117

A view of Garner Valley from Thomas Mountain West Road

This hike completes the trio of hikes on Thomas Mountain (see also Hikes 84 and 85) and offers spectacular vistas of Lake Hemet early on, the San Jacinto Mountains to the north, the Santa Ana Mountains to the west, and the expansive Anza Valley to the south.

DIRECTIONS

FOLLOW THE DIRECTIONS for Hike 68, but after driving 27 miles from Hwy. 111 in Palm Desert, continue another 4.5 miles until you see on your right the brown sign indicating Thomas Mountain Road. This road is just east of Lake Hemet by almost a mile. Turn left off Hwy. 74 and park where convenient. Like all trails in the Santa Rosa/ San Jacinto Mountains, this trail requires a National Forest Adventure Pass (NFAP).

After parking, begin this hike on the western side of Thomas Mountain, climbing to the top by following the dirt road you drove in on. After 0.75 mile, you can see Lake Hemet below you. This hike is especially scenic in spring (April or May), depending on what kind of winter it has been and how much rain has fallen. Abundant flowers fill the green, grassy fields and pastureland of Garner Valley to the north if rainfall has been adequate. Depending on the year, small pestering flies can be a nuisance.

After 3 miles the trail begins to access the denser forested areas. Views of Anza Valley soon greet you looking south, while the mountains east of Hemet rise to the west. If you continue 5 miles from the trailhead, you will be hiking on the south side of Thomas Mountain with Anza Valley dominating your view. However, another 0.75 mile will lead you into the thick pine forest at the top. This is a good turn-around spot; or if you want to push it, continue for another mile to see the east-facing view of the mountain. If your party is large enough, you can make a 13-mile shuttle hike one-way by parking vehicles at the trail ends of both East and West Thomas Mountain roads, exchanging car keys along the way. This hike makes for a great full moon ramble in spring or fall, with views of Lake Hemet shimmering beneath you for the first 1.5 miles.

Hikes 87 – 89

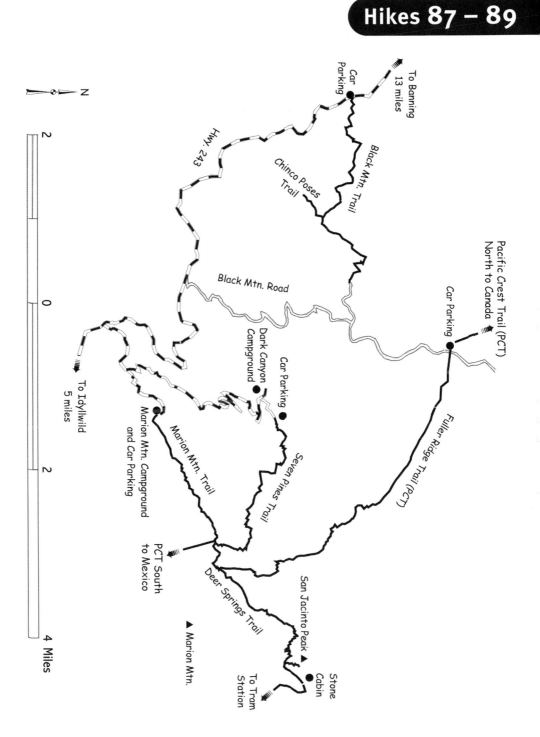

N

2   0   2   4 Miles

To Banning
13 miles

Car Parking

Black Mtn. Trail

Chinco Poses Trail

Hwy. 243

Black Mtn. Road

Pacific Crest Trail (PCT)
North to Canada

Car Parking

Fuller Ridge Trail (PCT)

Dark Canyon Campground

Car Parking

Seven Pines Trail

Marion Mtn. Campground
and Car Parking

To Idyllwild
5 miles

Marion Mtn. Trail

PCT South
to Mexico

Deer Springs Trail

▲ Marion Mtn.

San Jacinto Peak ▲

Stone Cabin

To Tram Station

87 Seven Pines Trail to Marion Mountain Camp (see map on page 173)

LENGTH: 6.5 miles

HIKING TIME: 5 hours

ELEVATION GAIN: 2,300 feet

DIFFICULTY: Strenuous

SEASON: May to October

INFORMATION: USDA Forest Service, Idyllwild, (909) 382-2922 or (951) 659-2117

This is a shuttle hike and one of the few hikes in the San Jacinto Mountains which travels alongside a river. This trip gives the hiker great views of Fuller Ridge to the north, Hemet Valley to the west, and the cooler western side of the San Jacinto Mountains. Cars need to be parked at both the Seven Pines Trailhead and the Marion Mountain Trailhead.

DIRECTIONS

FROM THE U.S. FOREST SERVICE OFFICE in Idyllwild, take Hwy. 243, going 5 miles west to the Allandale station. Turn right for the Marion Mountain Campground and park at the trailhead just before the campground. Take the other cars back toward Hwy. 243 but turn right before reaching the highway at the sign for Dark Canyon Campground. Continue through the campground and up the hill until you reach the trailhead for Seven Pines.

This trail climbs swiftly up through forest and granite boulders, with the looming, craggy wall of Fuller Ridge dominating the northern horizon. After more than a mile you are treated to the beautiful North Fork of the San Jacinto River. The trail crosses it through a magnificent grove of incense cedar and other pines. This makes a good rest stop and is so beautifully serene that it tempts hikers to go no farther. For this reason the short hike to the river makes a perfect summer picnic outing.

Hardier souls (and remember, you parked the cars at the other trailhead) push on and upward through more lush pines and boulder outcroppings. As you climb the 2,300 feet to the junction of Marion Mountain, you crisscross a series of gullies. The trail, unfortunately, has been badly eroded from past runoffs and can be quite rocky and steep in places.

Once you reach the Marion Mountain Trail, turn right and down the mountain for the 2.5-mile trek back to your vehicles. The views will continue to amaze you, but this section of trail is especially steep, with many sections burdened by 2-foot drop-offs. Those who have done this loop prefer to travel up the river-and-fern canyons of Seven Pines Trail to avoid having to haul themselves up the steeper Marion Mountain Trail.

Many hikers are captivated by the beauty of Dark Canyon Campground, which they must pass through to reach the Seven Pines Trailhead. The "dark" refers to the generous population of incense cedar and other thickets of pine that make this campground a welcome relief from the hotter lowlands surrounding San Jacinto Mountain.

88 Fuller Ridge Trail to San Jacinto Peak
(see map on page 173)

LENGTH: 15 miles

HIKING TIME: 10 hours

ELEVATION GAIN: 3,200 feet

DIFFICULTY: Strenuous

SEASON: June to November

INFORMATION: USDA Forest Service, Idyllwild, (909) 382-2922 or (951) 659-2117

As visitors to the Coachella Valley drive through the San Gorgonio Pass near Cabazon, they can look south to San Jacinto Peak and see a massive granite ridge emerging from the heights above the north face of San Jacinto Mountain and thrusting westward before descending sharply to the foothills beyond. This is the rugged Fuller Ridge and along its granite mass runs the Pacific Crest Trail, known through this section as the Fuller Ridge Trail. The views from near the top are magnificent, highlighting the San Gorgonio Mountains and peak to the north, and the spreading deserts stretching like a carpet between the two mountain ranges. This demanding hike and its weather can be tricky. A hike has been known to begin at 7 a.m. with 40 degree temperatures, only to end the day in the high 80s. The ascent to San Jacinto Peak further tests your endurance, but is worth the additional effort!

DIRECTIONS

TO REACH THE TRAILHEAD, drive 7 miles north from Idyllwild on Highway 243 or 17 miles south from Banning on Hwy. 243. Go east on Black Mountain Road almost 8 miles to the trailhead and park. This road can be quite rough on anything but a 4WD vehicle, so plan accordingly.

Snow often persists on San Jacinto's nearly 11,000-foot peaks through June, when the temperature 10 miles away on the valley floor may be well over 100 degrees.

From the trailhead you quickly climb to where granite outcroppings abound and the views begin to spread your horizon in all directions. After 3 to 4 miles you can look down the north face of San Jacinto Mountain into the plunging granite abyss of Snow Creek Gorge . . . this dropview alone is worth the hike! The ridge travels up and down, climbing relentlessly through pine, cedar, and fir until after 5 miles the trail joins with the Deer Springs Trail. From here, turn left and proceed for 2.6 miles up to the peak of San Jacinto Mountain before returning. An easier but more logistically difficult feat is to have someone drop your group off at the Fuller Ridge Trailhead, and instead of backtracking, you can continue down the eastern side of the mountain to the Mountain Tram Station and take the tram into Palm Springs before being picked up. This will shave almost 3 miles off the hike and about 1,000 feet of additional climbing.

89 Black Mountain Trail

(see map on page 173)

LENGTH: 7 miles

HIKING TIME: 4 hours

ELEVATION GAIN: 2,600 feet

DIFFICULTY: Strenuous

SEASON: Year-round

INFORMATION: USDA Forest Service, Idyllwild, (909) 382-2922 or (951) 659-2117

This trail climbs up Black Mountain to give the hiker superb views of the desert valleys below, and Banning Pass and the San Gorgonio Mountains to the north. Black Mountain is the northernmost peak in the San Jacinto Range, and one of the first hikes along the Banning–Idyllwild Road.

DIRECTIONS

TO REACH THE TRAIL, drive south from Banning on Hwy. 243 for 13 miles until you reach Black Mountain Trail, just 1.25 miles past the Vista Grande Ranger Station.

The trail winds through a burned area left from the Soboba fire in 1974, with some charred remains still visible. After 2.5 miles you will meet the Chinco Poses Trail, where'll you continue left up the mountain before reaching the Black Mountain Lookout Road. From here, hike the remaining distance to the lookout tower for sweeping views before returning to your starting point.

This trail can be cooler than you might expect in summer if onshore Pacific breezes are blowing that day. For this reason, this trail is a favorite with desert hikers seeking to cool off without driving all the way to Idyllwild.

Tahquitz Peak from Apple Canyon Road

90 North Fork of the Pacific Crest Trail to Live Oak Spring (see map opposite)

LENGTH: 14 miles	**SEASON:** Year-round
HIKING TIME: 8 hours	**INFORMATION:** USDA Forest
ELEVATION GAIN: 2,000 feet	Service, Idyllwild, (909) 382-2922
DIFFICULTY: Strenuous	or (951) 659-2117

The North Fork of the Pacific Crest Trail (PCT) offers the hiker a scenic, meandering, gradual climb to the Desert Divide Ridge overlooking the Coachella Valley with the added treat of visiting a beautiful grove of massive oak trees surrounded by grassy meadows and vine thickets, all fed by the rushing waters of Live Oak Spring. The Desert Divide Ridge is accompanied all the way to Idyllwild by the PCT. It offers a cool escape from the sweltering desert below and stunning vistas of the Coachella Valley; Santa Rosa and San Jacinto mountain ranges; and the Salton Sea Basin on the eastern horizon.

DIRECTIONS

THE TRAILHEAD DIRECTIONS are the same as for the South Fork PCT (Hike 102), taking Hwy. 74 from Palm Desert 23 miles to the parking area, or 0.5 mile east of the Hwy. 371 junction.

The trail begins with a massive mileage sign and description of the PCT system found in this area. The trail winds slowly down a hillside covered with manzanita, yucca, juniper, and pine. Along with offering spectacular vistas, the vegetation's scents are invigorating in the cool morning air. The trail makes its way into a boulder area for several miles, then climbs alongside a low mountain. The views reveal working ranches below, as well as the Mount Palomar Observatory to the southwest. You will pass through a variety of pine and high-desert scrub brush, with some small streams running from January to March.

After 5 miles the trail crosses a small dirt road. Look for the rock ducks that indicate the trail continues on the other side of this road. You will now hug a rocky mountainside for the last mile before reaching the top of the trail at Desert Divide. This is exactly 6 miles from where you began. Continue down for another mile to Live Oak Spring. The spring area offers a quiet, green lunch stop. It reminds many hikers of the oak-covered hillsides in Northern California. The two oak tree systems found at Live Oak Spring are massive because of the perpetual source of running water. If you continued 5 miles down the mountain you would intersect Palm Canyon.

Take care to carry enough cold water. In these parts you often begin a hike with cool temperatures but end the afternoon pushing 90 to 100 degrees.

Hikes 90 – 94

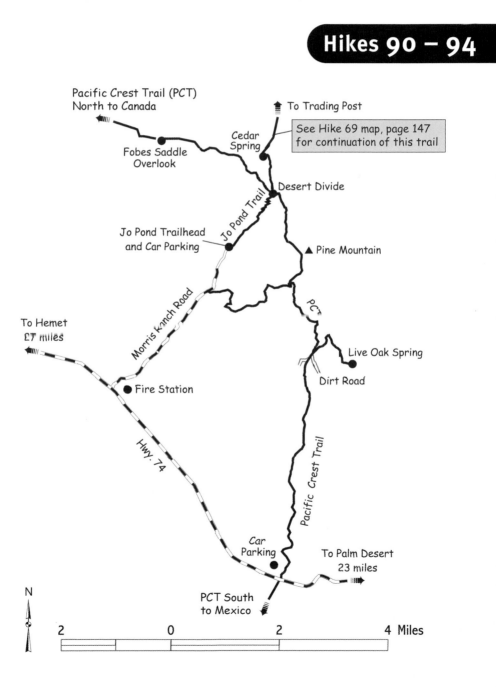

Pacific Crest Trail (PCT)
North to Canada

To Trading Post

Cedar Spring

See Hike 69 map, page 147
for continuation of this trail

Fobes Saddle
Overlook

Desert Divide

Jo Pond Trail

Jo Pond Trailhead
and Car Parking

Pine Mountain

Morris Ranch Road

To Hemet
27 miles

PCT

Live Oak Spring

Dirt Road

Fire Station

Hwy. 74

Pacific Crest Trail

Car
Parking

To Palm Desert
23 miles

N

PCT South
to Mexico

2   0   2   4 Miles

91　North Fork of the Pacific Crest Trail to Jo Pond Trailhead (see map on page 179)

LENGTH: 14 miles

HIKING TIME: 5 – 6 hours

ELEVATION GAIN: 1,700 feet

DIFFICULTY: Strenuous

SEASON: March to November

INFORMATION: USDA Forest Service, Idyllwild, (909) 382-2922 or (951) 659-2117

This hike takes you up to the Pacific Crest Trail (PCT), west along the spine of the Desert Divide section of the San Jacinto Mountains, then back down the mountain for a scenic hike offering spectacular vistas of the Coachella Valley, Thomas Mountain, the Palomar Mountains, and the Santa Rosas.

DIRECTIONS　Follow the directions for Hikes 90 and 93.

Begin by hiking the North Fork of the PCT, heading north toward the San Jacinto Mountains. The hike first rambles through thick chaparral along a winding hillside dominated by ribbonwood and manzanita, with a scattering of pinyon pine. After 2 miles you will begin to climb into a rocky area, and then for the next 1.5 miles you'll make your way through granite/sand composite rock fields with views toward the west. The trail then drops down onto a flat area before again climbing up the hillside to the east. After another 2.5 miles you will reach a gate where you must turn left up the mountain in order to stay on the PCT.

The trail heads west on top of the mountain until reaching the area near Pine Mountain. Here the trail climbs up the mountainside, tops along the mountain, crests again, then connects with the Jo Pond Trail after 2 miles. At this junction, turn left southward down the mountain and hike 2 miles until returning to where your vehicle is parked at the Jo Pond Trailhead.

Pond near Thomas Mountain, Garner Valley

92 Jo Pond Trail and Pine Mountain Loop

(see map on page 179)

LENGTH: 10 – 11 miles

HIKING TIME: 5 hours

ELEVATION GAIN: 1,500 feet

DIFFICULTY: Strenuous

SEASON: March to November

INFORMATION: USDA Forest Service, Idyllwild, (909) 382-2922 or (951) 659-2117

If you do this hike with more than one vehicle, park one car at the Jo Pond Trailhead parking area, and the other 1 mile farther south on Morris Ranch Road, just across or next to the county road marked by a wooden sign on the right as you drive in. This shuttle cuts the hike's length from 11 to 10 miles and avoids a return walking on the pavement.

DIRECTIONS   Follow the directions for Hikes 93.

This hike allows you to access the Pacific Crest Trail (PCT) hike toward Pine Mountain (almost 7,000 feet high), and loop back to your parked cars. Begin by walking from your car 100 yards north to the sign for Cedar Spring. After passing through the gate, continue uphill for 0.25 mile until you come to the trail sign that shows a left turn and takes you into a thicket of oak trees. The trail soon meets the Jo Pond Trailhead sign, and you will follow along a flowing stream if winter rains were generous enough. Along this trail section I have actually seen bobcat. The trail soon passes through another gate, over a meadow area made especially beautiful in spring and fall by appropriate colors and flowers, and up to yet another trail sign.

From here the trail makes its last touch with green undergrowth before climbing the high hillside for a 1,200-foot elevation gain over 1.5 miles. At the top of the mountain the trail joins with the PCT. Explore for a few minutes the Cedar Spring section going down the other side toward the Coachella Valley for some great vistas, then return to where you meet the PCT at the top and turn east. For the next several miles the trail offers you spectacular views of the surrounding mountains, valleys, and the San Jacinto Range upon which you are hiking. Eventually the trail follows a sharp turn south toward some small peaks. Note the peak due east, with large rocks scattered about its flank; this is Pine Mountain.

The trail then drops down the other side of the mountain, cutting down the wind on a windy day, before meeting up with a wide dirt road trail at a small

Some Pacific Crest Trail markers provide more than just directions.

saddle. To the left you can plainly see the trail heading toward Pine Mountain, but do not travel left. Rather, when you join this wider trail, turn right through a fence post area, and continue on this trail section as it takes you through a scenic area marked by grasslands and pine trees.

This section offers stunning views of the spine of the mountain heading southeast, reminding many of the Blue Ridge Mountains. The trail will gradually turn down and veer right to a major trail split. Turn right or westerly here, and follow the trail past more pine, a small reservoir, and the first indications of civilization. You will eventually come to a large gate; it either will be open or you must climb over. The Forest Service has informed me that this "trail" is open to hikers; it's just not well marked as such.

The trail continues down and up over small hills, eventually skirting a Girl Scout camp development before finally returning to Morris Ranch Road.

The views and quiet scenery along the way are well worth the effort, especially the swing down the mountain, with the cool pine forests and fragrant smells having a magical impact in April and May.

93 Jo Pond Trail to Cedar Spring

(see map on page 179)

LENGTH: 7 miles	**SEASON:** Year-round
HIKING TIME: 4 hours	**INFORMATION:** USDA Forest
ELEVATION GAIN: 1,700 feet	Service, Idyllwild, (909) 382-2922
DIFFICULTY: Moderate	or (951) 659-2117

In 1994 the Jo Pond Trail connecting Palm Canyon in Palm Springs to the south terminus at the Cedar Spring Trailhead was completed. This magnificent 13-mile trail allows hikers to climb either the Pacific Crest Trail (PCT) in the San Jacinto Mountains at Desert Divide and drop down into Palm Canyon along the West Fork Trail, or to reverse direction. The best times of the year are late October to late November and from mid-winter to April. The Jo Pond Trail treats the hiker to spectacular vistas of the Coachella Valley and surrounding mountains and, like its cousin the Pines-to-Palms Trail, provides a variety of desert and mountain flora to enjoy along the way.

DIRECTIONS

TO REACH THE SOUTH TERMINUS TRAILHEAD for the Cedar Spring section, take Hwy. 74 south from Palm Desert off Hwy. 111, driving 28 miles to Morris Ranch Road in Garner Valley. Turn right at the fire station and continue 3.5 miles to where the road ends and a sign indicates to park off-pavement.

Park here and follow the road, on foot, for 100 yards until you see the sign for the Cedar Spring Trail. Within minutes you will be walking along a delightful stream in a grove of beautiful oak, provided you hike sometime between January and April. You will soon see the large sign indicating the Jo Pond Trail with mileage to various highlights along the way. The trail continues through a meadow, green and well flowered from April to May, then climbs for 1.5 miles up a series of switchbacks until reaching the top of the PCT at Desert Divide. This first 3-mile section can be very hot during the late spring through summer. Hikers need to assess whether a Pacific onshore breeze is blowing. During these times it can be 110 in the desert below, but 65 degrees on this section of the trail. Also, watch for ticks.

Winter comes to the Pacific Crest Trail above Cedar Spring.

Hikers have several options when they reach the top of the crest. I suggest you first take the right fork to the east and explore for a mile or so; then return to the crest and continue down the desert side for 1 mile until you reach Cedar Spring. This is a beautiful lunch spot or rest area. Many hikers choose to camp here before exploring nearby trails. You will find a generous number of incense cedar and black oak, with running water nearby. The return trip offers views of the Palomar Mountains to the south.

94 Jo Pond Trail to Fobes Saddle Overlook (see map on page 179)

LENGTH: 9 miles

HIKING TIME: 5 hours

ELEVATION GAIN: 1,200 feet

DIFFICULTY: Moderate

SEASON: Year-round

INFORMATION: USDA Forest Service, Idyllwild, (909) 382-2922 or (951) 659-2117

DIRECTIONS To reach the trailhead, follow the directions for Hike 93.

The Pacific Crest Trail (PCT), which follows the ridgeline of the San Jacinto Mountains, takes the hiker through many scenic sections that yield spectacular views of the Santa Rosa Mountains to the southeast and the San Jacinto Mountains as they run northwest and culminate at San Jacinto Peak. Always drawing the hiker's attention along this section is the Coachella Valley, which sprawls beneath the mountains and ends at the Salton Sea Basin. This grand vista hike—the PCT along the San

Jacinto Range —also offers the hiker an opportunity to see terrain that suggests some-place other than the harsher desert conditions below. Valley residents can quickly escape by accessing the PCT at the Jo Pond Trailhead's south terminus and then can enjoy an invigorating hike through pine forests found by hiking west where the Jo Pond Trail intersects the Desert Divide. This section eventually takes you to an expansive over-look that shows the entire eastern flank of the San Jacinto Mountains.

Once you begin the hike it is 2.5 miles to the Desert Divide ridge and the PCT. Here, turn left up the mountain. As you climb, look often to the rear and take in the views of the many mountains due east—the Santa Rosas as well as Martinez Mountain. This section makes a marvelous "snow hike" from January to March. The snow is sometimes only 4 to 6 inches deep, but you will still come away with the feeling that you have experienced real winter conditions.

You will crest the mountain after only 0.5 mile. Beneath you is the long, thin trail of Palm Canyon coming out of Palm Springs to the north and ending in the Santa Rosa Mountains to the south. As you continue west you will be amazed by the spectacular peak system of the San Jacintos, a feature that fills the entire western skyline. This view is made more beautiful if the winter snows have been generous. Hikers taking this trail in late October and early November are treated to the fall colors of the thick stands of oak found along the ridge.

After 1.5 miles along the ridge, you will come to a sign that indicates the trail going down into a thick pine forest. Before taking this trail, go another 25 yards to the rocky point south of this sign. This makes a great lunch spot with magnificent views of the eastern flank of the San Jacinto Mountains. Continue through the pine forest and eventually you'll reach Fobes Saddle Overlook, which reveals the low saddle along the ridge trail as you look down and westward. The return hike treats you to more spectacular mountain vistas, with the Santa Rosa Mountains filling the eastern horizon.

The Coachella Valley from the Pacific Crest Trail

95 Keenwild to South Ridge Trail

(see map on page 187)

LENGTH: 8 miles

HIKING TIME: 4 hours

ELEVATION GAIN: 1,750 feet

DIFFICULTY: Moderate

SEASON: Year-round if no snow

INFORMATION: USDA Forest Service, Idyllwild, (909) 382-2922 or (951) 659-2117

This hike is especially scenic and enjoyable from late September to late October and from April through May. In a good rain/snow year, spring hiking is accented by running streams crossing or moving alongside the trail and colorful vistas highlighted by flowers and flowering bushes.

DIRECTIONS

FROM HWY. 111 in Palm Desert turn left (if coming from Indio) or right onto Hwy. 74 (if coming from Palm Springs) and drive 36 miles to the town of Mountain Center, then right on Hwy. 243 towards Idyllwild. After almost 0.5 mile turn right onto a paved road just after passing the large Keenwild Station (Forestry/Firefighting) sign. Park after 0.1 mile in the parking lot of the fire equipment/training bldg.

The hike begins by walking up the road past the stop sign indicating authorized vehicles only. Disregard the first "South Ridge trail" sign, and continue walking another 0.25 mile up the road until coming to the gated crossing that leads to the heliport. Instead turn right off the road where a trail sign indicates the beginning of a dirt trail marked as 5S02, heading down and to the right of the paved road.

Flowers found in the San Jacinto Mountains

After another 0.5 mile you will see the well-marked trail sign on your left indicating the trail to South Ridge marked as 3E08.

The trail is narrow at first, then gradually widens as it passes small streams and negotiates thickets of brush and pine. The trail slowly climbs the mountain, going east and offering many beautiful scenic vistas of the valleys below and mountains nearby. After 1.5 miles from the trail sign you cross May Valley Rd. Follow the signed trail to South Ridge through the meadowlands then up the ever-steeper side of the mountain. The flat meadowlands offer scenic vista views of Tahquitz Peak to the north and Red Tahquitz to its right, as well as the massive San Jacinto Mountains ridgeline, highlighted by Spitler Peak due east. After arriving at the South Ridge Trailhead, return to your vehicle the same route you came up or make a shuttle out of the hike by having someone pick you up (see South Ridge Trail to Tahquitz Peak Overlook). Try an even easier hike by being dropped off at South Ridge Trailhead and hiking the 4-plus miles back to Keenwild.

Hike 95

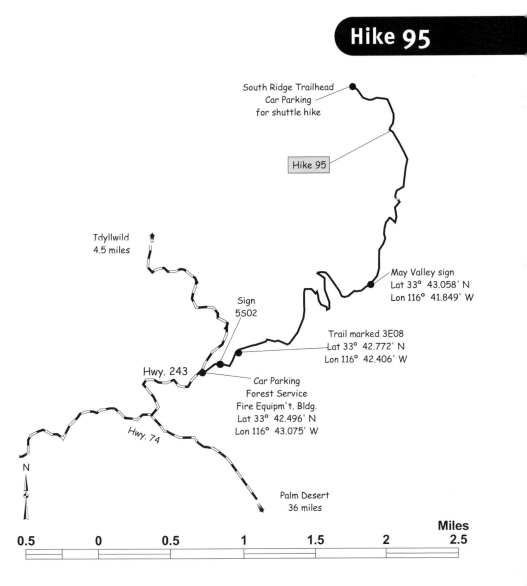

South Ridge Trailhead
Car Parking
for shuttle hike

Hike 95

Idyllwild
4.5 miles

May Valley sign
Lat 33° 43.058' N
Lon 116° 41.849' W

Sign
5S02

Trail marked 3E08
Lat 33° 42.772' N
Lon 116° 42.406' W

Hwy. 243

Car Parking
Forest Service
Fire Equipm't. Bldg.
Lat 33° 42.496' N
Lon 116° 43.075' W

Hwy. 74

N

Palm Desert
36 miles

Miles

0.5   0   0.5   1   1.5   2   2.5

Santa Rosa Mountains

HIKES 96 – 102

The Santa Rosa Mountain Wilderness area is a world apart from the desert surrounding it. This is a land of high chaparral, pinyon pine, yucca, juniper, agave, manzanita, ribbonwood, and prickly pear. The southern horizon is dominated by the twin massifs of Santa Rosa and Toro peaks, 8,000 and 8,700 feet high, while to the northwest the hiker can see the San Jacinto and San Gorgonio mountains filling up the sky.

Hikes 96 – 102 Trailhead Locations in the Santa Rosa Mountains

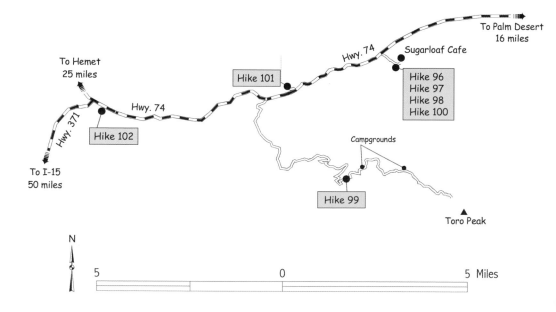

96 Horsethief Creek via Cactus Spring Trail

(see map on page 190)

LENGTH: 5 miles

HIKING TIME: 4 hours

ELEVATION GAIN: 900 feet

DIFFICULTY: Easy/moderate

SEASON: October to May

INFORMATION: USDA Forest Service, Idyllwild, (909) 382-2922 or (951) 659-2117

A favorite and easy way to explore this wild country is to hike the length of the Cactus Spring Trail, which penetrates deep into this wilderness area. The first segment of this hike is the beautiful Horsethief Creek section.

DIRECTIONS

TO REACH THE TRAILHEAD, turn south from Hwy. 111 in Palm Desert onto Hwy. 74. Proceed up the mountain for almost 16 miles until you pass Sugarloaf Cafe, where you will take the first paved road to the left. A sign on Hwy. 74 indicates the Cactus Spring Trailhead. Go 0.25 mile, then turn left into the large parking area. Park in the flat area north of the trash disposal. From Hemet, the trailhead is 8 miles east of the junction of Hwy. 371 and Hwy. 74.

After parking, hike east down the dirt road, then right (south) when you come to the larger dirt road heading up the mountain. After 100 yards you will see the Cactus Spring Trail sign to the left. Begin down the trail and be careful to turn, as it veers right after 0.25 mile. You will begin making your way through a thicket of vegetation, cacti, and pinyon pine. Within minutes the trail opens onto the remains of an abandoned dolomite mine. Continue east. The trail is a roller-coaster, up-and-down journey with a bias toward the down side. Be careful of fine loose rock when heading downhill. Sturdy hiking boots will help cushion this rocky trail.

As you head east, Martinez Mountain will fill the horizon. The trail is often washed by several streams, so you should be cautious of slippery rocks. By April, though, most of the streams have dried up. Hikers are often amazed by the large size of plants due to the abundant runoff during winter.

After more than 2 miles, look to your left, slightly downhill and off-trail, for the remains of an old corral made of dried manzanita. Cowboys once kept their herds penned here because of the water supply at Horsethief Creek.

The trail takes you to a rise above Horsethief Creek in a dramatic fashion. From this vantage point you can view the beautiful cottonwood and sycamore trees lining the creek bed for the better part of a mile. In late October, the canyon creek area is ablaze with bright yellow—a scene one might expect more in Pennsylvania than California. Drop down into the creek and you can explore upstream for a mile, although there is no trail to lead you; just follow the water through thickets of vines, trees, and bushes. Many hikers come to Horsethief Creek for a reprieve from the sweltering desert heat below, and are well rewarded. After returning to their vehicles, some hikers opt for a visit to Sugarloaf Cafe, where they will find friendly service, good food, and a pleasant atmosphere.

A multitude of vegetation thrives along Horsethief Creek.

Hikes 96 – 98

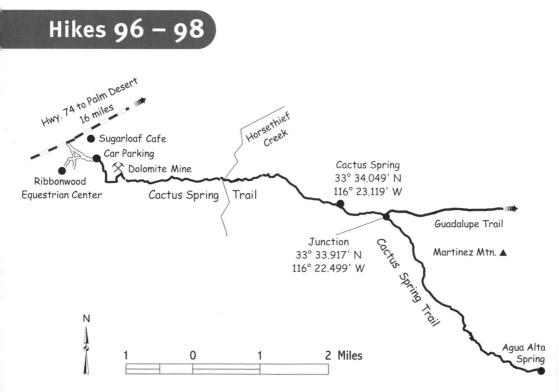

97 Cactus Spring Trail

(see map opposite)

LENGTH: 9 miles

HIKING TIME: 5 hours

ELEVATION GAIN: 1,200 feet

DIFFICULTY: Moderate

SEASON: October to May

INFORMATION: USDA Forest Service, Idyllwild, (909) 382-2922 or (951) 659-2117

The trail to Cactus Spring brings the hiker into even closer contact with the Santa Rosa Wilderness. This is a continuation hike from Horsethief Creek, traveling an additional 2 miles to a spring that, unfortunately, is often dry. Still, this trail provides some scenic vistas of Martinez Mountain and chaparral covered slopes of the vast watershed known as Horsethief Creek. If the winter rains have been abundant, then the hiker is treated to a scattering of mini-waterfalls cascading from the northern face of the Santa Rosa Mountains which form the boundary of the hiker's southern horizon.

DIRECTIONS   Follow the directions for Hike 96.

The trail continues on the eastern side of the creek with a steep climb up a sometimes slippery slope. You reach the top after climbing 400 feet and can then see the wide mountain vistas of the Horsethief Creek Basin. After hiking 0.25 mile at the top, you drop down into a delightful, small canyon that slowly winds itself ever higher and deeper into the wilderness. Sometimes a stream runs the length of this wash and helps nurture the abundant plant life.

The trail emerges from the canyon through a dense thicket of juniper and pinyon pine. It follows the wooden-post trail markers onto a level plateau. Here, the spacious views allow you to see the wilderness area, hidden from the desert dwellers below by the cover of the lower foothills. Martinez Mountain grows ever larger as you approach Cactus Spring. You will know you're there when to your left you see a dense

Along the Cactus Spring Trail

cover of grasses flowing down into the wash. Other than that, in the dry season Cactus Spring is only a name.

I am especially fond of this hike because of the clean, crisp air, heavily scented with juniper and pine mixed with the aroma of the more arid desert plants. Along the final mile, the hike feels energizing and wild. The wilderness shows no sign of human presence and the sprawl of the Coachella Valley below is completely hidden from view. Weather-wise, October and March seem to be the best times to visit, with early spring offering hikers plenty of blooming cacti and wildflowers.

98 Agua Alta Spring
(see map on page 190)

LENGTH: 22 miles

HIKING TIME: 11 hours

ELEVATION GAIN: 2,400 feet

DIFFICULTY: Strenuous

SEASON: October to April

INFORMATION: USDA Forest Service, Idyllwild, (909) 382-2922 or (951) 659-2117

The trail to Agua Alta Spring is the last part of the Cactus Spring Trail that can be hiked in a day, and it is a strenuous, long one. This segment takes the hiker into the farthest reaches of the Santa Rosa Wilderness. It conjures up images and feelings of a forgotten past, when the Cahuilla Indians roamed the canyons and slopes surrounding Martinez Mountain, gathering pinyon pine nuts and edible cacti to survive the harsh Sonoran desert lifestyle. The views in the recesses of upper Martinez Canyon are ones of desolate slopes and sheer rocky canyon walls, with the searing desert floor in the distance. It is a journey worth taking, challenging the hiker's inner spirit to make peace with the empty stillness of this unique wilderness environment.

DIRECTIONS Follow the directions for Hike 96.

You will continue from Cactus Spring, heading left into the large wash and following the wooden-post trail markers. After more than a mile, the trail turns slowly right and winds its way up toward the saddle that separates Martinez Mountain from Horsethief Creek Basin.

The trail continues down through several dry washes. Magnificent views of the surrounding canyons will awe the hiker, as well as the 6,500-foot Martinez Mountain to the left. At any rate, in the vicinity of the southern back side of this mountain, you can choose to climb to its top, but there is no trail and

San Jacinto Mountains near Pine Mountain Loop

the rock scrambling can exhaust even the hardiest hiker. If you continue past Martinez Mountain you will reach Agua Alta Spring at a point 8 miles from Horsethief Creek. This trail section is faint in places and requires some bushwhacking. The hike back to the trailhead is long and hot in the late spring, so I suggest you carry at least 4 quarts of water. Once the trek is finished, the hiker can seek refreshments at the Sugarloaf Cafe.

99 Santa Rosa Peak/Mountain Road Traverse (see map on page 194)

LENGTH: 10 miles

HIKING TIME: 5 hours

ELEVATION GAIN: 1,000 feet

DIFFICULTY: Moderate

SEASON: September to may

INFORMATION: USDA Forest Service, Idyllwild, (909) 382-2922 or (951) 659-2117

This hike traverses the northern flank of Santa Rosa Mountain along a dirt road that ends at the base of Toro Peak, offering incredible views of the San Jacinto Mountains to the west, the Coachella Valley below and to the north, the Salton Sea to the east, and the Anza-Borrego Desert to the south. You can easily summit Santa Rosa Peak along the way, however Toro Peak is on Indian Reservation land and is off limits to hikers. Please do not attempt to summit Toro Peak out of respect for the privacy of the land. April, May, and October are the best months to enjoy this scenic hike.

DIRECTIONS

TO REACH THE BEGINNING OF THIS HIKE, turn south off of Hwy. 111 in Palm Desert onto Hwy. 74. Continue up the scenic, steep, winding grade for 20 miles, and look to your left for a green sign for Santa Rosa Mountain at the beginning of the dirt road. (The green sign is 4 miles past the Sugar Loaf Cafe, if you come up from Palm Desert.) Head up this road (be careful of the rocks and potholes) for almost 9 miles. The road will eventually enter a dense forest area just after treating you to vistas of the Anza-Borrego Desert south of Santa Rosa Mountain. Park in the first convenient area to the left of the road. The road is your trail for this hike.

Hikes 99 – 100

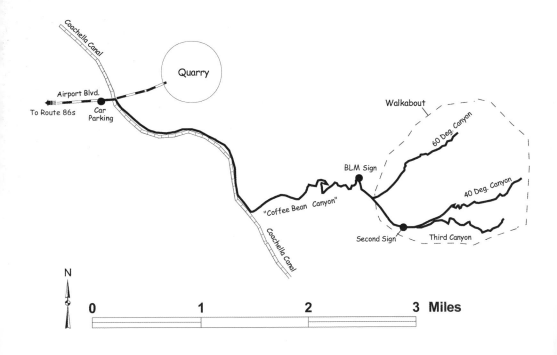

As you walk up the wide dirt road, you will be treated to vistas of the San Jacinto Mountains to the west, and when the trail bends to the east, the entire Coachella Valley will come into view. The forest is cool, green and a welcome relief from the warmer desert below.

After almost 2 miles, you will see a signed trail to your right, leading up a modest grade towards Santa Rosa Peak. You can summit the peak in less than 0.5 mile, enjoying great views of Toro Peak to the east and expansive vistas to the south. Return to the main trail and continue heading east along the northern face of the mountain. In a few more miles, the trail heads up and to the right (avoid smaller trails coming off the main road, going left). Higher up, you will see Martinez Mountain beneath you to the north/northeast. It seems as if you could reach out and touch it on a clear day!

As the trail continues higher, you will see the Salton Sea and eventually

Spring runoff in the Santa Rosa Mountains.

the Anza-Borrego Desert area to the south/southeast. This hike ends just below Toro Peak at the fence. Your return route west and down the mountain rewards you with additional vistas. A definite 5-star hike, one gets the feel of the old west and high-country adventure on this trail!

100 Sawmill Road Trail

(see map on page 194)

LENGTH: 10 – 18 miles

HIKING TIME: 4 – 8 hours

ELEVATION GAIN: 2,500 – 4,500 ft

DIFFICULTY: Strenuous

SEASON: March to November

INFORMATION: USDA Forest Service, Idyllwild, (909) 382-2922 or (951) 659-2117

The Sawmill Road Trail currently provides the only access up the north-facing slope of Toro Peak and the Santa Rosa Mountains. Hikers enjoy spectacular views by looking west toward the San Jacinto Mountains, northeast down Deep Canyon, and east toward Martinez Mountain.

DIRECTIONS

TO REACH THE TRAILHEAD, follow the directions in Hike 96 for Horsethief Creek Trail. After parking and heading east down the dirt trail, the hiker connects to a larger dirt road heading up the mountain. This is Sawmill Road Trail.

The trail winds relentlessly up the mountain. As it does, it gives the hiker magnificent views of the Coachella Valley and perhaps the only good view of the impressive Deep Canyon that borders Hwy. 74 to the east all the way up to

The San Jacinto Mountains from upper Highway 74.

Sugarloaf Cafe. Sawmill Road presents a quick ascent into the cooler pine forests near Santa Rosa Peak and provides a great exercise/cardiovascular workout.

After almost 5 miles straight up, you will arrive at the treeline and encounter the stone remains of a kilnlike structure. At this point hikers can turn around, having done a good 10-mile round-trip jaunt. A more strenuous hike continues just right and beyond the kiln and picks up the newly constructed "connector trail," which will take you to the top of Santa Rosa Mountain, connecting you to the Santa Rosa Road after a 2-plus mile hike. From here, turn left and continue east along the road for roughly 4 miles to the Toro Peak area. Please do not summit Toro Peak, as it is on private Indian Reservation land and the structures atop the peak are off limits. The views from beneath the peak are spectacular, with the Salton Sea Basin to the east and the Anza-Borrego Desert to the south.

Should you for some reason fail to find the connector trail, hike ⅛ mile farther past the kiln and bear left until you see an old sign indicating a trail up to the top of Santa Rosa Road. Upon connecting to the road, turn left and continue several miles until reaching the Toro Peak area.

101 Palm Canyon Pines-to-Palms Trail

(see map on page 199)

LENGTH: 16 miles

HIKING TIME: 8 hours

ELEVATION LOSS: 3,200 feet

DIFFICULTY: Strenuous

SEASON: October to April

INFORMATION: USDA Forest Service, Idyllwild, (909) 382-2922 or (951) 659-2117

This is a five-star hike, a must for serious hikers wanting to visit, in one day, flora and fauna ranging from piñon pine to Mexico's Sonoran deserts. The time of year is critical for doing this hike. It may start out cool if not cold at the top (4,000 feet), but end in blistering heat of 90-plus degrees in the lower reaches of Palm Canyon's desert area (800 feet). This hike is also best taken with hikers who have done the trail before, and should not be attempted alone. This is because the trail follows much of Palm Canyon's sandy bottom, exits at places easy to miss, and can be washed out or seriously eroded if the winter rains have been heavy. In 1994 a fire ravaged the entire area, burning almost 5 miles of this 16-mile hike. This further eroded what was once a well-maintained trail used by both hikers and mountain bikers.

DIRECTIONS

TO REACH THE TRAILHEAD, turn south onto Hwy. 74 from Hwy. 111 in Palm Desert. After 18 miles you will reach the Ribbonwood area. Turn to your right at Pine View Drive and proceed to its end, 0.1 mile from the highway. The Forest Service has another trailhead that originates in the Pinyon Flats Campground. I prefer this trailhead, however.

After parking, begin hiking down the road and veer right (after approximately 100 yards) when you see the small metal sign. Even if you miss this, the trail is an obvious downgrade along the ridge of themountain. For the next several miles you will encounter mesquite, sage, yucca, and pinyon and juniper pines. The views are fantastic, looking north, west, and east. A "valley" of mountains sprawls before you in all directions and you get a clear overview of the Palm Canyon watershed plunging into the long, deepening form of the canyon itself.

After 1.5 miles, you will be on a ridge above Palm Canyonon your left. Here you will see a sign indicating a ridge route. Take this ridge route for another 2 miles to avoid dropping into the canyon too early. Once in the canyon, follow the wash to the left where it joins up with the main canyon.

When you reach the main body of Palm Canyon, turn right and follow the combination wash and trail. Always stay on the right side of the canyon. Over the next several miles you will do several 10- to 20-foot climbs above the canyon. This

Prickly pear cactus

trail continues through washes and up the canyon side for several more miles until you reach the sign indicating Live Oak Spring. The trail then continues up the right side of the canyon. You can measure your distance easily enough by noting the mileage markers that tell how far you are from Hwy. 74. After the marker says 6 miles, and you continue for another 2 miles or so, look for the mountains to the west to begin forming some steep drops into Palm Canyon. In this section of the hike, the canyon narrows and deepens. Water in late winter rushes through the rocky gorges, and several waterfalls grace the slopes above the canyon. This area is known as Upper Paradise and makes a good lunch stop. Trees and pools of water are abundant, with the first fan palms now beginning to appear. From this point, the Indian Trading Post in Palm Canyon (the northern end of this spectacular hike) is only three hours away.

As the trail continues toward Palm Springs, the San Jacinto Mountains increase in size and dominate the western view. You are literally hiking through a

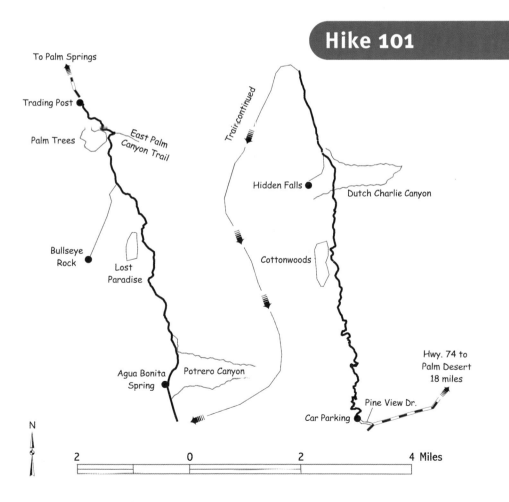

Hike 101

To Palm Springs
Trading Post
Palm Trees
East Palm Canyon Trail
Trail continued
Hidden Falls
Dutch Charlie Canyon
Bullseye Rock
Lost Paradise
Cottonwoods
Agua Bonita Spring
Potrero Canyon
Hwy. 74 to Palm Desert 18 miles
Pine View Dr.
Car Parking

N

2   0   2   4 Miles

valley of mountains. The trail connects with a wash that takes you several miles until you see another rock duck to your right. You will know you are at this junction because the trail drops down from the right and continues across the wash and to the left. Take the trail up the right side of the hill and continue the last several miles until you finally drop down into the thick grove of Washingtonian palms that gives Palm Canyon its name. You are now just a mile from the trading post. Wind your way to the left while staying to the right of the stream. The trail follows the stream, veers right, and passes a large side canyon on your left. Stay right, cross the stream where it's safe, and follow the trail to the trading post.

You have just finished an all-day adventure that, for many, opens up the natural wonders and beauty of this desert playground like nothing else can ever do. I suggest that any hiker unfamiliar with the trail contact the Coachella Valley Hiking Club at (760) 345-6234. This hiking group will gladly furnish you with any information you need. To make this hike in one day, have someone drop you off at the upper trailhead on Hwy. 74 and pick you up at the trading post in Palm Canyon (also known as Hermit's Bench). If you are a strong hiker and begin hiking at 7 a.m., you will reach the Indian Trading Post no later than 3 to 4 p.m.

102   South Fork of the Pacific Crest Trail
(see map opposite)

LENGTH: 11 miles

HIKING TIME: 6 hours

ELEVATION GAIN: 800 feet

DIFFICULTY: Strenuous

SEASON: September to May

INFORMATION: USDA Forest Service, Idyllwild, (909) 382-2922 or (951) 659-2117

The Pacific Crest Trail (PCT) is the western answer to the eastern Appalachian Trail. Each runs south to north along the predominant mountain ranges found inland from both oceans. Both are over 2,000 miles in length. The PCT crosses near the Coachella Valley at the junction of Hwy. 74 and Hwy. 371 in Garner Valley. The trail reaches out and climbs to the ridge above the desert known as the Desert Divide, proceeds west along the ridge to the mountains above Idyllwild, and drops down the northwest side of San Jacinto Mountain into Banning Pass, crossing over I-10 before heading north toward the Big Bear/Lake Arrowhead area. The South Fork is that section heading south toward Mexico, where the PCT meets Hwy. 74. It is a world apart from the North Fork, which is just across the highway and not nearly as warm and desertlike as its southern counterpart.

DIRECTIONS

TO REACH THE TRAILHEAD for both the South and North Forks, take Hwy. 74 out of Palm Desert (south at the Hwy. 111 junction) and proceed 23 miles. Or, from Hemet, drive 0.5 mile east of the Hwy. 371 junction. There is a PCT sign on the right indicating a parking area. Park and cross the highway to the south, where you will come to a gate that opens onto the trail. The sign here indicates mileage south of this point. The South Fork described here goes 0.75 mile beyond Table Mountain Road.

Hike 102

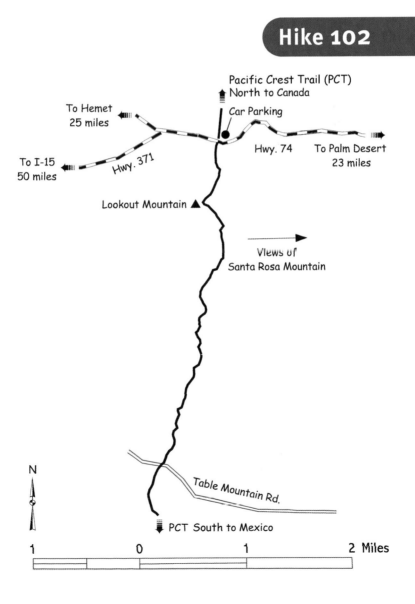

Pacific Crest Trail (PCT)
North to Canada

Car Parking

To Hemet
25 miles

To I-15
50 miles

Hwy. 371

Hwy. 74

To Palm Desert
23 miles

Lookout Mountain ▲

Views of
Santa Rosa Mountain

Table Mountain Rd.

N

PCT South to Mexico

1   0   1   2 Miles

The trail first takes you through sage and low brush, up a mountainside and along a low ridge. From here you can see the mountainous terrain that makes up the northern PCT route, and the magnificent vista of San Jacinto Mountain. The trail swings alongside the mountain for 2 miles. To the left you will eventually see a steep canyon network that marks the northern watershed for the Anza-Borrego Desert, 20 miles to the southeast. You will also glimpse row after row of distant mountain ranges, while to the right rise low hills whose deep green winter color suggests a hike in Wales. Passing through a flat meadow area, the trail begins a series of down-and-up wash crossings and alternating hill climbs. To the east this hike shows you the best view of Santa Rosa Mountain's southwestern flank.

After 4.5 miles the PCT reaches Table Mountain Road. Continue on for another 0.75 mile for a great view of Anza Valley. More important, in late March and early April the trail turn-around point is a field of brilliant golden California poppies that can serve as a colorful and restful lunch stop. Please note the weather conditions, as this trail can get very hot (100 degrees) in September or April if no Pacific onshore winds are blowing.

Ranch house at Mission Creek

Joshua Tree National Park

HIKES 103 – 114

Trailhead Locations in Joshua Tree National Park

Hikes 103 – 114

29 Palms

Joshua Tree   Hwy. 62

Yucca Valley

Din Ho Restaurant

Oasis Visitors' Center

West Entrance

Desert Hot Springs and I-10

La Contenta Road

Quail Springs Rd.

Hike 103

Hike 104

Hike 105

Hike 106

Hike 107

Pinto "Y" Jct.

(not to scale)

Hike 108

Hike 111

Hike 110
Hike 112
Hike 113

For Hikes 112 and 113, see page 218 map.

Cottonwood Visitors' Center

Hike 109

Hike 114

To Dillon Rd., Indio 20 miles

I-10

Chiriaco Summit Exit

To Mecca

N

5   0   5   10 Miles

103 Long Canyon to Chuckawalla Bill's Ruins (see map opposite)

LENGTH: 12 miles	**SEASON:** October to May
HIKING TIME: 6 hours	**INFORMATION:** Joshua Tree
ELEVATION GAIN: 1,800 feet	National Park, Twentynine
DIFFICULTY: Strenuous	Palms, (760) 367-5500

This hike takes you from the Joshua Tree National Park area through interesting, scenic Long Canyon and finally to the remains of prospector Chuckawalla Bill's roofless stone cabin. The hike through the wash can be quite tiring wherever you reach sand, although much of this trail is on hard wash bottom, so be sure to carry enough cool water and food.

DIRECTIONS

TO BEGIN THIS HIKE, drive west on I-10 to Hwy. 62, turn and travel north until you reach Yucca Valley. There, turn right on Joshua Lane, right at Warren Vista, and drive until you reach the corner of Andreas Road. The pavement ends here and a 4WD vehicle is recommended (high clearance). Turn right onto the dirt road and go 0.5 mile, then left onto the next dirt road (after 1.2 miles you will see a barbed wire fence indicating the national park boundary). Proceed another 0.5 mile, turn left, and go up the road toward the radio tower. Park after 0.3 mile at a row of five metal culverts beside a stone drainage ditch.

Head south 100 yards to the trailhead, down about 0.5 mile of rocky trail, over a 15-foot rock scramble, and into the bottom of Long Canyon Wash. There are many side washes but this will not pose a problem if you mark your way with arrows and rocks for your return as you head down the main wash in a southerly direction. Continue south, down Long Canyon Wash to reach Chuckawalla Bill's Wash. The distant Santa Rosa Mountains, to the south, will assist you in finding your way. You will eventually pass through a slick rock chute where the Santa Rosa Mountains shortly become visible before disappearing, then reappearing at the point where the wash widens. Here, vehicle tracks are often seen, and the Joshua trees thin out dramatically. After you have hiked 1.5 miles from the rock chute, on the left side is a 2-foot rock cairn and on the right side the earth has washed away from the hillside, exposing rusty brown soil and rocks. This wash heads west to take you to Chuckawalla Bill's cabin.

You will find scattered metal and wood pieces in the wash as you walk up to the roofless stone cabin. There is a spring about 100 yards past the cabin, which is visible after a wet spell.

This is an interesting "wilderness"-type hike, but first-time hikers might think of going with someone familiar with the trail and all its intricacies.

Hikes 103

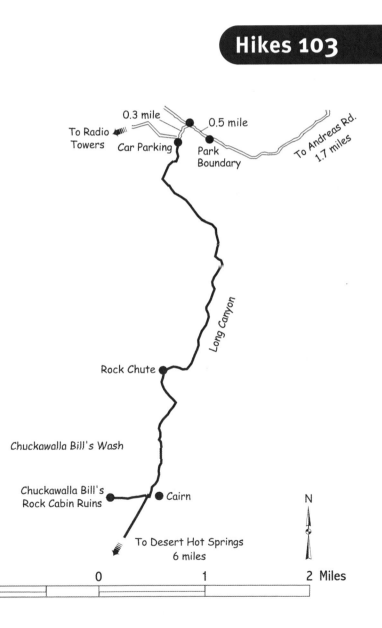

104 **Eureka Peak Loop**
(see map opposite)

LENGTH: 10 miles

HIKING TIME: 6 hours

ELEVATION GAIN: 1,500 feet

DIFFICULTY: Strenuous

SEASON: September to May

INFORMATION: Joshua Tree National Park, Twentynine Palms, (760) 367-5500

Eureka Peak, at 5,518 feet, commands a dominating view of the western boundary of Joshua Tree National Park, including the lower Coachella Valley, San Jacinto Mountain, and San Gorgonio Peak. For this reason it is well worth the effort of struggling up sandy washes and over steep ridges to gain the heights and subsequent views afforded by Eureka Peak. The hike itself offers the flora of high desert (4,000 to 5,000 feet) in a myriad of small canyons and washes leading up to the peak. In spring the hiker is treated to cooler temperatures compared to the searing heat below, and the vegetation after a wet winter is abundantly green.

DIRECTIONS

BEGIN THIS HIKE by driving from I-10 to Hwy. 62, north into Yucca Valley. Just past Yucca Valley take the road to the right, Joshua Lane, at the junction with Hwy. 247, and continue into Black Rock Canyon Visitor's Center. The trail begins north of the visitor's center, east of the parking area.

The trail sign at this point indicates the California Riding and Hiking Trail, marked by brown posts. Stay on this trail for 2 miles until the trail enters a large wash and forks. Take the right fork (south) marked by an orange post. In about 0.5 mile the wash forks again. Take the small wash right, to where it ends at a small gully. Another orange marking post will direct you to the left for a climb over a ridge. From here, head to the south side of Eureka Peak, almost 5 miles from your starting point. Even if the trail appears poorly marked, tracks from previous hikers will help you find your way.

To return, after you've taken in the wonderful views from the top, head east and down perhaps 0.5 mile until you reach the junction with the California Riding and Hiking Trail. Turn left and follow this trail all the way back to your starting point. The route is mainly flat and down, through a series of washes and small valleys. It's a good idea to inquire at the visitor's center before you start the day's hike as to the condition of the trail and any improvements made in marking it.

Hikes 104

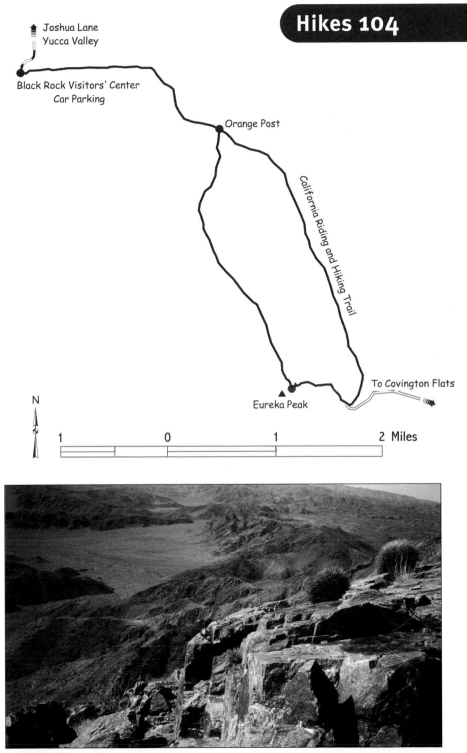

Joshua Lane
Yucca Valley

Black Rock Visitors' Center
Car Parking

Orange Post

California Riding and Hiking Trail

To Covington Flats

Eureka Peak

N

1   0   1   2 Miles

Joshua Tree National Park vista

105 Covington Loop Trail

(see map opposite)

LENGTH: 6 miles

HIKING TIME: 4 hours

ELEVATION GAIN: 400 feet

DIFFICULTY: Moderate

SEASON: October to June

INFORMATION: Joshua Tree National Park, Twentynine Palms, (760) 367-5500

The Covington Loop Trail is an easy but scenic introduction to the backcountry of Joshua Tree National Park. This hike makes a loop through Lower and Upper Covington Flats, past some of the largest Joshua trees in the park, with a good offering of high-desert vegetation, including juniper, yucca, and pinyon pine.

DIRECTIONS

FROM PALM SPRINGS drive west on I-10 until you reach Hwy. 62. Turn right (north) toward Joshua Tree National Park and drive about 25 miles to Yucca Valley and La Contenta Road. Turn right at La Contenta Road, going to road's end at Yucca Trail and La Contenta Road. Continue across Yucca Trail to the dirt road in front of you and proceed 1.75 miles to the Covington Flat Area sign. Here turn left and drive another 5-plus miles until you reach a sign that indicates a picnic area to the left. Take this road left for another mile or so and park near the picnic tables (a distance of 6.5 miles from the first Covington Flat Area sign).

The trail starts in back of the trail sign just east of the parking area. Head down this trail southeast through a rather extensive burn area. The trail will cross into a wash and rise onto a plateau, but is marked by signposts along the way. After 2 miles you will reach another metal sign indicating Keys View Road and Covington Flats. Turn right in a northeasterly direction and soon you will be climbing out of the burn area and up into a green, high-desert hill region covered in pinyon pine. Enjoy the cooler green plateau that sharply contrasts with the burn area you just left.

After almost 2 miles you will reach another parking area with a backcountry map/register sign. Just in back of the sign a small path makes its way down and into a larger wash. Head northeast (left) into the large canyon in front of you. As you enter the canyon keep to the right. You will be forced to bushwhack through overgrown vegetation and scramble down many small, dry, rock waterfall formations. Even when the route appears impassable, keep to the right and carefully slide down the rock formations to pick up the canyon trail along the canyon bottom. This canyon is fun to negotiate and contrasts with the flat sections of the hike. After 1.5 miles the canyon will lead you back into the open area you first hiked through. As the canyon empties into the wash, bear left and eventually you will meet the signposts you passed as you first negotiated the

A cottonwood wash, Joshua Tree National Park

wash. Once you're at this juncture, turn left along the trail and head back to the parking lot where you first came from. Spring (March-May) should reward the hiker with flowers in the canyon and wash areas, provided enough rain has fallen.

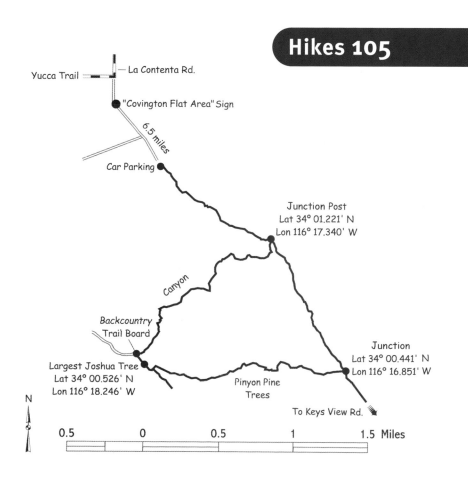

Hikes 105

Yucca Trail —— La Contenta Rd.

● "Covington Flat Area" Sign

6.5 miles

Car Parking ●

Junction Post
Lat 34° 01.221' N
Lon 116° 17.340' W

Canyon

Backcountry
Trail Board

Largest Joshua Tree
Lat 34° 00.526' N
Lon 116° 18.246' W

Pinyon Pine
Trees

Junction
Lat 34° 00.441' N
Lon 116° 16.851' W

To Keys View Rd.

N

0.5   0   0.5   1   1.5 Miles

106 Barker Dam Loop

(see map opposite)

LENGTH: 1 mile	**SEASON:** October to June
HIKING TIME: 2 hours	**INFORMATION:** Joshua Tree National Park, Twentynine Palms, (760) 367-5500
ELEVATION GAIN: 0 feet	
DIFFICULTY: Easy	

Joshua Tree National Park is a maze of huge boulders, uplifted mountains, and exotic high-mountain desert plants. One of the key areas in the park for viewing the sometimes strange and unique rock formations is the Wonderland of Rocks, where a man-made dam has captured water and runoff and created a small but unique lake. The area boasts interesting boulder formations, and the hike, while short, makes a good diversion from the more strenuous hikes the park has to offer.

DIRECTIONS

TO REACH THE WONDERLAND OF ROCKS AREA, take Hwy. 62 off I-10, north to Joshua Tree. Continue through town until you come to the turnoff to the right for the park entrance. Once at the fee station, drive another 10 miles to the Hidden Valley Campground, where a dirt road leads you another 2 miles to the Barker Dam parking area.

From north of the parking area, take the signed interpretive trail, highlighting the local desert plant life, into the Wonderland of Rocks. The trail leads into the Barker Dam area, where it meanders along the lake. From here you can explore whatever strikes your interest before returning.

Pinto Basin, Joshua Tree National Park

107 Ryan Mountain Trail

(see map below)

LENGTH: 4 miles

HIKING TIME: 3 HOURS

ELEVATION GAIN: 700 feet

DIFFICULTY: Moderate

SEASON: October to May

INFORMATION: Joshua Tree National Park, Twentynine Palms, (760) 367-5500

The top of Ryan Mountain offers one of the best circular views of the surrounding scenic features found in Joshua Tree National Park. The views include the high summits of San Jacinto Peak and San Gorgonio Peak, Pinto Basin, Lost Horse Valley, the Wonderland of Rocks, and the Little San Bernardino Mountains, forming the northern border of the Coachella Valley. The well-maintained trail is considered a moderate hike, but if taken at a slow pace, can be done as an easy hike.

Hikes 106 – 107

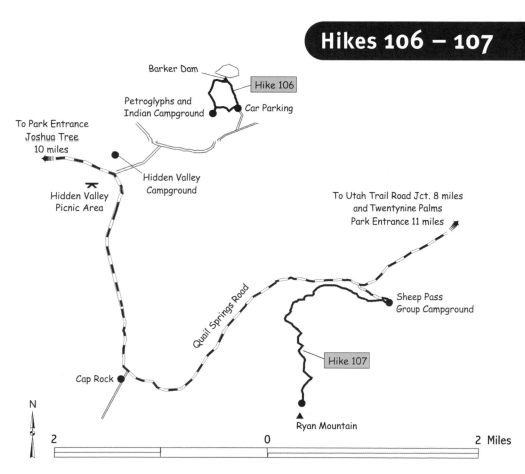

DIRECTIONS

TO BEGIN, drive south 3 miles on Utah Trail Road from the Joshua Tree National Park Visitors Center at Twentynine Palms. Stay right at the Pinto "Y" junction and drive 8.5 miles until you reach the Ryan Mountain Trailhead parking lot on your left. Do not park at Sheep Pass Campground as this is reserved for campers.

From the parking lot, take the Ryan mountain Trail as it heads west and eventually swings up the side of the mountain. This is a very straightforward hike to the top, but does offer you wonderful views of the surrounding extensive valleys for which Joshua Tree National park is famous for.

Ocotillo in bloom in Joshua Tree National Park

108 Lost Horse Mine Loop
(see map opposite)

LENGTH: 8 miles

HIKING TIME: 4 hours

ELEVATION GAIN: 600 feet

DIFFICULTY: Moderate

SEASON: September to June

INFORMATION: Joshua Tree National Park, Twentynine Palms, (760) 367-5500

Located near the center of Joshua Tree National Park, the Lost Horse Mine Loop Trail combines three hikes into one—offering hikers a visit to a once-successful working gold mine, spectacular desert-mountain vistas in Southern California, and a delightful meander through a gentle wash filled with Joshua trees, yucca, juniper, and many other high-desert plants. Add to these the views looking south toward the Coachella Valley and you have the makings of a really fine day hike that introduces you to the stunning natural beauty of Joshua Tree National Park.

TO BEGIN THIS HIKING ADVENTURE, drive north on Hwy. 62, off I-10, just a few miles west of Palm Springs. Continue north into the town of Joshua Tree, where you will turn right at the sign indicating the Joshua Tree National Park entrance (Park Boulevard). Continue through a sparse scattering of homes until you reach the park entrance. After paying the fee, continue through the park to Cap Rock Junction, where you will turn right onto Keys View Road and drive for another 2.5 miles. On the left, look for the dirt road directing you to Lost Horse Mine.

After parking, begin hiking the trail found east of the parking lot and starting just past the interpretive display. The trail takes you up for 2 miles until reaching your first destination, the Lost Horse Mine. Here you can explore the remains of this mine and read about its history. Continue on the same trail you came in

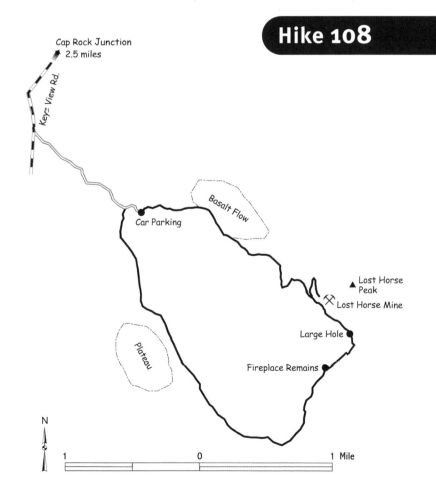

Hike 108

Cap Rock Junction
2.5 miles

Keys View Rd.

Basalt Flow

Car Parking

Lost Horse Peak

Lost Horse Mine

Large Hole

Fireplace Remains

Plateau

N

1   0   1 Mile

The Lost Horse Mine is the best preserved old mining operation in the park.

on, but be aware that from this point on there will be few hikers, as most choose to reach the mine and return to their vehicles before pushing on to another destination in the park.

Less than 0.5 mile from the mine, the trail climbs to a series of fantastic overlooks into Lost Horse, Queen, and Pleasant valleys, and even to the distant, jagged Coxcomb Mountains, marking the farthest eastern boundary of the park.

The trail begins a descent along a ridge and gives you a good feel for the rugged desert mountain environment. The trail winds alongside a mountain, offering spectacular vistas of the sweeping valleys below and the distant mountains. After 0.5 miles the trail turns right and down into a small valley to an old rock fireplace. From here the trail continues west, climbing onto a wonderful plateau that offers grand vistas of the distant Santa Rosa and San Jacinto Mountains.

In another mile, after you've exited a short, dry wash, you will reach a turn to the right, marked by rock cairns. For the next 1.5 miles you will be hiking through a flat but delightful valley, making your way over sandy trails marked sporadically by cairns. This section of trail takes you directly back to the parking lot. You will find that the trail bears right at any junction and keeps you in a desert wash bordered on both sides by low mountains.

109 Carey's Castle

(see map on page 216)

LENGTH: 8 miles

HIKING TIME: 5 hours

ELEVATION GAIN: 1,400 feet

DIFFICULTY: Strenuous

SEASON: October to May

INFORMATION: Joshua Tree National Park, Cottonwood Spring Visitor's Center (760) 367-5500

Joshua Tree National Park is the home to many abandoned mines and ruins of former prospectors. None compare, however, to "Carey's Castle." Sometime around 1940, a prospector by the name of Carey dug a mine shaft in the southern, desolate, rugged low mountains bordering Joshua Tree. He built his home (castle) under a huge boulder, as a single-room shelter, and finished the front with stonework, framing a small wooden doorway. His mine is located just 0.25 mile west of the castle. The hike up to this ruin is adventurous, as you must negotiate a series of beautiful canyons and dry falls, with plenty of big boulder hopping and scrambling. This hike is best taken with someone who knows the way, as no real trail exists to the "castle."

DIRECTIONS

THE ADVENTURE BEGINS by driving on I-10 for almost 26 miles east of the Dillon Road exit in Indio. Take the Chiriaco Summit exit, turning left toward the General Patton Museum. Drive on the dirt road found between the museum and the coffee shop (the sign reads "RV Parking") for 0.5 mile until you reach the aqueduct road at the large "T" intersection. Turn onto this road, driving almost 3.5 miles. To your left, look for a rock cairn marking a small parking area.

Cholla cactus, Joshua Tree National Park, near Pinto Basin

Head north up the desert wash, through beautiful blooming flowers, cacti, and ocotillo in March and April.

After 1 mile take a right at the first large canyon. Hike up this canyon until reaching the first main canyon where you turn left, then left again where it is next possible. This section lasts about 1 to 1.5 miles and includes a lot of boulder scrambling. The canyon eventually reaches another main branch. Here, take the smaller canyon to the right. You will gradually climb out of the canyon and onto the plateau area of Carey's Castle, the shelter built beneath the large boulder found to the right of the canyon's end. Head west on the dirt trail for about 0.25 mile to see the remains of the mine shaft. Both the views and the feeling of the place are rugged, wild, and captivating. Boulder-flanked mountains dominate the landscape and invite further exploring.

Hikes 109

Mineshaft
Lat 33° 44.372' N
Lon 115° 41.133' W

Carey's Castle
Lat 33° 44.398' N
Lon 115° 41.016' W

Right Turn
Smaller Canyon
Lat 33° 43.911' N
Lon 115° 41.264' W

Left First Main Canyon
Lat 33° 43.179' N
Lon 115° 41.087' W

First Right
Canyon
Lat 33° 42.740' N
Lon 115° 41.482' W

Wash

Car Parking

3.5 miles (not to scale)

0.5 mi.

Chiriaco Summit Exit

I-10

N

1   0   1   2 Miles

110 Lost Palms Oasis Trail at Cottonwood Spring (see map on page 218)

LENGTH: 8 miles

HIKING TIME: 4 hours

ELEVATION GAIN: 400 feet

DIFFICULTY: Moderate

SEASON: September to May

INFORMATION: Joshua Tree National Park, Twentynine Palms, (760) 367-5500

On the southernmost boundary of Joshua Tree National Park, several minor earthquake fault lines, branches of the San Andreas fault line 20 miles southwest, cut through the low mountains overlooking I-10. By doing so, the fault encourages water to seep to the surface. At one such point a large, lush growth of California fan palms can be explored and admired for their stately beauty. This particular grouping of fan palms has come to be known as Lost Palms Oasis, and makes a beautiful day hike through washes and over plateaus, offering stunning views of the surrounding mountains and valleys, including the distant San Jacinto Mountains to the west.

DIRECTIONS

TO REACH THE LOST PALMS OASIS TRAILHEAD, travel almost 20 miles past Indio, heading east on I-10. Exit at the Joshua Tree National Park off ramp, turn left on the road leading into the park, and drive the 8 miles to Cottonwood Spring Visitor's Center. There you will find additional material about the national park as well as a campground.

The best time for this hike is early spring (February to April) or October to November. It can get hot in the afternoon during those renowned warm times of year for this desert region, so carry an ample supply of cool water.

The trail begins east of the visitor's center. You head immediately up a gradual rising slope, then pass through a series of washes. Look for the brown trail markers as you

Cottonwood spring in autumn, Joshua Tree National Park

pass through the sandy washes. In springtime the flowers and astonishingly rich plant life will entice you to stop and enjoy the flora. As you climb, look to your rear for beautiful views of the valley and mountains surrounding this part of the park.

The trail takes you to a plateau, found at the 3-mile marker. Gaze due south for stunning vistas of the Salton Sea Basin . . . almost primeval in its rugged wilderness look. You will soon come to several small washes, out of which you'll climb until finally reaching the overlook for Lost Palms Oasis.

You can explore the oasis by dropping down the indicated trail, or you can just admire the beauty of both the palms and the magnificent mountains to the east. The hike on the Lost Palms Oasis Trail is more relaxing than many others because it has little elevation gain—it feels more like a walk through a nature park and gives you an intimate feel for the mixture of rugged mountains and flowering desert found especially along this trail.

Hikes 110 – 113

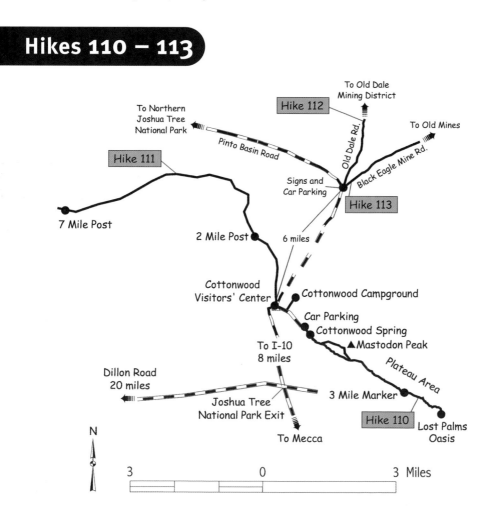

111 Pinkham Canyon Walkabout

(see map opposite)

LENGTH: 14 miles

HIKING TIME: 6 hours

ELEVATION GAIN: 100 feet

DIFFICULTY: Moderate/strenuous

SEASON: September to May

INFORMATION: Joshua Tree National Park, Twentynine Palms, (760) 367-5500

This hike should be done in the early morning to take advantage of the lighting on the colorful rock formations seen off in the distance and to the right of the trail. This "trail" is actually a jeep road that crosses a flat space of land and continues more than 14 miles west from the visitor's center into the Pinkham Canyon area.

DIRECTIONS

FROM THE DILLON ROAD exit off I-10, drive 21 miles east on I-10 to the Joshua Tree National Park turnoff. Turn left at the stop sign, and drive north 8 miles until you reach the Cottonwood Spring Visitor's Center. Park there and walk across the street to the dirt road located just west of the visitor's center.

The hike first heads north, then west. Behind you to the east, Eagle Mountain —at 5,350 feet—dominates the horizon.

I find this hike good for "getting away from it all," feeling free in the wide-open spaces, and, when gripped by curiosity, bushwhacking up to the nearby hills for views

Mountains north of Pinkham Canyon

of the surrounding areas. Although no spectacular canyon experience awaits you at the trail's end, the flat length of this hike allows for an all-day nondemanding outdoor exercise experience.

You can turn back at any time to make the hike shorter without losing some of the benefits of being outside, or you can go more than 20 miles round-trip into the backcountry before calling it a day. Spring and late fall when skies are blue are the best times for this hike.

112 The Old Dale Road/Mines Walkabout (see map on page 218)

LENGTH: 5–10 miles

HIKING TIME: 4–7 hours

ELEVATION GAIN: 50–300 feet

DIFFICULTY: Moderate

SEASON: October to May

INFORMATION: Joshua Tree National Park, Twentynine Palms, (760) 367-5500

I classify this as a walkabout because you can choose to hike along any or all of 10-mile Old Dale Road, or simply drive to the road's end and begin hiking into the Old Dale Mining District from there—a 5-mile hike. I advise you to purchase a copy of "The Recreation Map of Joshua Tree National Park" at one of the Visitor Centers, or something comparable.

DIRECTIONS

FOLLOW THE DIRECTIONS for Hike 110. After paying your entrance fee at the Cottonwood Visitor Center, continue north into the park for almost 6 miles. You'll know you are getting close to the trailhead when you pass through Smoke Tree Wash. As the road begins to turn west, look for the large turnout/parking area next to the signs to your right indicating the junction of two jeep roads: Old Dale Road to the left, and Black Eagle Mine Road to the right. Park near the signs, or continue up Old Dale Road to the mine site.

Once you've arrived at the Old Dale Mining District, you will come across the remains of more than 30 abandoned mines. (The recreation map mentioned above shows the relative location of the mines.)

Why do I recommend hiking along a desolate dirt road as it crosses the wasteland known as Pinto Basin? Because just after dawn, in fall and early spring, magic

Mine site in Old Dale Mining District

happens to the surrounding Pinto Mountains to the west and the jagged Coxcomb Mountains to the east. The new light, at first a deep yellow, begins to draw out the mauve, purple, cream and rust colors washing the mountain landscapes.

Solitude enfolds you as you trek across the wasteland, reveling in the silence and the evocative odors of the alkaline desert mixing with the sage, creosote, and other desert plants. In a world all to yourself, your thoughts unfold with the new day. The only effort you'll exert is during the first mile of walking through soft sand; after that the road begins to firm, allowing the desert-scape to draw you into its quiet beauty.

This hike gets warm upon your return, so do bring several quarts of cold drink and perhaps a camera to capture the unique landscape.

113 Black Eagle Mine Road Walkabout (see map on page 218)

LENGTH: 8–12 miles

HIKING TIME: 4–7 hours

ELEVATION GAIN: 100–300 feet

DIFFICULTY: Moderate

SEASON: October to May

INFORMATION: Joshua Tree National Park, Twentynine Palms, (760) 367-5500

DIRECTIONS Follow the directions for Hike 112.

While similar to the Old Dale Road/Mine Walkabout, this hike offers a different feel and experience, for most of the trail is in the foothills. The walkabout can be any length; drive your jeep or car as far as you like, and continue hiking until you enter the low mountains east of the trailhead.

Spring floral display, Joshua Tree National Park

There are 5 or 6 old mine sites to discover in these foothills, and you might want do this relatively flat hike at an easy pace, taking time out to examine artifacts along the way. You'll feel like an old prospector looking for your claim!

This hike can be quite warm later in the day during early fall and late spring, so bring several quarts of water.

114 "South" Pinkham Canyon Trail

(see map on page 223)

LENGTH: 10–14 miles

HIKING TIME: 4–6 hours

ELEVATION GAIN: 500 feet

DIFFICULTY: Moderate

SEASON: October to April

INFORMATION: No information number available

DIRECTIONS

FROM I-10 (Interstate 10) at Washington St. in Palm Desert, drive 23.9 miles east on I-10, turning right and off the highway at Frontage Road. Loop right and back under the road, parking just in front of the BLM post marker indicating Pinkham Canyon Trail.

This hike can be done several ways. To make it longer, park as in the directions and begin hiking on the dirt road west, following as it turns north, then after 2 miles, west again. A car can do this section, but the road is somewhat rough in places. Continue west for another 1.8 miles past the large wash (Pinkham Canyon Wash) and turn right at the BLM signpost indicating Pinkham Canyon Trail. To make this hike more direct, drive to this point and park alongside the road before beginning the hike at the post marker.

Old Dale Road into the mining area

Hikes 114

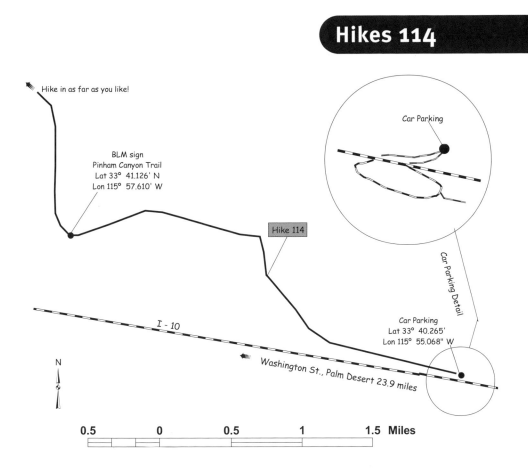

Hike in as far as you like!

BLM sign
Pinham Canyon Trail
Lat 33° 41.126' N
Lon 115° 57.610' W

Car Parking

Hike 114

Car Parking Detail

I - 10

Car Parking
Lat 33° 40.265'
Lon 115° 55.068" W

Washington St., Palm Desert 23.9 miles

N

0.5   0   0.5   1   1.5 Miles

This hike is best done in the early morning, allowing you to see the sun glistening off the Salton Sea to the south and the shades of desert colors on the surrounding mountains. The trail stays left of the wash, approaches the low foothills at the left, then enters the wash, as the wash and the trail merge back and forth. Just by staying in the large wash at this point you are hiking Pinkham Canyon. Eventually the wash narrows in the canyon, and the canyon trail continues to wind up into the northern Little San Bernardino Mountains. Back in the canyon one feels "away from it all," and you can actually hike for many miles (15 miles in one direction). Most hikers doing this section go in 5 –7 miles and return the same way they came in. It is somewhat exhilarating exiting the canyon in late afternoon sunlight, seeing the wide expanse of the Salton Sea Basin to the south and the far-flung stretch of mountains towards the east, as the openness frees you from the more confining inner canyon. A great hike to escape the valley!

San Gorgonio Pass and Nearby

HIKES 115 – 129

Hikes 115 – 129   **Trailhead Locations in San Gorgonio Pass and Nearby**

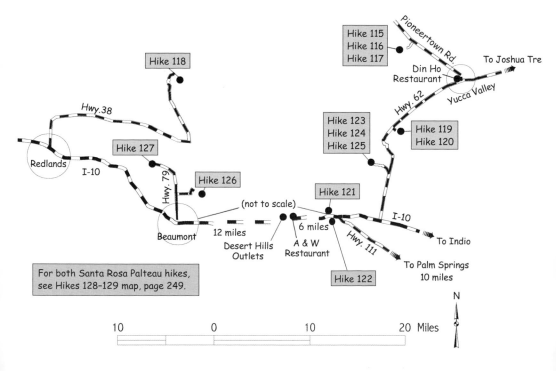

Hike 115
Hike 116
Hike 117

Pioneertown Rd.

To Joshua Tre

Din Ho Restaurant

Yucca Valley

Hwy. 62

Hike 118

Hwy. 38

Hike 123
Hike 124
Hike 125

Hike 119
Hike 120

Redlands

Hike 127

Hike 126

Hike 121

I-10

I-10

Hwy. 79

To Indio

(not to scale)

Beaumont

12 miles

6 miles

Desert Hills Outlets

A & W Restaurant

Hwy. 111

To Palm Springs
10 miles

For both Santa Rosa Palteau hikes, see Hikes 128–129 map, page 249.

Hike 122

N

10   0   10   20 Miles

Pipes Canyon/Indian Loop

115

(see map on page 226)

LENGTH: 7 miles	SEASON: September to May
HIKING TIME: 4 HOURS	INFORMATION: The Wildlands
ELEVATION GAIN: 900 feet	Conservancy, Desert Field Office
DIFFICULTY: Moderate	(760) 369-7105

Pioneertown Mountains Preserve is a conservation area of over 27,000 acres, and one of several preserves managed by The Wildlands Conservancy. Located at 4,450 feet, this canyon/ mountainous area supports a riparian woodland in the canyon, nourished by a flowing stream from the surrounding mountain snowmelt runoff. Pinyon pine, Joshua trees, goldenbush, Mojave yucca, and a generous offering of other plant species combine with bighorn sheep, mule deer, rabbits, coyote, and other animals to present the hiker with a dynamic, beautiful nature preserve accessible by three different hikes. Fire, unfortunately, has greatly damaged this Preserve. Be prepared to see its affects.

DIRECTIONS

FROM I-10, just west of Palm Springs, turn north onto Hwy. 62 toward Joshua Tree National Park. After 19 miles, in the town of Yucca Valley, turn left at Pioneertown Road, then turn left after 5 6 miles at the Pipes Canyon Road intersection marked by a Pioneertwown Mountains Preserve sign. Drive west for 0.6 miles over a seasonal stream crossing and veer right at the next sign for Pioneertown Mountains Preserve. Continue 0.4 miles to the entrance gate and parking area.

The Canyon Loop hike begins just past the entry gate. Continue walking through the canyon, sometimes crossing the stream if it's present (in a dry winter the stream can be found only after a mile of hiking), observing the variety of flora and any animals that might be about. After a mile or so you will come to a narrowing of the canyon. On your right, look for the stone house remains of an earlier settler. Soon the canyon forces you to hike in or near the water before it widens out, revealing groves of cottonwood and rushes.

As the trail enlarges, look for a desert area veering to your left, about 0.5 miles from the stone ruins. The trail is marked "Indian Loop Trail" on a wooden post. Turn left and head up the trail through the first major canyon. The trail then climbs steeply up the side of this canyon ravine until topping out on a saddle above the canyon. Follow the marked trail which continues up the hill to the left.

For the next 1.5 miles the trail meanders up and down through undergrowth and small pinyon pine. After 0.75 mile by looking to your left and down toward the valley, you can see the three magnificent mesas you drove through: Flat Top, Burnt Hill, and Black Hill . . . reminders of a New Mexico landscape. Near 1.5 miles from the saddle above the canyon, look for a distinct trail junction, accented by rock cairns. Take the left down turn and go 0.75 mile, noting the lava and basalt rock scattered throughout the area. This trail rises to a small

Hikes 115 – 117

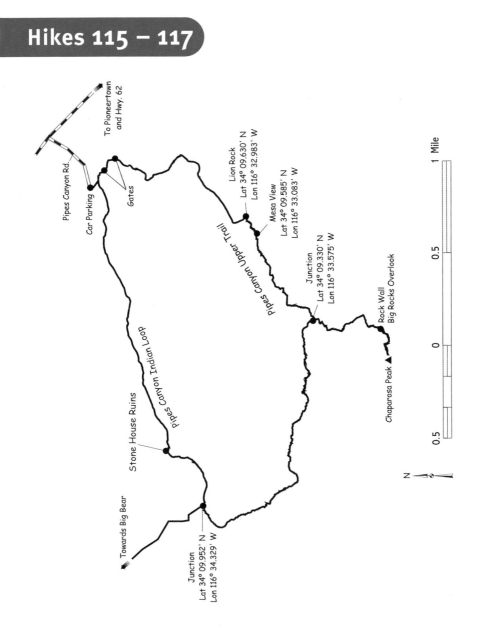

hilltop before proceeding down to a major trail junction. At the junction turn left, and in 0.5 mile negotiate around a closed gate by going right. The trail then continues down a hillside before coming to the bottom, marked by two gates within yards of each other.

At the first gate go right around it, then left and uphill to the second gate, then veer left back toward the parking lot, past a large house, then down a small incline to your vehicle.

Flat Top, Burnt Hill, and Black Hill mesas are easily viewed from the Pipes Canyon Indian Loop Trail. (After the fire)

116 Pipes Canyon to Chaparrosa Peak
(see map opposite)

LENGTH: 6 miles

HIKING TIME: 3 hours

ELEVATION GAIN: 1,300 feet

DIFFICULTY: Moderate

SEASON: September to May

INFORMATION: The Wildlands Conservancy, Desert Field Office (760) 369-7105

DIRECTIONS   Follow the directions for Hike 115.

At the parking lot follow the road bed (lined with stone walls) up a small hill to the south. Continue on the road marked by a trail post, past the gated private residence, heading southeast (left) for 150 yards to the "Indian Loop trailhead" sign. Walk south on the trail marked with rock cairns until you reach the chain link fence. Turn right and follow the trail into the small drainage where it crosses the stream.

Follow the cairns as the trail winds up the hillside with a few more stream cross-ings. The trail will then join the jeep trail and continue up the steep hillside (pass-ing by a residence of trailers on your left at the bottom of the hill). Continue past two gates to reach a high rocky area with a small distinct trail marker, a lion point-ing right on a flat, etched stone. (Note: an old roadbed lies to the left.) Turn right.

Take this trail up the hillside and enjoy magnificent views of the valley below as well as Flat Top, Burnt Hill, and Black Hill mesas. The trail then proceeds down into a raised valley, offering a variety of unique rock formations to enjoy, and more lava pieces to examine. After a mile the trail meets a major junction. Turn left and continue on this trail as it winds its way through washes, up ravines, and along hillsides before topping out in a spectacular vista of what I call the Rock Wall and Window Rock, a cut-out section of mountain that frames Toro Peak in the Santa Rosa Mountains to the distant south. Also look for Halloween Face, a unique placement of three holes in the rock wall in front of you which resembles a carved pumpkin face.

The trail continues from window rock 0.5 miles up to Chaparrosa Peak, where at an elevation of 5,541 feet, you get a great view of the surrounding landscape. The views from the top are stunning, especially of San Jacinto Mountain, most especially if it has a good covering of snow. Return to your vehicles the same way you came.

Parellel Canyon, Orocopia Mountains

117 Pipes Canyon toward Big Bear
(see map on page 226)

LENGTH: 14-plus miles

HIKING TIME: 7 hours

ELEVATION GAIN: 2,000 feet

DIFFICULTY: Moderate/strenuous

SEASON: September to May

INFORMATION: The Wildlands Conservancy, Desert Field Office (760) 369-7105

DIRECTIONS Follow the directions for Hike 115.

After entering Pioneertown Mountains Preserve, hike for a mile-plus until passing the stone house, and continue through the narrow section of the canyon until the trail suddenly widens and becomes a full-fledged jeep trail. In a wet winter, the months of April and May bless this section of trail with flowering lupine, wildflowers, and greening cottonwoods. After the trail leaves the wetland area and widens, it makes a sharp right turn and begins a 20-plus mile climb toward the Big Bear mountain area. Large pinyon pines accent the trail as it climbs toward the cooler mountain heights. You will also pass a developed mountain cabin and other reminders that civilization is not too far away.

This trail is easy to follow, is gradual in its climb, and offers a great view of the higher mountain slopes ahead. Keep in mind that, though it becomes cooler as you climb, the lower portion of the canyon trail remains quite warm on a typical late spring day. This environment seems a

San Gorgonio Mountains and the Beaumont Hills, early spring

wilderness area all your own, as foot traffic is rare and vehicle traffic almost nonexistent. Strong hikers can go a long way before turning back, enjoying a section of Southern California backroads rarely visited.

118 San Bernardino Peak Trail to Columbine Spring (see map opposite)

LENGTH: 9 miles	SEASON: June to October
HIKING TIME: 5 hours	INFORMATION: USDA Forest
ELEVATION GAIN: 2,100 feet	Service, Mentone, (909) 794-1123
DIFFICULTY: Strenuous	

The San Gorgonio Wilderness has been described as an "Island of Wilderness in a Sea of Civilization," embracing over 59,000 acres of well-timbered slopes covered with sugar, limber, and Jeffrey pine; white fir; incense cedar; black and live oak; and a generous scattering of Douglas fir. Small meadows, lakes, and the rocky slopes of the tallest mountain in Southern California, San Gorgonio Peak (11,502 feet), highlight this area of the San Bernardino Mountains. A permit is required to hike in the wilderness and can be obtained by calling the above number.

The San Bernardino Peak Trail gives the hiker a great introduction to the many trails crisscrossing the San Bernardino Mountains, and is easily accessed from the Coachella Valley. The hike itself takes you up to 8,000 feet, affording spectacular views of the valleys below, but also shows a clear sweep of mountain ridges looking north toward Lake Arrowhead and Big Bear Lake.

DIRECTIONS

TO REACH THE TRAILHEAD, drive to Redlands and head north on Hwy. 38. Continue to Mentone and on to the Mill Creek Ranger Station. Wilderness permits can be obtained there, but should have been called for well in advance of busy weekends. Drive 20 miles farther to the town of Angelus Oaks, turn right at the fire station, and look for the sign that indicates San Bernardino Peak Trail. Follow the dirt road to the small parking area; the trail begins at the north end of the parking lot.

The trail climbs steeply up switchbacks and through forests of pine, oak, and fir. As you ascend, the sharp rocky ridges across the valley assert themselves and dominate the horizon. After several miles, the trail begins to traverse a glorious plateau of manzanita and chaparral. From here, you can see the distant ridges of the northern San Bernardino Mountains.

The views will continue to be astounding. After almost 4.5 miles you will arrive at a side trail for Columbine Spring. You can continue down to the spring or hike farther up the trail toward Limber Pine Branch and ultimately

San Bernardino Peak (10,624 feet). The hike back down the mountain gives you the added beauty of seeing sharp mountain ridges to the west. Take a good supply of cool water during the summer, as the lower slopes near Angelus Oaks can be quite hot.

Hikes 118

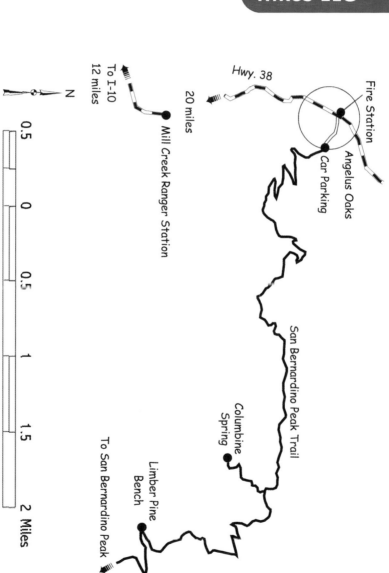

119 Big Morongo Canyon Trail

(see map opposite)

LENGTH: 10 miles

HIKING TIME: 4 hours, roundtrip

ELEVATION GAIN: 1,000 feet

DIFFICULTY: Moderate

SEASON: October to May

INFORMATION: (760) 363-7190, bigmorongo.org

Big Morongo Canyon Trail first shows hikers a lush riparian oasis—almost too rich in vegetation to be associated with the nearby desert—then plunges them through the wide, stream-fed wash of Big Morongo Canyon before bringing them to the desolate southern canyon northwest of Desert Hot Springs.

At this time, please check with the preserve to see if the south exit portion near Desert Hot Springs is open, or whether the fence that has been built still blocks the trail.

DIRECTIONS Follow the directions for Hike 120.

High desert vegetation above Big Morongo Canyon Trail

After parking, begin the trail by the interpretive displays and follow the trail/road along the creek for a mile until coming to a small dam. Up to this point the trail astounds the hiker with a look reminiscent of the Maryland wetlands, rather than the farthest reaches of the great Sonoran Desert. But this trail quickly empties you into the canyon proper, where, during the spring, you will follow a stream for almost 3 miles. Take care crossing the slippery rocks, which are often not securely anchored to the bottom. The canyon trail is really the canyon floor. Make your way as best you can, following the path of least resistance downstream past the rock- and dirt-enclosed walls of Big Morongo Canyon—where flowers are abundant in early spring—until the canyon ends 5 miles from where you began this adventure.

Hikes 119 – 120

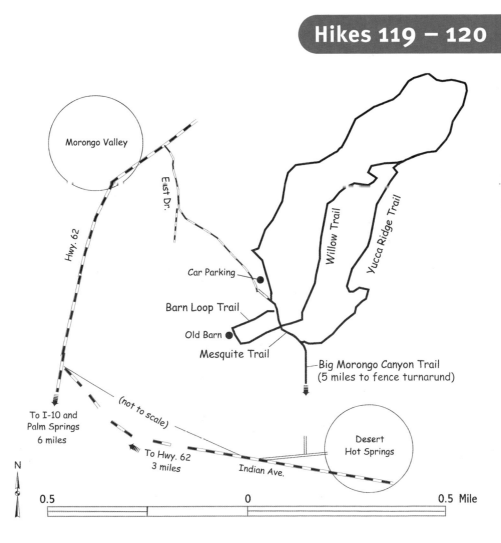

Morongo Valley

East Dr.

Hwy. 62

Willow Trail

Yucca Ridge Trail

Car Parking

Barn Loop Trail

Old Barn

Mesquite Trail

Big Morongo Canyon Trail
(5 miles to fence turnarund)

To I-10 and
Palm Springs
6 miles

(not to scale)

To Hwy. 62
3 miles

Desert
Hot Springs

Indian Ave.

N

0.5   0   0.5 Mile

120 Big Morongo Canyon Preserve
Walkabout (see map on page 233)

LENGTH: 3 miles

HIKING TIME: 2 hours

ELEVATION GAIN: 200 feet

DIFFICULTY: Easy

SEASON: Year-round, 7:30 a.m. to sunset

INFORMATION: BMC Preserve, Morongo Valley, (760) 363-7190; bigmorongo.org

The Big Morongo Canyon area was active as a "ranch stopover" for weary travelers as far back as 1873. In recent times a partnership between The Nature Conservancy, Bureau of Land Management (BLM), and San Bernardino County Regional Parks has helped preserve and develop more than 29,000 acres for a modern-day hiking, scenic, historical, and bird-watching oasis, where lush vegetation can thrive in a riparian setting fed by mountain snowmelt.

The Big Morongo Canyon Preserve is truly seasonal. Serving as a transitional zone between the Mojave and Sonoran deserts, it offers the visitor a rich landscape suggestive of New Mexico hill country. An explosion of cottonwoods, red willows, cattails, bulrushes, and other riparian species contrasts sharply with the barren desert landscape nearby. In fall, the yellow cottonwoods scent the air with the musty odor of approaching winter, whereas in spring, vibrant, crisp shades of green reemerge to color the canyon once again.

The preserve is a favorite escape of mine—its clear, cool morning air complementing majestic San Gorgonio Peak to the west, while the mountains slope down from on high with their verdant forests. Spring is the most inviting of seasons, as more than 250 species of birds are found in the canyon. So different is this area from the nearby lower deserts that in just a few miles the visitor has traveled back both in time and in place, refreshed by the brilliant foliage and colors, odors, flowing water, and wildlife. No pets, smoking, or camping is permitted in the preserve. The area remains a true sanctuary of serene natural beauty—peaceful and refreshing to the spirit. Trail maps, birding information, and other useful materials are available on the property.

DIRECTIONS

FROM I-10 turn north onto Hwy. 62, just west of Palm Springs. Drive for 11.5 miles into the town of Morongo, turning right on East Drive, then left into the Big Morongo Canyon Preserve.

From the parking lot, after you read the available trail and wildlife brochures, begin discovering Big Morongo Canyon by walking east toward the trees. Five trail systems interlink, allowing for a 3-plus mile hike around the immediate canyon area. The Desert Willow Trail offers a look into nearby wetlands; the Yucca Ridge Trail climbs above the wetland and wooded areas, offering a spectacular view of the Big Morongo Canyon and San Jacinto and San Gorgonio peaks; the Barn Trail crosses grassy fields to an old barn from the 1920s ranching era; the Mesquite Trail guides you into the heart of the riparian wetlands, over boardwalks and alongside flowing streams; and the Canyon Trail takes you alongside the stream and eventually down into the Desert Hot Springs area.

The Big Morongo Canyon Preserve features 3,900 acres of beautiful terrain.

Visitors will be amazed at the year-round contrast between lush wetlands and surrounding desert slopes —and following a wet winter in March and April, those slopes support a colorful display of wildflowers and blooming cacti. Pack a picnic lunch, take your camera, leave your stressful worries behind, and let the Big Morongo Canyon Preserve work its magic on you during every season of the year!

121 Pacific Crest Trail (PCT) North from I-10 (see map on page 237)

LENGTH: 4–7 miles

HIKING TIME: 3–5 hours

ELEVATION GAIN: 700 feet

DIFFICULTY: Moderate

SEASON: October to May

INFORMATION:
No information

This section of the PCT takes you in back of the hills fronting Interstate 10 in the "Pass" area, then along a canyon wash, up hills and down again into the Whitewater Wash. In a wet winter, this is a great "green grass & flowers" hike in March or early April.

DIRECTIONS

ON I-10 drive 8 miles west past Indian Avenue until reaching Haugen-Lehmann Way. Turn right off the Interstate, then right at the overpass onto Haugen-Lehmann Way. In a few hundred yards turn left at Tamarack Rd., then right after 0.1 mile onto Cottonwood Rd. Drive for 1.2 miles through a scattering of homes, being sure to stay on Cottonwood and not veer off onto the side roads that merge out of Cottonwood. After 1.2 miles you will come to a divide. Take the left thinner road for 0.2 mile until you see the wood post on your right indicating the PCT. You can either park here or if you have a 4wd, continue 0.4 mile to the parking lot where the PCT is picked up just east of the parking area, indicated by another post marker.

The trail leads towards the low hills to the east, enters the canyon in back of the higher hills where windmills are located, and continues through the canyon for several miles until turning left in a northerly direction. The trail is most scenic in a wet winter when green grass, bushes, and flowers accent your way.

After turning north the trail stays between the foothills before turning left and climbing west by northwest. The higher you climb, the more spectacular the views of the Coachella Valley to the east. After a steep slope to the top of a hill, the trail heads north and down in a rather isolated hilly area before reaching the Whitewater Wash Area. From there it parallels the wash, heading north, and crosses Whitewater River Canyon near the Red Dome Area. It continues on into the hills near the Mission Creek area. You are free to go as far as you like, or even overnight. If time permits, when the trail leaves Whitewater Wash and continues for at least 1.5 miles into the hills north, you can visit the Mission Creek area, with its picnic tables and bathrooms, by turning right at the trail juncture that heads east.

By taking the Whitewater Canyon Road from I-10, you can reach the Whitewater Canyon Preserve approximately 5 miles north of the highway. From there, you can access the PCT by using the connector trail from the preserve parking lot and heading north. This gives you a shorter hike and easier access to Whitewater Canyon. For more information on the Whitewater Canyon Preserve, please see the appendix.

Hike 121

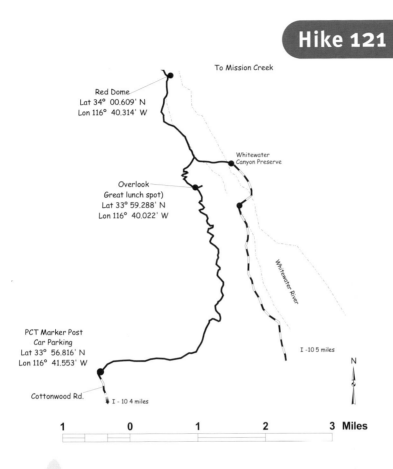

To Mission Creek

Red Dome
Lat 34° 00.609' N
Lon 116° 40.314' W

Whitewater
Canyon Preserve

Overlook
Great lunch spot)
Lat 33° 59.288' N
Lon 116° 40.022' W

Whitewater River

PCT Marker Post
Car Parking
Lat 33° 56.816' N
Lon 116° 41.553' W

I -10 5 miles

N

Cottonwood Rd.

I - 10 4 miles

1   0   1   2   3 Miles

122

Pacific Crest Trail (PCT) South
from I-10 (see map on page 238)

LENGTH: 10 miles

HIKING TIME: 5 hours

ELEVATION GAIN: 2,000 feet

DIFFICULTY: Strenuous

SEASON: October to May

INFORMATION:
No information

The Pacific Crest Trail (PCT) comes down the north face of San Jacinto Mountain, spilling over into the San Gorgonio Pass, across I-10, and northward up the slopes of the San Bernardino Mountains. The easiest access to this section of the PCT is from I-10, where you cross the flat desert before reaching the low foothills of San Jacinto Mountain and eventually the higher elevations at 9,000 feet above Snow Creek Canyon.

Hike 122

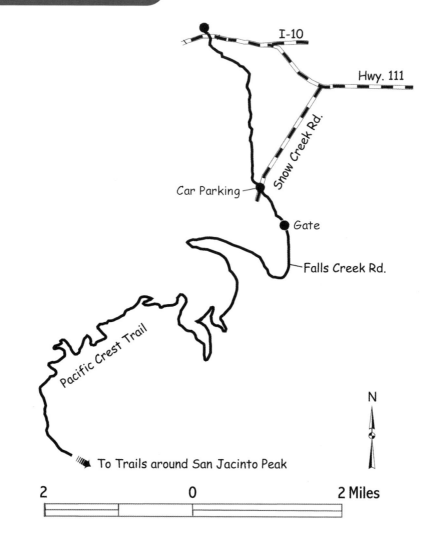

I-10

Hwy. 111

Snow Creek Rd.

Car Parking

Gate

Falls Creek Rd.

Pacific Crest Trail

To Trails around San Jacinto Peak

N

2   0   2 Miles

DIRECTIONS

TO REACH THE TRAILHEAD drive west on I-10 for 8 miles past the Indian Avenue exit to Haugen-Lehmann Way. Turn right, then left over the overpass and reconnect to I-10 going east. After a mile take the Palm Springs Hwy. 111 exit to Palm Springs. Turn right after another mile onto Snow Creek Road, then park along the road at its junction with Falls Creek Road, in front of the sign on the right that indicates no parking beyond the sign. Walk onto Falls Creek Road to your left, past the gate, and continue up the paved road for almost 2 miles until you reach the PCT sign to your right.

Hike to your right, as the trail soon begins climbing up the mountain, making steep switchbacks for nearly 16 miles to the top, where it connects with the trail systems near San Jacinto Peak.

I recommend doing the first 5-7 miles of this trail, then turning around if you want just a moderate to strenuous day hike that offers you spectacular views of the desert below, as well as the San Gorgonio Mountains across the valley to the north.

123 Mission Creek to the Pacific Crest Trail North (see map on page 242)

LENGTH: 8 miles

HIKING TIME: 5 hours

ELEVATION GAIN: 1,300 feet

DIFFICULTY: Moderate

SEASON: October to April

INFORMATION: The Wildlands Conservancy, Desert Field Office, (760) 369-7105

The Mission Creek Preserve is a new watershed hiking area east of San Gorgonio Mountain and west of Desert Hot Springs. This is one of the best flower hikes in the entire Palm Springs area providing winter rains have exceeded 4–5 inches. Plan to hike in late March in order to hit peak bloom time.

DIRECTIONS

FROM I-10 north of Palm Springs, turn north onto Hwy. 62, going to Joshua Tree National Park. After 5 miles, and just west of Desert Hot Springs, look for the sign indicating Mission Creek Road. Turn left (west) and drive until you come to the gated access. Once through the gate, drive on the improved dirt road several miles to its end at a parking area. **Contact the number above for permission to enter the Wildlands Conservancy and the combination to the locked gate.**

If you have not secured a parking permit, and lock information ahead of time, walk the 1.5 miles past the entrance gate to the stone ranch house. The trail begins west of the houses on the preserve property, following a small streambed toward San Gorgonio Mountain. In spring, following a wet winter, this area is lush with flowers and offers great views of San Jacinto Mountain to the south. A fire caused some damage to the canyon that the trail passes through. Be prepared for a stretch of almost a mile of rough trail conditions. After several miles the trail connects to the Pacific Crest Trail (PCT). Turn right (north) at this trail juncture and continue winding your way along the foothills for several more miles to see beautiful ridge views from the top.

The payoff for this hike is the wildflowers found after wet winters and springs. If little rain has fallen, this trail tends to be somewhat desert-

Indian paintbrush after a wet winter

like. You can hike as far as you please on the North Fork of the PCT before turning around and hiking back to your vehicle.

124 Mission Creek to Whitewater River Canyon Walkabout (see map on page 242)

LENGTH: 12 miles

HIKING TIME: 5 – 6 hours

ELEVATION GAIN: 600 feet

DIFFICULTY: Strenuous

SEASON: October to April

INFORMATION: The Wildlands Conservancy, Desert Field Office, (760) 369-7105

DIRECTIONS   Follow the directions for Hike 123.

After reaching the PCT, turn left and wind your way along the foothills until the trail climbs up and over the low ridge overlooking the expansive Whitewater Canyon. The trail then drops down the other side and into the canyon. A jumble of large granite boulders forms the bottom of this wide canyon, where the Whitewater River flows down from San Gorgonio Mountain. The "trail" is still recognizable for some distance as it makes its way across the canyon floor. The actual route will change depending on the flood runoff from the surrounding San Gorgonio Mountains.

Pick the easiest and safest route that will eventually follow west/northwest along the Whitewater River. Boulder jumping, avoiding side streams, observing the lay of the land in front of you—these are necessary skills on this walkabout! In wet winters you will negotiate trees and other debris, uprooted and driven downstream during peak runoff.

As the trail begins to enter the narrowing canyon, the landscape changes to a more riparian environment. You will lose sight of the peaks but gain the lush low-lying forests, willows, and grasses that are found along the banks of the river. The hiking can be slow if you need to avoid large obstacles that may be blocking the trail, but the river walk will take you into the back recesses of the canyon and offers the feel of a real wilderness adventure. To return to your vehicle, you will backtrack the same way you came in, noting familiar landmarks from the journey into the canyon.

San Gorgonio Peak, also known as Old Grayback, is the highest point in Southern California.

Hikes 123 – 125

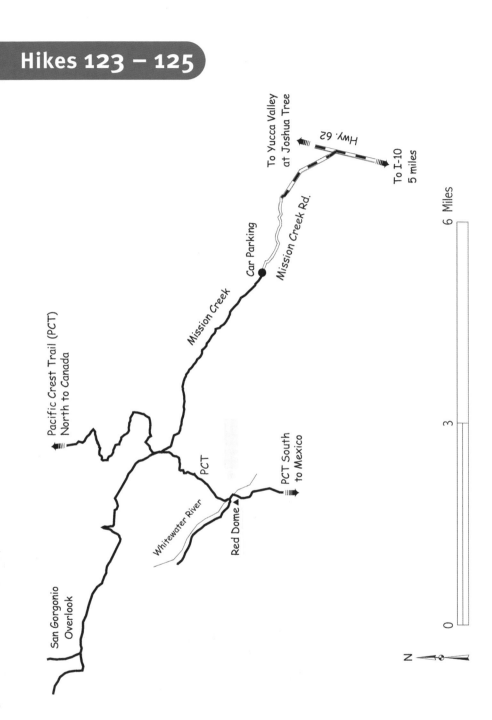

125 Mission Creek to San Gorgonio Overlook (see map opposite)

LENGTH: 13 miles

HIKING TIME: 6 hours

ELEVATION GAIN: 1,000 feet

DIFFICULTY: Strenuous

SEASON: October to April

INFORMATION: The Wildlands Conservancy, Desert Field Office, (760) 369-7105

This hike is an adventure that takes you into exotic landscapes and wild, rugged country. It seems hardly possible to be in the midst of wilderness, with Palm Springs just minutes away! The hike is best done just after dawn in order to capture the rich color of the mountains and surrounding desert.

DIRECTIONS Follow the directions for Hike 123.

The trail begins at the sign south/southwest of the parking area and the stone buildings. For the first 2 miles, you'll slog through desert brush country, with nice views of the surrounding mountains. Continue west on this trail as it crosses the Pacific Crest Trail, which looks like an old wagon road. After a bit more than a mile, the trail turns right and descends into a valley, and the appeal of this hike becomes even more clear. Mount San Gorgonio, an 11,500-foot granite-covered pyramid, looms to the west. Its powerful presence in the midst of the hill-country is mystifying.

After crossing the desert-like valley known as Catclaw Flat for 2 miles, the trail rises above an expansive boulder-strewn watershed to the west. Enjoy the views from here before heading back the way you came, or take some time to explore some of the other trails in this area.

Flowers displayed along Mission Creek Trail

Hikes 126 – 127

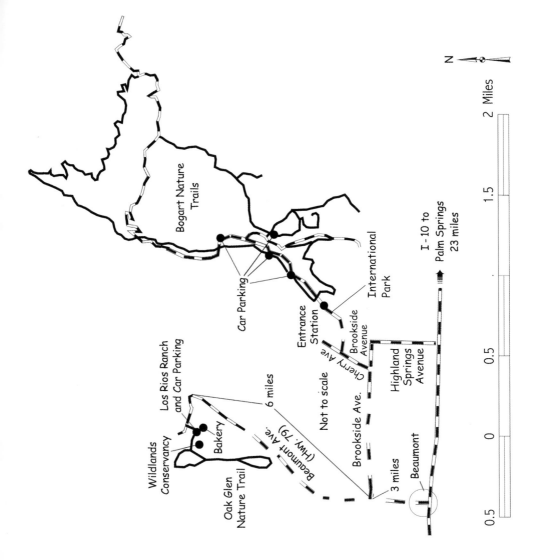

126 Bogart Park Walkabout

(see map opposite)

LENGTH: 4 – 5 miles

HIKING TIME: 3 hours

ELEVATION GAIN: 500 feet

DIFFICULTY: Easy

SEASON: Year-round

INFORMATION: Bogart Park, Beaumont, (951) 845-3818

DIRECTIONS

FROM THE PALM SPRINGS AREA, drive on I-10 to Beaumont, a small town 23 miles west of Palm Springs, and turn north on Hwy. 79 (Beaumont Avenue). After 3 miles turn right on Brookside Ave. and continue to the stop sign at Cherry Ave. Turn left and continue for over a mile until reaching the park entrance.

Bogart Park is, for me, one of the real undiscovered treasures of Southern California. Tucked away in the lower San Gorgonio Mountain foothills, this verdant escape offers 414 acres of refreshing flora and fauna that combine the look of "old California" with a mix of cherry trees, elm, pine, and cottonwood suggestive of the hill country of Pennsylvania. All four seasons come to Bogart Park—late March through mid-May is especially inviting, when cherry trees blossom and a light green foliage returns to the trees. Camping, hiking and equestrian trails, some fishing, and an expansive meadow for picnics are available, and a serene out-of-the-way atmosphere pervades the park.

The park is open daily but closed Tuesday and Wednesday, with a host at the entrance to collect fees on weekends. I often journey here to walk in the cool, quiet morning air as yellow sunbeams illuminate the grasses beneath the groves of California oak. The upper area of the Meadows is another favorite walk of mine, offering glimpses of the western face of towering San Jacinto Mountain to the southeast and the high granite snow-swept face of the San Gorgonio Range to the north. Next to this Meadows section of the park hiking trails lead either around a quiet pond which graces the lower east side, or extend up a nearby hill, accompanied by a rambling stone wall suggestive of Irish country. From the top of the hill, great vistas to the south and west dominate the skyline.

On your own you can follow the Bogart Nature Trail found ⅛ mile past the entrance at the Oaks parking lot. An interpretive brochure is available at the entrance station, pertaining to the trail as it follows along Noble Creek, offering the visitor a look at both riparian and oak woodland habitats. Other hiking trails begin just east of the entrance station and meander into the surrounding hill country. A small trail map is available on weekends at the fee collection station.

Another favorite hike in the park is found by walking on the road to the north end of the park, the equestrian area, and picking up the trail that winds through the

Pond along Oak Glen Nature Trail

grass and trees and which sometimes crosses the small creek. After .25 miles stay on the lower smaller trail that veers slightly left from the larger "road type trail" that climbs up the hills to your right. By staying on this lower trail you will be treated to a mile of creek bed, lush tree groves and scenery a bit like an eastern forest. Follow this trail until it ends up a hillside, then return the same way that you came. A great spring or fall section of Bogart Park!

You can best experience the true rejuvenating power of Bogart Park alone or with a friend. During the week you'll have the place mostly to yourself. Explore the trails, view the peaceful pastoral settings found throughout the park, and enjoy a picnic lunch in the Meadows. Desert dwellers from the Palm Springs area will find Bogart Park both a cool, refreshing experience, and a glimpse into the magic of the seasons mostly absent from the hot desert environment. After your visit, return to Hwy. 79, turn right and continue up the mountain 7 miles to Oak Glen, famous for its apples, gourmet foodstuffs, scenic views, and gentle mountain and country people.

127 Oak Glen Nature Trail

(see map on page 244)

LENGTH: 2 miles

HIKING TIME: 1 – 1.5 hours

ELEVATION GAIN: 100 feet

DIFFICULTY: Easy

SEASON: Year-round

INFORMATION: The Wildlands Conservancy, (951) 797-8507

The Wildlands Conservancy's nature trail is open to the public on Saturdays and Sundays from 9a.m.–4:30p.m., and the conservancy offers a naturalist-guided night hike on the third Saturday of each month. The best time for the day hike described here is mid-October through mid-November, and April through May.

DIRECTIONS

FROM PALM SPRINGS, go west 23 miles on I-10 to the town of Beaumont, and turn right onto Hwy. 79. Drive north for almost 9 miles, passing through Cherry Valley and climbing into the high foothill country known as Oak Glen, a very scenic region that resembles the orchard country of Pennsylvania or Virginia. After reaching the first few apple orchards, the road will turn left (west). Park at the Los Rios Rancho apple orchards, where you will find a gift shop and a great bakery specializing in apple crisp and pie. The Wildlands Conservancy's office and nature trail are just west of the parking lot.

This short nature hike is a great getaway from the crowded city or the hot desert. Children love this hike, and adults enjoy the beautiful layout of the trail. The hike leads past a working apple orchard and has a California Trees side trail that highlights many of the state's native species. A lovely, secluded pond provides a quiet place to reflect before the trail heads down through a wooded area next to a stream. The flora is rich and exotic. The trail splits as it heads down a glen, loops back on itself, and returns to its starting point. Take the boardwalk wetlands section on the way back for a different feel.

A grove of oaks in a park-like setting south of the buildings provides a perfect place to enjoy a picnic, and a petting zoo just a short drive to the west appeals to the younger set.

Please take time to visit the Wildlands Conservancy office to learn about the wonderful work they are doing to preserve important habitat. Oak Glen is a natural island in the sea known as Southern California!

Oak Glen in late spring

128 Santa Rosa Plateau Walkabout

(see map opposite)

LENGTH: 5 – 10 miles

HIKING TIME: 3 – 4 hours

ELEVATION GAIN: 200 feet

DIFFICULTY: Easy/moderate

SEASON: Year-round

INFORMATION: Santa Rosa Ecological Reserve (951) 677-6951

Another jewel of natural beauty, this plateau invites discovery and offers a serene "old California" setting of chaparral, oak woodlands, and the state's finest remaining bunchgrass prairie. Also located on the reserve is Riverside County's oldest building, an early 1800s adobe ranch house that accents the entire area's ambiance. Here is a glimpse into how California looked before it was settled en masse by the Americans, when old Spanish Land Grant rancheros held sway over the land, and civilization had yet to leave its mark.

Covering almost 7,000 acres, the Santa Rosa Plateau is located at the southern end of the Santa Ana Mountains, just 10 miles north of Temecula. Over 2,000 feet of elevation changes influence the land, with its undisturbed flora, fauna, and habitat, including vernal pools, spring wildflowers, sycamore, willow, and coast live oak trees, sagebrush, California buckwheat, bluegrass prairie, rabbit, coyote, quail, golden eagle, and bobcat. To visit in October or November is to see a twin to the landscape of Northern California's Sonoma and Santa Rosa area, with dried yellow grasslands highlighted by dark green California oak. March and April reveal a lush, verdant explosion of colorful spring wildflowers woven through rolling green prairie, running streams, and rich woodlands. No dogs are permitted on the reserve, and the visitor's center offers brochures about the plateau that day hikers who choose to "walkabout" from trail to trail will find helpful.

Santa Rosa Plateau early spring

DIRECTIONS

ON I-15 drive to Clinton Keith Road, about 10 miles north of Temecula. Turn west (right, if coming down I-15 from Palm Springs or LA) and proceed several miles until you come to the road taking you to the visitor's center.

After parking, pick up a trail map at the visitor's center and walkabout at your own pace and leisure. Many trails loop back on themselves, so the length of your hike is determined only by your time allowance. Early morning is best to view the magnificent surrounding mountain ranges and to absorb the full effect of the area.

Hikes 128 – 129

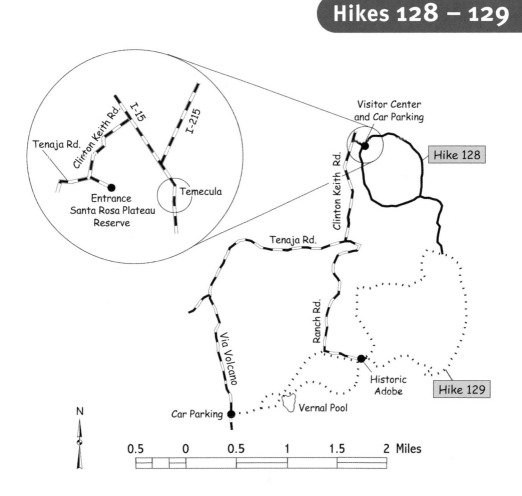

129 Santa Rosa Plateau Loop

(see map on page 249)

LENGTH: 9 miles

HIKING TIME: 4 hours

ELEVATION GAIN: 1,000 feet

DIFFICULTY: Moderate/strenuous "Adventure Hike"

SEASON: Year-round

INFORMATION: Santa Rosa Ecological Reserve, (951) 677-6951

DIRECTIONS

FOLLOW THE DIRECTIONS FOR HIKE 128. Continue on Clinton Keith Road past the visitor's center until you come to the junction of Tenaja and Via Volcano roads. Turn left onto Via Volcano Road until you can see the preserve sign to the left indicating a hiking trail, the Vernal Pool area. Park along the road and hike into the preserve.

In a short while you will come to the Trans Preserve Trail on the left. Turn left onto this trail and proceed for 1.25 miles. As you ramble through the hill country you will be treated to spectacular vistas of the surrounding mountains, the San Gorgonio, Santa Rosa, San Jacinto, and Palomar ranges, made more majestic in early spring if winter snows are still covering the peaks. Spring (mid-March through April) will offer a generous display of wildflowers, including lupine. Some streams will be running, and as you make your way down into the valley, every once in a while your eye will "frame" an incredible picture of pastoral beauty—prairies, mountain backdrops, and green hills that once dominated the Southern California landscape.

In time the trail meets with Hidden Valley Road. Turn right onto this trail/road and follow it past tranquil prairie grasslands where, in places, orange California poppies burst through the green grasslands. After 0.75 mile you will come to the historic adobes, where you can rest, explore the ranch and surrounding lands, and picnic on a bench alongside the adobe ranch house. Look inside through the windows for a glimpse of "old California" before resuming your adventure.

The trail continues right of the barn area, indicating the Lomas Trail. In a few yards turn right off the Lomas Trail onto the Adobe Loop Trail, continue through an extended thicket of old oak trees, and follow the somewhat magical-looking flowing stream. The trail continues until it meets with the Punta Trail. In less than a mile this trail junctions with the Mesa Trail. Turn left onto the Mesa

This early 1800s adobe ranch house is the oldest building in Riverside County

Trail as it follows a drainage below the large Mesa de Burro to the right. You will continue climbing along this trail, treated to scenic views of nearby valleys, until connecting with Monument Road. Turn left up the hill, enjoying a vista landscape of the many Southern California mountain ranges that are within easy view of the plateau. At the next junctions, turn left each time until you are back on the Lomas Trail again heading down toward the historic adobes. Once there you can return to your vehicle by heading back on Hidden Valley Road for a short while before meeting the Vernal Pool Trail. Turn left onto this trail and follow it up the ridge for the next mile, then turn right as it tops out and swings back toward where you parked your vehicle. This section of trail can be very flowery in a good spring. Hikers need to take plenty of cool drinks, since the plateau can suddenly warm up, even if the morning starts off cool.

Santa Rosa Plateau

Orocopia Mountain Wilderness and the Chuckwalla Mountains

HIKES 130 – 140

NOTE: *Hikes 132–140 are often accessible by 4wd only!*

Hikes 130–140

Trailhead Locations in the Orocopia Mountain Wilderness and the Chuckwalla Mountains

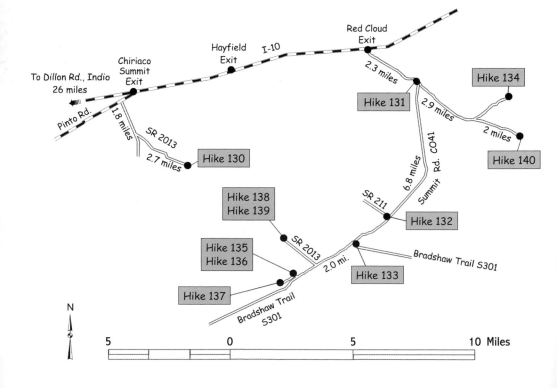

Gold fever struck the Colorado River Basin south of Blythe, California, in the early 1860s near La Paz, Arizona. For shipment supplies from the coast, the Bradshaw Road was constructed through both the Orocopia and Chuckwalla mountains. The road still exists, now known as the Bradshaw Trail, and provides 4WD enthusiasts a jeep road just north of the Salton Sea that leads all the way to Arizona.

The name Orocopia is Spanish for "much gold." The mountains east of Box Canyon, stretching 25 miles to the Bradshaw Road, are these Orocopia Mountains . . . minus any real gold. A scattering of played-out mines dots the landscape, but the real "treasure" is the wilderness experience this area affords hikers who want to access a spot in Southern California that still hints of the Old West.

To my knowledge the trail descriptions in this book are the most extensive yet written about this area. From the very first time I headed into this wilderness, I knew that I had found a place to rejuvenate and release the cares of the world— a place where I could feel like a visitor to a far-off time when the thrill of being the

first person to visit "somewhere new" was still a possibility. The Red Canyon area suggests southern Utah and Moab like no other place in California. The plateau valley that separates the Orocopia and Chuckwalla mountains offers spectacular vistas of multiple mountainranges, mysterious rocky upthrusts to the east, and grand shimmering "blue moun-

The entrance to Painted Canyon

tains" on the far southern horizon . . . a visual sweep of almost 100 miles. The land itself draws you into it in such a way that the "child explorer" in each of us joyfully surfaces and delights in the clean open spaces. Exotic winding canyons, abandoned old mines, red rock formations, and a vast openness that stretches to colorful mountains on every horizon are reason enough to brave the elements and discover the Orocopia Wilderness and Chuckwalla Mountains for yourself!

Most of the "trails" are in fact jeep trails, with considerable opportunities for off-trail rambles into endless canyons and mountain recesses. The hiker just needs to mentally mark his or her return. October and November yield blue autumn skies, and in a wet year, March and April surprise the visitor with abundant and rare flowers, ocotillo in bloom, yellow-flowering palo verde trees, multitudes of ironwood trees, desert tortoise, and red-tailed hawk.

130 Upper Red Canyon Walkabout

(see map opposite)

LENGTH: 8 miles

HIKING TIME: 4 hours

ELEVATION GAIN: 200 feet

DIFFICULTY: Easy/moderate

SEASON: October to April

INFORMATION: BLM Office, Palm Springs, (760) 251-4800

Red Canyon cuts through the eastern section of the Orocopia Mountain Wilderness and offers the hiker entry from both the north or south. This northern route shows the hiker hints of the more stunning red rock formations found at the southern end of the canyon, and it offers majestic vistas of the valley to the east.

DIRECTIONS

TAKE I-10 EAST 26 miles from the Dillon Road exit just beyond Indio to the Chiriaco Summit turnoff. Turn off the freeway at the stop sign on the right, then right again on Pinto Road heading west for almost a mile. Turn left at the dirt road with a sign located several yards from the road. Off-road vehicles, jeeps, and trucks are recommended for accessing the trailhead. Passenger cars can reach the trailhead but only after a rough ride. Drive on the dirt road for 1.8 miles, noting the signpost to the right indicating Red Canyon Road/Trail, also designated SR 2013. Stay on the obvious main road as it makes its way after another 2.7 miles directly into the mountains. Park just before the road drops down into a wash.

Palo Verde tree near Upper Canyon

Hike 130

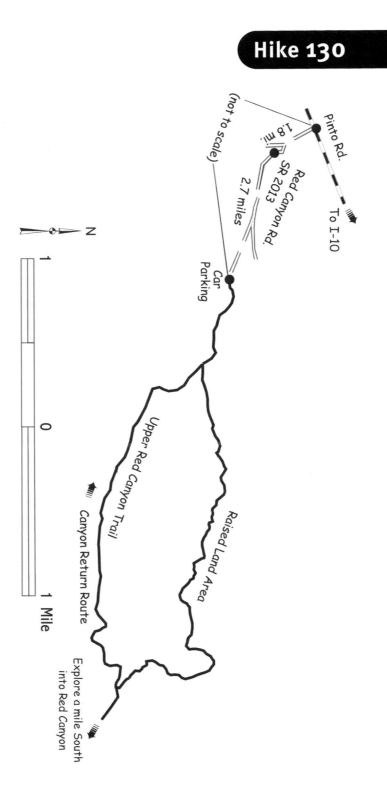

Pinto Rd.

To I-10

1.8 mi.

SR 2013

Red Canyon Rd.

2.7 miles

(not to scale)

Car Parking

N

1   0   1 Mile

Upper Red Canyon Trail

Canyon Return Route

Raised Land Area

Explore a mile South into Red Canyon

The hike follows this jeep trail for several miles, climbing onto raised land areas where quartz rock is abundant. Indeed, these mountains are awash in interesting mineral specimens, so keep a sharp eye out for another favorite rock to collect! When the trail leads you into a small canyon, it will take a turn up and out of the canyon and, in another mile-plus, lead you above a large canyon to your right—Red Canyon. Here I suggest you drop down into Red Canyon and explore it heading south (left) for a mile or so. Return north through the canyon and you will eventually intersect the same trail you hiked in on.

Throughout the hike a good roving eye will spot many nearby side trails that beg for exploring. Note, too, the geology of Upper Red Canyon and how it differs radically from that of Lower Red Canyon.

131   Summit Road to the First Mines
(see map opposite)

LENGTH: 6 miles

HIKING TIME: 3 hours

ELEVATION GAIN: 150 feet

DIFFICULTY: Easy

SEASON: October to April

INFORMATION: BLM Office, Palm Springs, (760) 251-4800

This hike leads to several abandoned mines in the northeastern portion of the Orocopia Mountains. It also offers many side canyons that the more curious hiker might explore.

DIRECTIONS

FROM THE DILLON ROAD EXIT just beyond Indio, take I-10 east for 35 miles and continue to Red Cloud Road exit, the second exit east past Chiriaco Summit. Turn right onto Red Cloud Road, right at the stop sign, then 0.3 mile to the wide jeep road to the left. This dirt jeep road is one of the main access roads into the Orocopia Mountain Wilderness. Passenger cars can negotiate this road but will experience a bumpy washboard ride. At this northern terminus of Red Cloud Road, look for the large map sign to the right of the road.

Continue 2.3 miles south along this road until you come to the junction where the road splits into three. Take the middle fork, known as CO Road 41 or Summit Road. Just as you ease onto this road, take a sharp turn down the road to the right, crossing the railroad tracks, and park in the large flat area just off the road to your left.

Begin your hike west on this dirt road for almost 2 miles until you come to a large wash. Be sure to stay left, as the road splits to the right 0.5 mile from the wash. Just before entering the wash, note the side trail branching off to the left and crossing the wash just left of a large ironwood tree. Follow this trail as it crosses the wash and then becomes a jeep trail winding into the backcountry, which is filled with exotic mountains. This road/trail leads farther into the mountains for almost a mile, with great vistas of the Eagle and Coxcomb Mountains to the northeast. The trail continues above and into a canyon wash, with opportunities to explore several inviting canyons to the left of the trail.

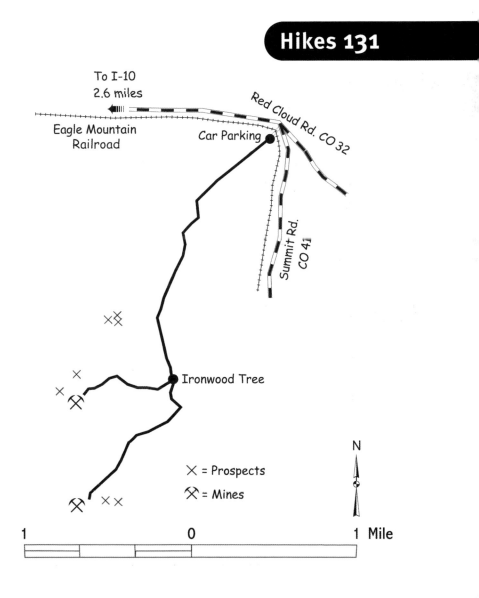

Hikes 131

To I-10
2.6 miles

Eagle Mountain
Railroad

Red Cloud Rd. CO 32

Car Parking

Summit Rd.
CO 41

Ironwood Tree

X = Prospects
⚒ = Mines

N

1   0   1 Mile

Hikers follow Summit Road into the Orocopia Wilderness.

Eventually the trail ends at the base of a mining area. Climbing up the side of the excavations and remaining woodworks, hikers may get lucky and view some artifacts from an earlier day.

To reach the second mine, retrace your steps to where the trail enters the first wash at the large ironwood tree. Turn left down the wash and bushwhack along the wash as it winds its way around and into the nearby mountains. In less than a mile you will see the trail leading left up to another abandoned mining area.

This easy exploratory adventure gives one the feeling of always being on the verge of some great discovery, and in March and April, after a wet winter, the landscape is surprisingly green with flowers, bushes, and trees, especially the palo verde. Time of day can impact the aesthetics of this hike; I recommend early morning, especially since it warms up to the 80s by midday in spring.

132 Summit Road to the Wood House

(see map on page 260)

LENGTH: 10 miles

HIKING TIME: 4 – 5 hours

ELEVATION GAIN: 100 feet

DIFFICULTY: Moderate

SEASON: October to April

INFORMATION: BLM Office, Palm Springs, (760) 251-4800

This hike crosses a wide desert plain and ends in the eastern fringe of the Orocopia Mountains, where a lone wooden house structure stands and where an interesting canyon leads into the back recesses of the foothills.

DIRECTIONS

FOLLOW THE DIRECTIONS FOR HIKE 131. After turning off I-10 and onto Red Cloud Road, drive south and turn onto Summit Road. Then continue another 6.8 miles until you come to SR 211 (Amy's Wash Road) and park just after turning onto it.

The hike follows Amy's Wash Road 5 miles across desert flatlands into the mountains. You are treated to magnificent 360 degree sweeps of the Orocopia/ Chuckwalla Basin, nearby mountains, and often noisy flyby practice runs by F-14/F-16 fighter jets. As you cross the wide, upsweeping valley, note the change in vegetation. I have spotted desert tortoise along this route as well as beautiful flowering ocotillo bushes. After 5 miles you will spot an old wooden structure just west of the trail. This property is to be looked at only and its privacy respected. However, you are free to roam up to the nearby mountains and look for signs of past mining activity.

Continue southwest/west on the main trail. It will curve around the mountain and in less than 0.5 mile will take you above an interesting canyon before abruptly ending at the base of the foothills. This area invites exploration and gives you the feeling of isolation in a place "all your own."

Railroad tracks lead into the Orocopia Wilderness.

133 Bradshaw Trail Plateau

(see map below)

LENGTH: 10 miles

HIKING TIME: 4 – 5 hours

ELEVATION GAIN: 150 feet

DIFFICULTY: Easy/moderate

SEASON: October to April

INFORMATION: BLM Office, Palm Springs, (760) 251-4800

This hike takes you along a section of the Bradshaw Trail that crosses between the Orocopia and Chuckwalla mountains east toward Arizona. It offers a pleasant meander up the plateau, just north of the Chocolate Mountains Bombing Range, with beautiful views of the entire valley looking west. This hike is especially nice if you want to just "get away" to some far isolated spot that opens wide to the four horizons and doesn't tax your stamina.

Hikes 132–133

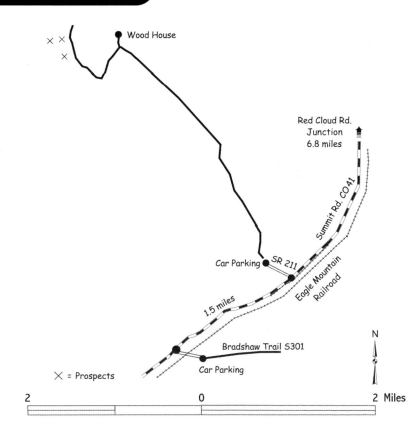

Wood House

Red Cloud Rd.
Junction
6.8 miles

Summit Rd. CO 41

Car Parking
SR 211

Eagle Mountain Railroad

1.5 miles

Bradshaw Trail S301

Car Parking

X = Prospects

N

2   0   2 Miles

DIRECTIONS

FOLLOW THE ROAD DIRECTIONS FOR HIKE 131. After reaching Summit Road, drive south on this road for 8.3 miles until you reach Bradshaw Trail marker S301. A map sign is to your right, but you can park in any accessible spots.

Begin the hike by hiking east on the Bradshaw Trail, which turns left off Summit Road. The trail slowly climbs above the valley, offering wide, expansive vistas of the entire valley and surrounding mountains. You will cross several washes along the way, and you may see desert tortoise. In a wet winter, flowering species of trees and bushes can be found along the route.

After 3 miles look right for the remains of old fuel pods and "bomblike" used devices.

The trail continues east for 50 miles before reaching Arizona, so your turn-around spot will be at your own discretion and desire to explore along the trail.

Do honor the signs that caution you away from the adjacent bombing range. On any given day you might also be buzzed by naval fighter jets on a training mission in the area.

Red Canyon viewed from the Bradshaw Trail

134 Red Cloud Road to the Radio Towers

(see map opposite)

LENGTH: 5 miles

HIKING TIME: 3 hours

ELEVATION GAIN: 1,700 feet

DIFFICULTY: Strenuous

SEASON: October to April

INFORMATION:
No information available

This hike challenges you with a straight-up workout, with some grades approaching 30 percent. You will follow a jeep road to the top of a mountain, where a large array of radio towers relays signals from across Southern California. The view at the top is magnificent and well worth the sweat; however, the "trail" is not the easiest to climb up or down!

DIRECTIONS

FOLLOW THE DIRECTIONS FOR HIKE 131, but after reaching Red Cloud Road where the sign shows the map of the area, continue south on the dirt road 2.6 miles to where Summit Road veers right off Red Cloud Road. Stay on Red Cloud Road, the left road, for another 2.9 miles to where the road splits again. Passenger cars can travel this road, but with difficulty. I recommend a 4WD vehicle or a truck. Take the road to the left that heads east toward the radio tower mountain, and park at the base of the mountain where convenient.

Spring flowers in Red Canyon

Hike 134

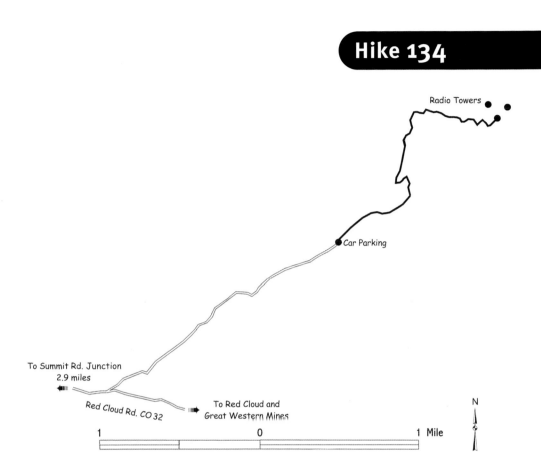

From here the dirt road/trail leads straight up to the top of the mountain, with several 30 percent grades that will have you slip-sliding your way up the steep incline. You'll get great views on the way up, but once you're at the top of the mountain, make your way around the towers for a spectacular vista overlook of the Chuckwalla and Orocopia mountains, a view that just may include Arizona to the east. When I hiked this road I was passed by a service truck that gave me a friendly hello, so I believe the road is accessible to hikers. Of course, respectful treatment of the property at the top is a given. This strenuous workout is challenging enough to entice only the most sturdy of hikers.

135 Lower Red Canyon Walkabout

(see map opposite)

LENGTH: 4 – 6 miles

HIKING TIME: 3 – 4 hours

ELEVATION GAIN: 0 feet

DIFFICULTY: Easy

SEASON: October to April

INFORMATION: BLM Office, Palm Springs, (760) 251-4800

This hike takes you to the heart of the Orocopia Mountain Wilderness, the large 10- to 12-mile long canyon known as Red Canyon. This area is highlighted by a parallel system of canyons more suggestive of the Moab, Utah, red rock country than any place in Southern California. A network of jeep and hiking trails criss-crosses the canyon area, allowing side trips during a long hike to at least one other adjacent canyon.

DIRECTIONS

FOLLOW THE ROAD DIRECTIONS for Hike 131. Once on Summit Road, drive south 10.6 miles to the signpost marked Red Canyon. The entrance to the canyon is marked by a massive rock cliff formation. Drive into the canyon and park.

Along Red Canyon

Begin this walkabout hike by first looking onto the cliff face to your right as you enter Red Canyon. You can sometimes spot a large red-tailed hawk's nest three-quarters of the way up the cliff. Continue hiking into the canyon and you will be able to examine a generous spring offering of flowers if winter rains were adequate. Desert tortoise have also been spotted in the bush areas near the canyon entrance.

After 0.75 mile the canyon splits, with a large canyon branch veering left (do not follow the smaller branches found during the first 0.25 mile). Follow this branch into a beautiful canyon where soft sculptured sand cliffs create a mystical landscape, highlighted by several "sand towers" along the way and

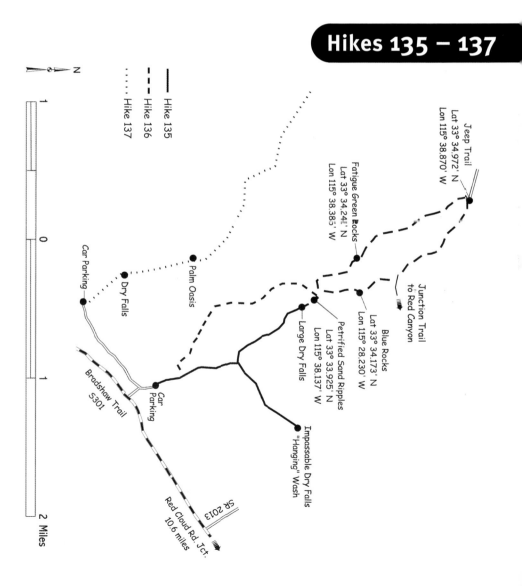

Hikes 135 – 137

N

Hike 135

Hike 136

Hike 137

0

1

2 Miles

Car Parking

Dry Falls

Palm Oasis

Jeep Trail
Lat 33° 34.972' N
Lon 115° 38.870' W

Fatigue Green Rocks
Lat 33° 34.24#' N
Lon 115° 38.38#' W

Junction Trail
to Red Canyon

Blue Rocks
Lat 33° 34.173' N
Lon 115° 28.230' W

Petrified Sand Ripples
Lat 33° 33.925' N
Lon 115° 38.137' W

Large Dry Falls

Impassable Dry Falls
"Hanging" Wash

Car Parking

Bradshaw Trail
S301

Red Cloud Rd. Jct.
10.6 miles

SR 2013

many small side canyons that invite exploring but do not lead far from the main branch canyon.

You will come to a large dry falls on your right after 0.75 mile. The trail continues to the left and eventually to several jeep trails leading steeply out of the canyon. This marks your turn-around spot. Return down canyon to the main section of Red Canyon, turn left, and walk up the canyon for another 0.75 mile until you reach a huge dry falls and "hanging wash" that blocks any further hiking on this route. Return to your vehicle the same way you came in.

136 Lower Red Canyon/Left-Hand Canyon Loop Overlook (see map on page 265)

LENGTH: 8 miles

HIKING TIME: 4 hours

ELEVATION GAIN: 800 feet

DIFFICULTY: Moderate/strenuous "Adventure Hike"

SEASON: October to April

INFORMATION:
No information available

This hike has it all. It first takes you into and then above Red Canyon; drops you down into a spectacular uplifted colorful rock canyon that looks more like Moab, Utah; takes you out of this canyon and back again above Red Canyon; drops back down into the colorful rock canyon, through massive stratified uplifted rock; and finally goes back through a side branch of Red Canyon.

DIRECTIONS   Follow the directions for Hike 135.

As you enter Red Canyon, hike for 0.25 mile until you come to the first small canyon to the left. Follow the trail up this canyon as it climbs the ridge to the south of Red Canyon. After 45 minutes of steady hiking, climbing ever higher hill crests, you will turn down and right off the ridge trail you've been following. Along this trail section you will be treated to spectacular vistas of the Red Canyon area, colorful explosions of rock outcroppings throughout the low mountains and hills to the south, views of the parallel canyons south of Red Canyon and—on clear days—even the Salton Sea.

Hike down off the ridge trail, following a jeep trail to the left for 0.25 mile until it drops down into a beautiful red rock Utah-like canyon I call Left-Hand

Canyon, because it lies just left (south) of Red Canyon proper. Colorful red, mauve, lilac, robin's egg blue, amber, and rust rock strata highlight this canyon and invite rock examinations often along the way.

As you drop down into the canyon, hike left up the canyon wash for a mile or more until you come to a jeep trail climbing out of the canyon to your right. (Do not take the jeep trails near where you first dropped down into the canyon.)

Climb out of Left-Hand Canyon up the steep jeep trail, noting the magnificent rock and canyon formations to the south and west. Hike down the other side of the hill to the jeep trail found at the bottom of the hill. Turn right, while enjoying the abundant mix of rocks found along this ridge portion of the hike.

Continue for 0.5 mile east along the ridge trail until the trail turns sharply to the left toward Red Canyon. Quickly turn to your right and bushwhack 40 yards to the fainter ridge trail that hugs the northern section of Left-Hand Canyon, following along but above the same canyon wash you hiked in on.

Follow this ridge trail, always staying to your far right just in from the canyon's edge, until you come to a

Hiking buddies, Lower Red Canyon Walkabout

light blue mass of broken rock pieces along the trail, about 0.5 mile from where you left the last jeep trail as you headed down into Red Canyon. Follow the sliver trail heading down 30 yards until widening into a faint jeep trail. Follow this trail just before it turns very steeply down into Left-Hand Canyon, almost at the exact place you first entered the canyon from the jeep trail above and south of the canyon. For a safer descent, negotiate the small rock wash leading down into Left-Hand Canyon, found just right of the steeper jeep trail.

Once in the canyon, turn left and enjoy a section of uplifted red rock strata, narrow canyon slots, and small dry waterfalls until you come to a massive, large drop of dry falls. Veer left around and down the rock face onto the canyon floor, and turn left. Sand cliffs and sculptured towers accent the canyon for the next 0.75 mile until it empties into Red Canyon. Turn right and follow the canyon back to your vehicle.

137 Parallel Red Canyon
(see map on page 265)

LENGTH: 8 miles

HIKING TIME: 4 hours

ELEVATION GAIN: 300 feet

DIFFICULTY: Moderate

SEASON: October to April

INFORMATION:
No information available

DIRECTIONS

AFTER FOLLOWING THE ROUTE FOR HIKE 135, turn left at the first signpost, just before entering Red Canyon. This dirt jeep road runs alongside the canyons for 0.8 mile until you can enter the first canyon on your right. This I call Parallel Red Canyon, because it parallels Red Canyon and offers spectacular red rock formations.

Rock strata, western Orocopia Mountains

After entering the canyon, park your vehicle. Proceed up canyon. Note the rich, exotic rock formations along the way, especially the abundant quartz deposits located in cracks in red rock strata. After 0.5 mile you will encounter a small, uplifted dry falls, which looks like it was actually built from cement. Continue hiking the canyon floor as it climbs slowly up canyon. After a mile you will come to a palm oasis where above, on both sides of the canyon, a light greenish rock strata erupts from the rock surface.

Further hiking takes you over several uplifted rock formations, but the main feature of Parallel Red Canyon remains the stunning red strata accented here and there by lilac, bluish-green, and rust-colored rock. If you feel energetic and curious enough, try bushwhacking over the canyon to gain a vista, or following the many branch canyons off to the left. As long as you know where you are in relation to Parallel Red Canyon, your land navigation skills will lead you safely back to your vehicle.

138) Lower Red Canyon via Upper Jeep Trail (see map on page 270

LENGTH: 8 miles	**SEASON:** October to April
HIKING TIME: 4 hours	**INFORMATION:**
ELEVATION GAIN: 500 feet	No information available
DIFFICULTY: Moderate	

The jeep trail designated SR 2013 climbs above Lower Red Canyon's north ridge for better than 10 miles, offering great vistas of the Orocopia Mountain Wilderness along the way while providing "side jeep trails" down into Red Canyon for exploration of the canyon bottom.

DIRECTIONS

FOLLOW THE DIRECTIONS FOR HIKE 131. After 10.3 miles, Summit Road meets SR 2013, the jeep trail that travels along the north ridge of Lower Red Canyon. Turn right off Summit Road and onto Red Canyon Jeep Trail SR 2013. Park where it's convenient, perhaps 0.25 mile in from the road.

The trail climbs the ridge above Red Canyon, sometimes quite steeply, while offering several side jeep trails down into Red Canyon to the left of the ridge trail. Hike for almost 2 miles before taking the left jeep trail (the third signpost you come to) down into Red Canyon. The trail is very steep, so caution going down and up is advisable. Once you're at the bottom, turn left for 0.5 mile until you come to the high drop-off that stops any further hiking down canyon. This

Colorful rock wall in Big Colorful Canyon

severe drop leaves part of Red Canyon on a "higher shelf," while isolating a lower section that leads back to Summit Road. Explore up canyon in a westerly direction before returning to your vehicle via the upper ridge trail.

Lower Red Canyon resembles the red rock country of southern Utah. Many spectacular side canyons branch off the main canyon floor, leading to exotic and colorful rock formations. Explore at your own leisure. The climb back out will be very steep and slippery, so caution is advisable.

Hikes 138 – 139

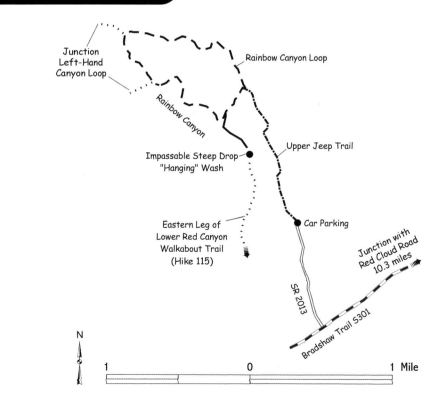

139 Rainbow Canyon/Lower Red Canyon Loop (see map opposite)

LENGTH: 7 miles

HIKING TIME: 3 – 4 hours

ELEVATION GAIN: 500 feet

DIFFICULTY: Moderate

SEASON: October to April

INFORMATION:
No information available

DIRECTIONS
Follow the directions for Hike 138.

Once parked, begin hiking on the jeep trail SR 2013 as it quickly climbs the north ridge above Red Canyon. During the next several miles the trail gradually rises, sometimes in steep upgrades, until leveling out on the north ridge of Red Canyon. Along the way you will view the entire Orocopia Basin as well as the pronounced, colorful surrounding mountain ranges. On a clear day you can also observe the deep blue ribbon of the Salton Sea to the south.

After almost 2 miles you will come to a signpost marking a left turn off the ridge trail and down into Red Canyon. (Any other signposts before 2 miles should not be followed.) This is the third signpost you come to. As you look south toward the southern edge of Lower Red Canyon, notice the colorful explosion of light green, red, and dark mauve rocks. This marks the part of Rainbow Canyon where you will soon be hiking.

The jeep trail down into Red Canyon is steep, so caution is advisable. Once you're on the canyon floor, turn right and note the small canyon with a narrow opening ahead on your left, branching off Red Canyon. This seemingly insignificant canyon holds a beautiful treasure of multicolored—almost rainbowlike—rocks and rock strata . . . Rainbow Canyon.

Hike slowly up this canyon, making your way in a stair-step fashion, examining the many colorful rock layers and individual rocks as you hike. Keep to the right, negotiating any short dry falls that you come to. The canyon winds up and westward for less than 0.5 mile. When the canyon truly ends, bushwhack up the left side until you gain the farthest, highest ridge. Hike farther south across the slope until you come to the next ridge of the next major canyon. There you will find your trail, a faint path/old jeep road. Turn right.

Hike west for 1 mile until the trail joins a very developed jeep trail veering down and to the right toward Red Canyon and away from the ridge you have just hiked along. Note the spectacularly colored rock formations nearby and in the mountains farther to the south. This developed jeep trail makes its way down into Red Canyon, where you will turn right and hike another mile before you get to the jeep trail that climbs left out of the canyon and back to your vehicle along the ridge trail you came in on. This climb out is steep and slippery, so use caution.

140 Red Cloud and Great Western Mine Tour (see map opposite)

LENGTH: 7 miles	**SEASON:** October to April
HIKING TIME: 4 hours	**INFORMATION:** BLM Office, Palm Springs, (760) 251-4800
ELEVATION GAIN: 300 feet	
DIFFICULTY: Moderate	

Although the Spanish name for this area, the Orocopia Mountain Wilderness, means "much gold," little gold was ever taken out of the Orocopias in the period between 1860 and 1930. However, several mines operated on the Chuckwalla Mountain side of the wilderness in the early part of the twentieth century. These were the Red Cloud and Great Western Mines. Only scattered remains mark the land that once supported a serious mining concern. The hike into the mining area is both scenic and hints at the romantic, nostalgic flavor of the "Old West."

DIRECTIONS

FOLLOW THE DIRECTIONS FOR HIKE 131. When Summit Road junctions with Red Cloud Road, continue left on Red Cloud Road CO32 for 2.9 miles until you come to the split in the road. Veer right at the signpost to stay on Red Cloud Road and continue driving for another 2 miles until you come to a wide turnout parking area to the right. Park there. Continue by hiking south on the road you drove in on.

The hike takes you into a canyon area that narrows after 0.5 mile. The trail leads past an old stone and cement structure that could have been a stamping mill. Other stone structures can be found on the left side of the canyon nearby. After another mile-plus, the trail follows the jeep road into the canyon where you will begin encountering your first "old mine" remains of Red Cloud Mine. To your right you'll see a cyanide leaching pit. Explore the trail going left off the main trail as it climbs a road to reveal several large slag piles with some old rusted iron structures still standing.

Return to the main trail and hike another 0.5 mile until you come to the Great Western Mine. Numerous side trails up into the surrounding hills and along

canyon bottoms offer adventure seekers plenty of opportunities for discovering the extent of this once large mining operation. A bush-whack 0.5 mile farther into the canyon due south will reveal a trail to the right which climbs into the mountains and ends in a gor-geous vista over-look of the whole Orocopia Mountain Wilderness Basin.

Pond at Upper Meadows, Bogart Park

Hike 140

Red Cloud Rd. to
Summit Rd. Jct.
2.9 miles

To Radio Towers

Split in Road

Car Parking

2 Miles
(not to scale)

Stamping Mill

Leaching Pit

Red Cloud Mine

Great Western
Mine

× = Prospects

⚒ = Mines

Vista Overlook

N

1   0   1   2 Miles

Appendix 1
Hikes According to Degree of Difficulty

Easy Hikes

Hike Number/Name	Miles	Page
1. Painted Canyon/Ladder Canyon Loop	5	19
2. Little Painted Canyon Walkabout	4–5	22
4. The "Big Split Rock" Slot Canyon Walkabout	6	25
13. "Pyramid Canyon"	6.5	43
14. Big Colorful Canyon	6	46
16. Slot Canyon Cave Trail	6.5	50
17. "Little Utah Canyon"	5	52
18. "Utah Canyons" Overlook	4	53
19. "Big Utah Canyon"	4.5	55
20. "Never Ending Canyon" Loop	4	56
21. The Meccacopia Trail to Salton Sea Overlook	7	57
25. Sheep Hole Oasis/Godwin Trail Shuttle	7	64
30. Pushawalla Palms and Canyon Trail	6	74
31. Willis Palms and West Mesa Trail	3	75
32. Coachella Valley Preserve Trails	6	76
38. Bear Creek Urban Trail, La Quinta	6	88
44. Mirage Trail (aka "Bump and Grind")	2	102
45. Homestead/Hopalong Cassidy/Gabby Hayes	2.5	104
47. Randall Henderson Trail	2.5	107
48. Fern Canyon	3.5	110
51. Lower Palm Canyon Trail	3–4	115
52. The Victor Trail/Fern Canyon	2.5–5	117
56. Andreas Canyon	2	123
59. Earl Henderson Trail	4	128
64. Tahquitz Canyon	2.5	135
70. The Ernie Maxwell Scenic Trail	5	149
80. Hurkey Creek Trail	3	163
96. Horsethief Creek via Cactus Spring Trail	5	189
106. Barker Dam Loop	1	210
120. Big Morongo Canyon Preserve Walkabout	3	234
126. Bogart Park Walkabout	4–5	245
127. Oak Glen Nature Trail	2	246

Moderate Hikes

Appendix 1 *(continued)*

Moderate Hikes *(continued)*

Strenuous Hikes

Strenuous Hikes *(continued)*

Appendix 2
The "Best of the Best" Hikes:
From Full Moon Walkabouts to Wildflower Excursions

This Appendix is my own way to especially assist the vacationing hiker who may be in the Palm Desert/Palm Springs area for a limited time. Read my own picks as "Best-of-the-Best" hikes, each following a certain theme. Subjective, yes…but as I've been around these parts for many years, I have seen other people's reactions to these hikes. It's my hope that you will enjoy these themed hikes that others, and I, have found. Some hikes will be mentioned more than once, as they fit several categories. All the better for you! I have not limited these selections to distance, so read driving directions in order to plan accordingly. If a 4wd vehicle is usually necessary, I'll so indicate. A double asterisk means that this is a truly special hike, one not to be missed.

Quiet, Meditative Places:

So you want to be somewhere special, scenic but quiet…perhaps a lazy afternoon escape hike to gather your thoughts and be touched by the special natural beauty and ambience surrounding you. Not focused on exercise or big challenges; just tranquil nature at her kindest. These hikes are best done early in the morning or mid-afternoon so you'll catch the lengthening sunlight on the way back. Also you may find that just the first several miles of the hike satisfies you, as you may be slowly walking these trails/areas to experience their full offering of peaceful beauty. My picks include:

Big Morongo Canyon Preserve Walkabout **
Bogart Park Walkabout/Oak Glen Nature Trail (fall, spring, & summer)**
"Little Utah Canyon"
The Meccacopia Trail to Salton Sea Overlook
Mission Creek to the Pacific Crest Trail North (park at gate and walk in)**
Palm Canyon Pines-to-Palms Trail, first 3 miles **
"Pyramid Canyon "**
South & North Fork of the PCT
Spitler Peak Trail, first 3 miles **

Colorful Rocks/Geological Formations

Nature offers hikers an abundance of color and geological interest in the Coachella Valley. These hikes and places will encourage you to bring the camera and a child-like wonder to enjoy these exotic, fascinating treks. Many of these hikes suggest Utah-like canyons and some are quite near the San Andreas Fault. One often encounters groups of geology students on field trips from nearby universities.

The variety and stunning presentations of these hikes makes for a welcome contrast to the more civilized amenities of the nearby desert resort cities.

Big Colorful Canyon
*The "Big Split Rock" Slot Canyon Walkabout ***
"Coffee Bean Canyon"
*The Grottos/2nd Grotto "Rainbow Rocks Walkabout" ***
The Grottos Overlook Trail
*Lower Red Canyon/Left-Hand Canyon Loop Overlook (4wd) ***
*Mystery Cairns Hike (4wd) ***
*Painted Canyon/Ladder Canyon Loop ***
*Palm Canyon Trail to the Stone Pools ***
Slot Canyon Cave Trail

High Adventure...Pushing the Envelope

These hikes are just that...high adventure, not for the faint of heart and usually strenuous but with big payoffs!

2nd Grotto/Rainbow Rocks/Hidden Springs Loop
Agua Alta Spring
Cactus to Clouds Hike
"Coffee Bean Canyon"/Mecca Hill Canyons Walkabout
*Fuller Ridge Trail to San Jacinto Peak ***
Guadalupe Trail to Sugarloaf Cafe
Jo Pond/Cedar Spring Trail to Palm Canyon Trading Post
*Lost Canyon via The Boo Hoff Trail ***
Magnesia Springs Canyon
*Pacific Crest Trail South from I-10 ***
*Palm Canyon Pines-to-Palms Trail ***
*Palm Springs Aerial Tramway to Saddle Junction Loop/ or to Idyllwild ***
San Bernardino Peak Trail to Columbine Spring
*The West Fork Trail to Andreas Canyon ***
*The Zen Center to Red Tahquitz Overlook ***

High Country Mountainous Scenery

Scenery with "green & trees" to contrast the desert below, with an escape from the desert heat as part of the draw.

The Ernie Maxwell Scenic Trail
*Deer Springs Trail to Suicide Rock ***
*Devil's Slide Trail to Tahquitz Peak Lookout Loop ***
*Keenwild to South Ridge Trail ***
*Palm Springs Aerial Tramway to Saddle Junction Loop ***
*Santa Rosa Peak/Mountain Road Traverse ***
Spitler Peak Trail

Appendix 2 *(continued)*

Fun-for-the-Kids (and the "Kid in You")

Want to be ten years old again? Want to treat your kids to someplace and some experience "special"? These hikes are sure to be fun for everyone...a great team or family builder, and nice hikes for a first date.

Andreas Canyon **
Big Morongo Canyon Preserve Walkabout **
The "Big Split Rock" Slot Canyon Walkabout **
The Grottos **
Lost Canyon via The Boo Hoff Trail
Lower Red Canyon/Left-Hand Canyon Loop Overlook (4wd) **
"Never Ending Canyon" Loop (caution on the ridge top...backtrack if necessary)
Painted Canyon/Ladder Canyon Loop **
Silt Canyon
Slot Canyon Cave Trail **
Tahquitz Canyon

Full Moon Rambles

Exotic full moon hikes offer a real change of pace from the daily grind or the "usual suspects" kind of hikes. Take a flashlight, get to the trailhead just before dark and know that you only have to hike for a few miles to get the effect.

Big Colorful Canyon
"Little Utah" Canyon
Painted Canyon/Ladder Canyon Loop **
   (park on the road two miles from the trailhead and walk in and out, just to the trailhead)
"Pyramid Canyon" **
Sawmill Road Trail...on warmer vs. cold evenings. **

Wildflowers

The operative word here is water...no rain means no flowers! Depending on the year, some hikes can overwhelm you with nature's bounty, but it's always iffy and each year must be taken on its own merits. After temperatures reach into the 90's, flowers fade quickly. Joshua Tree National Park hikes are higher up and so can be done later than the desert hikes.

Bogart Park Walkabout/Oak Glen Nature Trail
Horsethief Creek (April/May for flowering cactus...early morning)
"Little Utah" Canyon
Lost Palms Oasis Trail **
Meccacopia Trail to Salton Sea Overlook **
Mission Creek to the Pacific Crest Trail North (mid March–early April) **
Santa Rosa Plateau Loop/Walkabout **

Desert Canyons

Desert canyons are especially exotic to visitors from greener places. Our local canyons, especially in the Mecca Hills/Orocopia Mountain Wilderness, suggest Utah more than what one would expect in Southern California. These are friendly, usually flat, and best done either early morning or late afternoon.

2nd Grottos/Rainbow Rocks Walkabout **

Andreas Canyon

Big Colorful Canyon

"Coffee Bean Canyon"/Mecca Hill Canyons Walkabout

"Little Utah" Canyon

Lost Canyon

Lower Palm Canyon Trail **

Lower Red Canyon/Left Hand Canyon Loop Overlook (4wd) **

Painted Canyon/Ladder Canyon Loop **

"Pyramid Canyon" **

Tahquitz Canyon

"High, Wide and Handsome" Vistas

I enjoy a ridge from where I can see for miles and capture the essence of the surrounding land. These offerings give you just that. Not for the whole hike, but enough to get your aesthetic attention.

The Boo Hoff Trail to La Quinta **

Devil's Slide Trail to Tahquitz Peak Lookout Loop

Jo Pond Trail to Fobes Saddle Overlook **

Lost Horse Mine Loop

Lower Red Canyon/Left -Hand Canyon Loop Overlook (4wd) **

Palm Canyon Trail to the Stone Pools **

Palm Springs Aerial Tramway to San Jacinto Peak

Pipes Canyon Upper Trail to Big Rocks Overlook

Santa Rosa Peak/Mountain Road Traverse **

Sawmill Road Trail **

South Ridge Trail to Tahquitz Peak Overlook **

Thomas Mountain East & West Road Trails **

The West Fork Trail to Andreas Canyon **

The Zen Center to Red Tahquitz Overlook **

Palm Oasis

In the desert why not go for the water and their lush oasis greenery? These oases deserve your attention.

Andreas Canyon **

Lost Palms Oasis Trail at Cottonwood Spring **

Lower Palm Canyon Trail **

Murray Canyon Trail

Pushawalla Palms and Canyon Trail

Appendix 2 *(continued)*

Old Gold Mines

Not that you'll find any gold, but that the exotic feel of the place and the "Old West" throwback is definitely worth the trek!

Lost Horse Mine Loop (or just to the mine) **
The Old Dale Road/Mines Walkabout
Red Cloud and Great Western Mine Tour (4wd helpful) **
Summit Road to the First Mines

Secret Getaways and "a place of your own"

I enjoy the feeling of "this is my special place," usually a hike in an area that is infused with its own uniqueness, often suggesting "some other place I've been that I miss." Some of these hikes I'd do every week, just to be in their "special place." Often these hikes are best done weekdays, adding even more to their serene escape sanctuary.

Bogart Park Walkabout (closed Tues. & Wed.) **
"Little Utah" Canyon
Meccacopia/Little Box Canyon Loop
Mission Creek to the Pacific Crest Trail
     (park in front of gate, walk in 3 miles) **
North Fork of the Pacific Crest Trail to Live Oak Spring (first 3 miles) **
Oak Glen Nature Trail **
"Pyramid Canyon" **
Santa Rosa Plateau Loop **
Spitler Peak Trail (first 3 miles) **
Thomas Mountain East Road to Summit

Rivers, Creeks, Lakes, and Ponds

Not that this desert is blessed with many of the above! It's still all about winter rains and snow pack in the high country. But when rivers run, and where lakes of some sort exist...this is where you'll see them.

Andreas Canyon
Big Morongo Canyon Trail/Preserve Walkabout **
Bogart Park Walkabout/Oak Glen Nature Trail **
Horsethief Creek via Cactus Spring Trail
Lower Palm Canyon Trail **
Mission Creek to the Pacific Crest Trail North
Murray Canyon Trail
Palm Canyon Trail to the Stone Pools **

Appendix 3
Best Restaurants After a Hike

For years, members of the Coachella Valley Hiking Club and I have fellowshipped after a hike with either a late lunch or early dinner at restaurants that welcome hikers after a long day on the trail. We have appreciated considerate and fast service and the most excellent food for weary hikers with big appetites. If you are planning a lunch or dinner with a larger group, or to ensure timely seating, call ahead and find the times of operation and seating availability. Here are my best recommendations for fine restaurants that welcome hikers and whose food is exceptionally good:

All hikes east and south of Indio:
CIRO'S RISTORANTE & PIZZERIA, 81-963 Hwy. 11, Indio, (760) 347-6503
Pizza, lasagna, great food, great service.

TERESA'S CAFE, 45-682 Towne St., Indio, (760) 347-7411
The best Mexican home-cooked meals!

Desert Cities
FRENCH CORNER CAFE & BAKERY, Desert Crossing Center
72-423 Hwy 111, Palm Desert, (760) 568-5362

San Gorgonio Pass and nearby hikes:
A & W ROOTBEER, Cabazon, (909) 849-3301
A '50s-style restaurant with great food and fast service.

La Quinta:
EL RANCHITO
78-039 Calle Estado (off Desert Club Dr./Bermudas), La Quinta,
(760) 564-0061 *Great fajitas and carnitas.*

San Jacinto Mountains and Idyllwild hikes:
THE GASTROGNOME RESTAURANT
54381 Ridgeview Dr., Idyllwild, (909) 659-5055
A real "five star" presentation of fine dining, warm mountain atmosphere.

Appendix 3 *(continued)*

Joshua Tree National Park/Yucca Valley hikes:

DIN HO CHINESE RESTAURANT

56-098 29 Palms Hwy., Yucca Valley, (760) 365-4353

Chinese food at its best, comfortable atmosphere, and fast service.

"The Lodge" at White Water Canyon

Appendix 4
Dog-friendly Trails

Appendix 4 *(continued)*

Mt. San Jacinto from White Water Canyon Preserve.

Appendix 5
Helpful Information for Desert Visitors

Hiking Hints
Area Maps and the National Forest Adventure Pass (NFAP)

Visitors using this book who want to supplement and expand their knowledge of the area will find Desert Map & Aerial Photo (73-612 Hwy. 111, Palm Desert, [760] 346-1101) the perfect resource for topographic maps and resource materials and for purchasing the NFAP. This pass permits you to park at trailheads in the Santa Rosa and San Jacinto mountains, whether on a daily basis or for a longer time frame with a yearly pass. The owners who operate Desert Map know the area as well as anyone, and are very helpful in directing you to any local trails that would fit your needs.

Dirt Jeep Roads

All of the roads into the Orocopia Mountain Wilderness and Painted Canyon/ Mecca Hills are dirt jeep roads. If in doubt, contact the Bureau of Land Management at (760) 251-4800 to see if they are passable. Passenger cars usually can access the trails into Painted Canyon/Box Canyon, and along Red Cloud Road, and Summit Road.

Unmarked Trails and Signs

Most desert trails in the Coachella Valley are either not marked at the trailhead or marked sparingly along the way. This requires hikers to take extra care in hiking, noticing turnoffs and return points. If in doubt, and if you lack a topographic map or map-reading skills, or have a poor sense of direction, retrace your hike back along the route you came in on if you sense that you are losing your way. Only well-seasoned and skilled hikers should attempt bushwhacking in an unknown area. Too often, one canyon or trail begins to look exactly like all the others.

Weather

Hikers should be aware that early morning temperatures, especially after March 1 and before November 1, can be deceptive. Temperatures of 60–70 degrees at the trailhead can soon become 85–100 by afternoon. Always take a generous supply of cold drinks, 1 quart per 4 miles hiked.

Also, the temperatures in the Santa Rosa and San Jacinto mountains can be 40–50 degrees cooler than the desert floor, especially if a cold, moist marine layer of clouds has penetrated into the mountains and a strong, onshore flow or breeze is present.

Local Attractions

The Living Desert

Located in Palm Desert, this fine attraction offers informative exhibits and insights into the desert flora and fauna that you might see on one of your hikes. It is well worth visiting.

Palm Springs Aerial Tramway

Palm Springs Aerial Tramway gets you to the top of the San Jacinto Mountains/ Mount San Jacinto State Park. The tram runs most of the year and affords desert visitors a quick and scenic ride to the mountain trails above Palm Springs. A restaurant is also featured, with a ranger station just outside the Mountain Tram Station. By riding the tram, hikers can take longer hikes instead of spending valuable time driving. Please check with the tram for additional information at (760) 325-1391 or (760) 327-6002; www.pstramway.com. The tram is located on Hwy. 111, just at the northern edge of town.

San Jacinto Mountains from Garner Valley horse ranches

Appendix 6
Desert Resources/Events

"Whitewater Preserve"

The newly developed (2008) Whitewater Preserve is a 2,851-acre area surrounded by the BLM's San Gorgonio Wilderness. The jewel of the Preserve is a scenic 291-acre development at the end of Whitewater Canyon Road, located almost 5 miles north of Interstate 10 via the Whitewater exit. This smaller parcel includes ponds, a Ranger Station/Lodge that accommodates picnickers, and a connector trail that leads northwest from the parking lot and connects to the Pacific Crest Trail (PCT) .25 miles from the Ranger Station.

Picnic tables, bathrooms, and a peaceful green area accent the Preserve, making it especially people friendly. The Whitewater Canyon area is a serene scenic hideaway where colorful taupe, camel, green, and mauve rock walls suggest a Colorado or Utah-like environment highlighted by the majestic San Gorgonio Mountain/Peak Valley as seen from where Red Dome meets the Whitewater River Valley. Hikers can now hike this section of Whitewater Canyon via the PCT and explore upper Whitewater Canyon as it encounters the Red Dome rock formation 2 miles north of the parking lot.

The Preserve is open year-round, 8am-5pm. For information, please call (760) 325-7222.

See Map for Hike 121 "The Pacific Crest Trail North from I-10"

The Hike for Hope

Hike for Hope is a charity fundraising event supporting the City of Hope, held usually the 1st Sunday in March at the Palm Springs Indian Canyons. Their web site, www. hike4hope.com, provides detailed information as well as pictures and ways the public can support the event. This event is one of the premier charity hiking events in the nation and draws almost a 1,000 hikers annually. Weather is usually in the 70-80s, sunny, and as friendly as the enthusiastic crowd that participates yearly. For more information, please call (760) 202-3885.

Index

About the Author/Photographer

Philip Ferranti has hiked the western United States for over 30 years. He has spent much of that time exploring the trails in and near Palm Springs and the Coachella Valley. He founded the Coachella Valley Hiking Club in 1992, has written for *Backpacker* magazine, and is a frequent guest speaker at outdoor/hiking conventions. As president of Transformation Seminars since 1981, Philip specializes in seminars on stress management and hiking for health and wellness. He has written nine books, including *Hiking! The Ultimate Natural Prescription for Health & Wellness* (distributed by Westcliffe Publishers) and *Colorado State Parks: A Complete Recreation Guide.* Philip expanded the original bestseller, *75 Great Hikes in and near Palm Springs and the Coachella Valley* to include 25 more hikes in 2000. The book you hold is the revised version of *120 Great Hikes in and near Palm Springs.*

Philip is available for slide shows, lectures, seminars, and guided hikes both in and near Palm Springs, and for longer packaged hiking vacations in Utah, Colorado, and the San Francisco Bay Area. Phone him at (760) 345-6234, e-mail him at Pferran1@aol.com, or log on to www.philipferranti.com or www.stockinvestingstrategies.com.

About the Cartographer

Hank Koenig (1936–2008) was an avid hiker, trekking extensively in New England, the Northwest, and in Southern California. After retiring from a 30 year career with a major defense contractor, Hank immersed himself in his favorite pursuits: hiking and electronics. As a GPS specialist for the McKenzie Ranger District on the Willamette National Forest in Central Oregon, Hank developed data for map creation and trail inventories. Hank trained BLM and USFS staff in the practical uses of GPS. He and his hiking-partner wife, Sheila, were founding members of the Coachella Valley Hiking Club.

Hank was responsible for mapping many of the hitherto unknown trails that he and Philip Ferranti discovered while working on this book. This icon of the Southern California hiking community will be sadly missed, but he would be greatly pleased to know that future hikers will benefit from his work.